Questions in the
Psychology of Religion

Questions in the Psychology of Religion

KEVIN S. SEYBOLD

CASCADE *Books* · Eugene, Oregon

QUESTIONS IN THE PSYCHOLOGY OF RELIGION

Cascade Books
An Imprint of Wipf and Stock Publishers
199 W. 8th Ave., Suite 3
Eugene, OR 97401

www.wipfandstock.com

PAPERBACK ISBN: 978-1-4982-3881-6
HARDCOVER ISBN: 978-1-4982-3883-0
EBOOK ISBN: 978-1-4982-3882-3

Cataloging-in-Publication data:

Names: Seybold, Kevin S., 1956-, author.

Title: Questions in the psychology of religion / Kevin S. Seybold.

Description: Eugene, OR: Cascade Books, 2017. | Includes bibliographical references and index.

Identifiers: ISBN: 978-1-4982-3881-6 (paperback). | ISBN: 978-1-4982-3883-0 (hardcover). | ISBN: 978-1-4982-3882-3 (ebook).

Subjects: Religion and Psychology | Psychology, Religious | Brain—Religious aspects—Christianity.

Classification: BL53 S49 2017 (print) | BL53 (ebook).

Manufactured in the U.S.A.   03/01/17

In Memory of My Parents
J. Rolland and Ferne Seybold

Contents

Acknowledgments

This book is the result of conversations with colleagues, class lectures and discussions with students, and hours of reading and thinking in my office. I am grateful to Grove City College for granting me a sabbatical that enabled me to work extensively on this project. During that sabbatical semester, I was a visiting research scholar at Biola University's Center for Christian Thought, a research fellowship made possible through the support of a grant from the John Templeton Foundation. At the Center, I was able to study and work with a number of amazing people who expanded and enriched my understanding of the philosophical bases of many issues related to psychology, including Eric LaRock, Dan Speak, Robin Collins, Stewart Goetz, Nancy Duvall, Jason McMartin, J. P. Moreland, and Mike Sanborn. Particular thanks go to Tom Crisp, Gregg Ten Elshof, Steve Porter, Evan Rosa, and Rachel Dee who formed the leadership team for the Center. Thanks also to Peter Hill, Keith Edwards, and John Williams at Biola for their friendship and camaraderie while I was at the University. Of course, the opinions expressed in this book are mine and do not necessarily reflect those of either the Center for Christian Thought or the John Templeton Foundation.

I am also indebted to friends and colleagues here at Grove City College, in the psychology department and across campus, with whom I have enjoyed many conversations that have helped to focus my thinking on the questions raised in this book. Special thanks to Mark Graham, Paul Kemeny, Mike Coulter, Erik Anderson, Gil Harp, Christopher Franklin, Tim Homan, Warren Throckmorton, Gary Welton, Joe Horton, Kris Homan, Suzanne Houk, and many others who challenge me each day with questions, ideas, and viewpoints that make me rethink my own positions on issues in psychology, science, religion, belief, practice, etc.

The editorial staff at Cascade Books, led by K. C. Hanson, was extremely helpful in the writing of this book. Many thanks to them. Finally, I am thankful to my family for their consistent support, especially my wife, Ginny. I am also grateful to my parents, to whose memory I dedicate this book.

Introduction

The word 'integrity' itself has two meanings. The first is 'honesty' ... We have to be honest in facing our limitations, in facing the sheer complexity of the world, honest in facing criticism even of things which are deeply precious to us. But integrity also means wholeness, oneness, the desire for single vision, the refusal to split our minds into separate compartments where incompatible ideas are not allowed to come into contact ... An undivided mind looks in the end for an undivided truth, a oneness at the heart of things. And this isn't just fantasy. The whole intellectual quest despite its fragmentation, despite its limitations and uncertainties, seems to presuppose that in the end we are all encountering a single reality, and single truth.[1]

I teach undergraduate psychology courses at a Christian college in Pennsylvania. In some of these courses I include the above quote by John Habgood (born 1927) in the syllabus. Habgood studied natural science at Cambridge University and taught physiology and pharmacology there for several years. In 1954, he was ordained in the Anglican Church, eventually becoming Archbishop of York, a position he held until his retirement in 1995. As both a scientist and theologian, Habgood (The Lord Habgood as of 1995) has written several books and articles dealing with the integration of science and religion.[2] One of the objectives I have for the courses I teach is to develop in students the ability to see ways that science (psychological science in particular) and religion, both very important in our culture, can work together, instead of seeing them as fundamentally incompatible or in

1. Habgood, *Confessions*, 95.
2. Seybold, "Untidiness," 114–19.

conflict, a view, unfortunately, that many people hold. I want the students in my courses to read or hear about various ideas, findings, and theories coming from psychology and to honestly consider them, even if the ideas, findings, and theories might be thought "inconsistent" with what they have learned in church, Sunday school, or Christian high school. The students do not necessarily have to agree with these new ideas, but at least understand them, think about them, and to try to work out how the apparent "inconsistencies" or "incompatibilities" can be resolved.

In my classes, I follow what is typically called the Two Books approach, the origin of which can be traced back, at least, to Augustine (AD 354–430). According to this perspective, there are two books, Nature (sometimes called general revelation) and Scripture (sometimes called special revelation), that God provides for us. God, as Creator, gives us nature, and God inspired the authors of Scripture. Because God is the author of both books, both must be true. The information found in the book of Nature and in the book of Scripture is all true, and so cannot be contradictory or incompatible. What we learn in our study of nature is ultimately consistent with what we learn in our study of Scripture.

Of course, a book has to be read and interpreted. Scientists read and interpret the book of Nature by using the procedures we call science; scientists look for natural mechanisms revealed in the natural world. Psychological scientists study that part of nature involving human (and animal) behavior and mental processing. Psychologists look for natural mechanisms involved in why human beings act, feel, and think the way they do. When Christian psychologists study this aspect of nature, they believe they are investigating how God created human beings. What natural causes, biological, environmental, cognitive, and so forth did God use (or is God using) to make humans the way we are?

The Bible also has to be read and interpreted, and biblical scholars or theologians use procedures (e.g., learning the original languages, studying the original cultures, learning about different genres of literature) to try to correctly interpret what God is telling us in the scriptural revelation. Sometimes scientists make mistakes as they try to interpret nature, and theologians or biblical scholars make mistakes as they try to interpret Scripture. When this happens, there might appear to be some conflict between nature and Scripture, but the conflict is only apparent. Both nature and Scripture are true, so they cannot be, if correctly understood, in conflict.

The Habgood quote is intended to remind us that we need to study both nature and Scripture with integrity—honestly recognizing that as humans we are limited in what we know. We also need to be humble in recognizing that we might be wrong about what we think either nature or Scripture is saying. Both nature and Scripture are true, and as Christians we need to try to find that wholeness or unity—that single reality and truth. The chapters in this book are written in this spirit. Many theories, findings, and ideas are discussed in what follows. This information is based on some of the latest, and I hope best, research psychological science provides regarding certain issues at the interface between religion and psychology.

Chapter 1 begins with a look at the nature of religious thoughts, emotions, and behaviors. Are they different in some fundamental way from other thoughts, emotions, and behaviors that are not religious? Is religion something that can be studied by psychological science, or is it unique and unknowable via psychological investigation? I develop the perspective that religious behavior, experience, emotion, and so forth are not fundamentally different, so a psychological study of religion, as we might study nonreligious behavior, experience, emotion, and the like is legitimate and warranted.

Chapter 2 considers how America is changing religiously. Multiple recent surveys agree that there is a decline in the proportion of Americans who identify with Christianity. While much of this decrease is a continuation of a pattern that has been seen for decades in the more liberal Protestant denominations, the decline is now present in conservative denominations as well. This trend, coupled with an increase in the percentage of people who identify themselves as agnostics or atheists, or who are not affiliated with any particular religious group (the so-called nones), leads some to wonder if religion is on its way out as a major source of cultural and social influence. Perhaps the long-predicted death of God is finally here. Another perspective, however, suggests that while Christianity as it is currently understood and practiced in much of the West is changing, religion itself and belief in God are not going away. God is not dying. Evidence from psychology, neuroscience, biology, evolution, and other related fields suggests that there might be a biological basis for religion and that human beings (as a species) need religion—it might even be adaptive. With such close ties to our biological nature, religion is unlikely to "go away."

Chapters 3 and 4 elaborate on the suggestion that there is a "naturalness" to religion. Chapter 3 covers what is a relatively new approach to the study of religion known as the cognitive science of religion or CSR. The basic tenet of CSR is that belief in God (or in gods) is not something that has to be explained by invoking some unusual or unnatural psychological system or mechanism. These religious beliefs, just like many nonreligious beliefs, are formed by natural mental tools; they are a natural product of the way our brains work. Another area within psychology and neuroscience interested in the naturalness and universality of religious experience is the field known as neurotheology. The term is in some ways unfortunate in that *neurotheology* is not telling us anything about God. We are, however, learning about how the brain (as well as the entire body) is involved in mediating religious experience. We use our physical bodies to worship and experience God as we use our bodies in all of our experiences, religious or otherwise. All of our experiences are mediated via the brain, and chapter 4 reviews the literature in this field.

A fundamental question that links psychology with religion deals with the nature of human beings. What does it mean to be human? What are we? Are we merely physical creatures, or are we ultimately immaterial beings? The question of what it means to be human often focuses on the question of soul. Do we have souls? If so, what does that mean? Chapter 5 discusses what the soul is supposed to do, what functions it serves, and why many people believe we need an immaterial soul to be fully human. It also presents evidence from psychology and neuroscience suggesting that the functions many people have traditionally attributed to an immaterial soul are closely linked to the functioning of the very material brain. The chapter reviews ways that scholars approach the so-called mind/body or soul/body problem today: some argue for a kind of dualism, others for a type of monism or physicalism, and still others for something between these two positions.

Another central issue in religion deals with morality. What makes us moral? Is the capacity to act morally important in distinguishing humans from other animals? Various scientific disciplines, including psychology and evolutionary biology, have taken up the issue of morality in the past twenty years. Chapter 6 reviews the literature coming from these sciences that pertain to the origins of morality. What this research suggests is that the view that humans are basically immoral, selfish, evil creatures whose morality is only "skin deep" is fundamentally wrong. Morality (or at least the precursors of moral behavior) is found in animal behavior. The emotion of empathy and social behaviors such as altruism are found in lower animals suggesting that the roots of morality are found in our biology and basic social psychology. What impact does this research have for our understanding of moral codes as originating from religion? What, if any, role does religion have in maintaining moral behavior? What role does God play?

The final chapter in this book concerns what is called cultural cognition. It is often noted that America is becoming more and more polarized on political, social, and even religious issues. Why do self-identified conservatives typically take a pro-life, pro–death penalty, anti–gun control stance? Why do conservatives generally tend to be skeptics about climate change? Why are conservatives more likely to question the legitimacy of evolutionary theory and believe that Islam is incompatible with American values and the American way of life? Why do self-identified liberals typically take a pro-choice, anti–death penalty, pro–gun control stance? Why do liberals generally tend to be more open to climate science and evolution and believe that Islam is compatible with American culture? There seems to be an accepted "conservative" view and an accepted "liberal" view on various issues that have little in common (e.g., gun control and climate change). This chapter discusses the literature in psychology dealing with decision theory, information processing, dual-processing theory, and so forth that relates to why people make the decisions and adopt the opinions they do. These same psychological processes can also be used to help understand why "conservative" and "liberal" Christians who read the same Bible can come to such divergent views on gay marriage, abortion, care for the environment, and immigration. Given what we know about decision-making and information processing (including the important role of misinformation), how might Christians (and people of other religions or of no religion at all) become less polarized and more willing to work with others with dissimilar viewpoints? What are some of the findings from psychology that can implemented to help people reach consensus on the important issues of the day, in the church and out of it?

As I mentioned above, the material in these chapters represents some of the latest research findings in psychological science on these topics. One way to think of psychology from a Christian perspective is to understand it as trying to study the book of Nature, what God has created. Humans are part of God's creation, and psychological science is interested in finding the natural mechanisms mediating human behavior, thought, and emotion. Whether we are considering morality, religious experience, religious beliefs, the soul, or any other issue that is relevant to the relationship be-tween psychology and religion, psychology is looking for natural processes. There may be nonnatural mechanisms that are also involved. If there are, however, psychology will not find them. Science is limited to discovering natural causes, and psychology is limited to looking for the natural mecha-nisms of human behavior and mental processing. Identifying, for example, the natural processes involved in religious experience does not mean that religious experience has been explained away by these mechanisms. (There might also be supernatural explanations for the experiences.) Finding the natural processes merely recognizes that human behavior and mental ac-tivity are going to involve biological and psychological mechanisms, and psychology is interested in knowing what those mechanisms are.

There is a unity, an undivided truth, a oneness at the heart of things. Integrity, honesty, and humility. These are good virtues to pursue as we attempt to integrate psychological science with religion.

1

Psychology of Religion
Are Religious Thoughts, Emotions, and Behaviors Psychologically Different?

To the psychologist the religious propensities of man must be at least as interesting as any other of the facts pertaining to his mental constitution.[1]

As concrete states of mind, made up of a feeling *plus a* specific sort of object, religious emotions of course are psychic entities distinguishable from other concrete emotions; but there is no ground for assuming a simple abstract 'religious emotion' to exist as a distinct elementary mental affection by itself, present in every religious experience without exception. As there thus seems to be no one elementary religious emotion, but only a common storehouse of emotions upon which religious objects may draw, so there might conceivably also prove to be no one specific and essential kind of religious object, and no one specific and essential kind of religious act.[2]

M ost people, whether or not they are personally religious, have an opinion about what religion is, and for most people, religion consists

1. James, *Varieties*, 4.
2. Ibid., 33.

for most religion is a

of a set of beliefs, rules, and behaviors established by some kind of institution (e.g., a church, synagogue, or mosque). Even the nonreligious person
knows that beliefs, rules, and behaviors differ from one religion to another.
Many people might also know that even within a particular religion (like
Christianity) there are variations in how that religion is understood and
practiced. What many people might not understand, however, is why these
beliefs are held, why the particular set of rules are followed, or why certain behaviors are performed. This misunderstanding holds true not only
for the nonreligious as they look at religious people, but also for religious
individuals as they consider the personal religious beliefs and behaviors of
others. How is it the case that there are so many different religious traditions each, in many cases, claiming to be the one true religion?

Has religion always been this diverse and divided? Have people always
understood religion as we do now? Has there always been religion in some
form? Anthropologists tell us that something like religious practice has
existed for many millennia. The earliest examples of Neanderthals burying
their dead date back at least one hundred fifty thousand years ago, suggesting a concern for the spirits of the deceased. Burying the dead with
grave goods such as tools, ivory beads, and weapons is a practice that dates
to around thirty thousand years ago with the arrival of *Homo sapiens* and
also indicates a type of religious activity and thought. Cave paintings, such
as those on the island of Sulawesi in Indonesia and the Chauvet Cave in
France, date back thirty-five thousand years and are thought to represent
early humanity's understanding of self and personhood and how they related to the world around them. Some of these paintings are thought to
contain religious themes that concerned the people who entered the caves.
These examples of the religious human mind suggest that religion, in one
form or another, has been present since the earliest humans and has always
been a part of human culture and society.

But was religion always understood and conceptualized as is it today?
While we probably can never know what early humans were thinking when
they buried their dead one hundred thousand years ago, we do know that
the meaning of religion has changed over the past several centuries from a
conceptualization of religion as an interior virtue (training one's mind and
character) to an external function that consists of an accumulation of propositional statements and beliefs that represent particular doctrinal content.[3]

3. Harrison, *Territories*, 7–11.

If we consider just Christianity as an example, first-century followers of Christ would have understood belief or faith as trust and confidence in the person of Jesus. I believe in or have faith in my financial advisor. I have confidence that he has my best interests in mind as he makes financial decisions on my behalf. This was the understanding of *belief* two thousand years ago. The early Christians believed in Jesus. They had faith in the person of the Christ, and they followed him and tried to live their lives as Jesus did.[4] The early church fathers such as Augustine understood religion from this internal virtue perspective. Christianity was a way of training one's mind and shaping one's character.

By the sixteenth and seventeenth centuries, religion had assumed more of a cognitive character. Belief became understood as giving intellectual assent to a set of propositional statements. Belief in Jesus (faith or confidence in Jesus) became belief that certain propositions about Jesus are true.[5] Understood propositionally, the truth of a particular religion can be established and compared to the falsity of other religions. Religion can also be studied as an explanation for certain events, such as why people think, behave, or feel the way they do. This way of viewing religion opens it up to be studied by the cognitive, psychological, and even the evolutionary sciences.

Developing psychological or other scientific accounts for religious beliefs, behaviors, and emotions, however, should not be thought of as explaining these religious experiences away. A better understanding of the psychological processes underlying religious beliefs, for example, does not make those beliefs less important, religious, or spiritual to the person who has them. Knowing the physiological mechanisms responsible for a particular religious action or emotion does not invalidate the behavior or emotion as a genuine religious experience. Providing an evolutionary perspective on the origin of religious ritual does not mean the ritual is not part of the worship of a true, living God.

4. Bass, *Christianity*, 103–35.

5. Harrison, *Territories*, 92–108. In his poem "The Incarnate One," Edwin Muir writes about the change in Christianity from an emphasis on the person of Jesus to a more intellectual perspective (Muir, "Incarnate One," 55).

RELIGION AND SPIRITUALITY

If the understanding of what religion is became more abstract and cognitive between the sixteenth and seventeenth centuries, at least in the West, how is religion conceptualized in the twenty-first century, and how is religion the same or different from *spirituality*, another term used a lot today? Religion and spirituality tend to be viewed in polarizing ways with religion understood by some as a fixed system of ideas (propositions to which one must assent), doctrinal, formal, institutional, authoritarian, outward, inhibiting of expression, rigid, and just plain bad. Spirituality, on the other hand, is seen as individual, emotional, inward, unsystematic, nondogmatic, and good, at least compared to bad religion.[6]

This neat division between religion and spirituality is more apparent than real, however. While there are certainly differences between the two concepts, there is overlap as well. Both religion and spirituality have cognitive, behavioral, emotional, and physiological components. Most people experience their spirituality (as a search for the sacred) in the context of religion, and both religion and spirituality can have good and bad qualities. In addition, while one can certainly have spiritual experiences when alone, most forms of spiritual expression take place in a social setting.[7] Finally, both religion and spirituality follow a developmental process over the life span of the individual, and both can have positive influences on mental and physical health.[8] (In this book, I am interested in questions and issues that arise at the interface of psychology and religion, but these questions and issues can be equally applied, I believe, to spirituality. As a result, I will use the terms interchangeably.) Given that religion/spirituality involves cognitive, behavioral, and emotional components, it is important to consider what psychological mechanisms might be involved in religion and spirituality. In addition, given that both religion and spirituality involve a search for the sacred, it is relevant to consider the psychological processes involved in finding the sacred.

6. Hill et al., "Conceptualizing"; Hill and Pargament, "Advances."
7. Hill and Pargament, "Advances," 4–6.
8. Hill et al., "Conceptualizing."

WHAT MAKES AN EXPERIENCE RELIGIOUS?

One way to think about religion is to conceptualize it as consisting of a specific set of unique qualities, a collection of experiences that is entirely unlike any other kind of human experience, a common core of characteristics that make religion special. This approach sees religion as *sui generis*, a Latin term that means of its own kind or in a class by itself. The elements, characteristics, and components that make up religion (i.e., beliefs, behaviors, emotions, and the like) are unique to religion; they are different in kind from the characteristics (beliefs, behaviors, emotions) that compose any other type of experience. An alternative model to seeing religion as *sui generis* is known as ascription. From this perspective, religious cognitions, behaviors, emotions, and experiences are not fundamentally different from nonreligious cognitions, behaviors, emotions, and experiences. Instead of a particular experience being uniquely religious, a person ascribes the experience as religious or deems it to be religious.[9] The *sui generis* model assumes that there are some experiences (behaviors, emotions, beliefs and so forth) and events that are inherently religious, that there are certain experiences that are always religious, and that these religious experiences can only be compared with other religious experiences and cannot be compared to any nonreligious experience or event. The ascription model, on the other hand, assumes that events, experiences, and the like are not inherently religious or nonreligious; that different things can be considered religious or not religious; and that the basic psychological processes that underlie religious experiences, behaviors, emotions, and such are the same processes that mediate nonreligious experiences and so can be compared.[10] If the ascription model is correct and the *sui generis* approach wrong, then it becomes possible to study religion from the perspective of psychology because the psychological mechanisms that mediate any religious experiences we might have are the same as the psychological mechanisms that mediate all of our experiences, emotions, and behaviors. A psychology of religion not only becomes possible but becomes imperative.

9. Taves, *Religious Experience Reconsidered*, 8–9.
10. Ibid., 18.

PSYCHOLOGY AND RELIGION

Psychologists, however, have not always been interested in religion as a variable that influences human behavior and mental processing. Following the founding of psychology as a separate discipline in the late nineteenth century, a number of psychologists did do research in what we would call today the psychology of religion. Key figures such as G. Stanley Hall and William James were instrumental not only in making the new discipline of psychology into a science, but also in investigating religion's role in the questions psychology asked. James in particular was a proponent of what we would today call the ascription model when he spoke of a common storehouse of human emotions rather than uniquely religious emotions in the quote at the beginning of this chapter. Following Hall and James, psychology tended to ignore religion and its role in human behavior and cognition for much of the twentieth century. The negative views of religion provided by Sigmund Freud and B. F. Skinner no doubt contributed to this neglect. Another factor that influenced the failure of psychology to study religion as a variable is the fact that psychologists, as a group, tend to be nonreligious in their personal lives, with around one-third reporting belief in a personal God.[11]

Despite these trends, psychology "rediscovered" religion in the later part of the twentieth century, and today there are many psychologists, whether or not they are religious themselves, who study religion and its role in human cognition, behavior, and experiences. These psychologist publish their research findings in journals devoted to religion and spirituality studies (e.g., *Psychology of Religion and Spirituality* published by the American Psychological Association) as well as in journals that are open to publications from a variety of psychology areas. For example, research dealing with the psychology of religion has been published in *Psychological Science, Perspectives on Psychological Science, Current Directions in Psychological Science, Personality and Social Psychology Review*, and *Nature*, among many others.

If there is nothing unique about religious experiences, if they are religious because the person having the experience deems them to be, how is it that people make these ascriptions? If religion (and spirituality) involve a search for the sacred, what are the psychological processes that are involved in deciding that something is or is not sacred, that some experience is or

11. Hill et al., "Conceptualizing," 52.

is not religious? One way of thinking about the sacred is to consider the sacred as something set apart from the nonsacred or profane. Ann Taves in her book *Religious Experience Reconsidered* writes about how humans seem to have a need to set all manner of things (events, experiences, places, and objects) apart, and in doing so we make them special. These special things might sometimes be protected by taboos or prohibitions—they might be considered sacred—but there is nothing *sui generis* that makes the special things sacred. The tendency to set things apart in this way is fundamental to being human; it is a natural function of the way our human minds work. The question for psychologists is, therefore, what are the psychological processes involved in "setting things apart"?[12]

Sacred things, from this perspective, represent a subset of all special things. Setting something apart is "a process that people use to designate things that they perceive as nonordinary."[13] These special things can involve a power that is perceived by people as extraordinary. Often this power is attributed to an agent with intentions and directions; in short, an agent with a mind. The psychology of religion becomes, in part, the study of the psychological processes involved in seeing something as special and set apart, perhaps even sacred.

The idea that religious experiences are fundamentally the same psychologically as any other experience means that the methods used by psychologists to investigate human behavior, thoughts, and emotions can be used to study religious experiences as well. This approach opens up the real possibility of a psychology of religion, trying to understand the psychological processes that mediate religious behaviors, emotions, beliefs, and experiences. As I mentioned above, psychologists during much of the twentieth century were not interested in the psychological mechanisms underlying religion, but that has changed dramatically over the past thirty years.

Religion is important for the majority of Americans and is part of what influences the way people behave and think and feel, the kinds of phenomena that psychologists study. Religion influences the moral decisions and judgments people make. For example, Christianity tends to emphasize the importance of thoughts as well as behavior in determining what is moral or sinful behavior. Judaism, on the other hand, is more centrally focused on the behavior itself, not so much on the cognitions that might go along with

12. Taves, *Religious Experience Reconsidered*, 28–48.
13. Taves, "Building Blocks," 144.

the behavior.[14] So, Christians are more likely to believe that lusting after another person (or committing adultery in one's heart as former U.S. president Jimmy Carter admitted in an interview) is a sin, just like the actual behavior of adultery. Jews tend to report that the behavior is more morally wrong that the thought or intention. Religion also influences how we relate to others. Forgiveness is emphasized in many religions, but there are behaviors (e.g., murder) that are unforgiveable in some religions. In addition, priming (exposing the person to ideas or words nonconsciously) thoughts of God increases prosocial behavior, particularly in those individuals who are already proreligious.[15]

How we see or understand ourselves is also affected by religion. Americans tend to have a more individual or independent perspective of the self compared to East Asians, who hold a more interdependent or communal view. Within American religious traditions, Protestants are thought to have a particularly strong independent view of the self, compared to Catholics, for example. This difference in religious tradition influences how Protestants and Catholics tend to interpret the behavior of other people. The fundamental attribution error (or fundamental error) is the tendency to attribute other's behavior to their internal dispositions or traits, not to the social context in which the behavior occurs, and American Protestants make these internal attributions to a greater degree than do American Catholics. This fact suggests a greater internal conceptualization of the self.[16] The work of Cohen and other psychologists suggests that an individual's psychology is greatly affected by that person's religion. If so, psychology should continue, or even increase, the amount of effort expended on studying the influence religion has on psychological phenomena.

MAKING ASCRIPTIONS AND ATTRIBUTIONS

Beginning to understand how a person ascribes or deems one experience to be religious and another experience nonreligious requires a brief discussion of attribution theory. As mentioned above, the fundamental error is when an attribution of the cause of a person's behavior is made to an internal reason rather than an external source. We tend to say that a person acted in a particular way because of something inside the person, ignoring possible

14. Cohen, "Religion's Profound," 78.

15. Shariff et al., "Religious Priming," 27.

16. Cohen, "Religion's Profound," 80.

external reasons why the person might have acted that way. We make these attributions to all manner of events, things, and people in part because doing so provides a kind of control over and meaning to the phenomenon. We like to believe that events have a purpose, that they are not random, and that the events can be controlled.[17] What kind of factors motivate a person to make a religious attribution or ascription for some event? If a religious experience is not *sui generis*, what are the considerations a person makes to lead them to deem the experience a religious one?

One set of factors involved in making ascriptions are situational, the location of the experience (e.g., in a church vs. in a football stadium); whether there are other persons there who might be religious (e.g., clergy); and, if there are other people present, what they are doing (e.g., praying).[18] There are also event factors such as whether the event is important or expected, whether the event is seen as positive or negative, and the nature of the event itself (e.g., is it a political, medical, or entertainment event). Medical events and occurrences that are positive and personally important are more likely to be ascribed as religious.[19] In addition to situational and event factors, qualities of the person such as religious background (or lack thereof), personality dispositions (e.g., locus of control and need for esteem), and cognitive factors (does the person have the necessary language to make a religious ascription) influence the kind of attribution or ascription a person makes as to the religious nature of the experience.[20]

APPLYING PSYCHOLOGY TO UNDERSTANDING RELIGION

What might we learn about religion by investigating the underlying psychological processes? Over the past twenty-five years, the kind of psychology interested in the mental processes of thinking, memory, and decision-making (cognitive psychology) has come to understand that much of how we perceive and think about the world around us is influenced by our bodies.[21] There is an interconnection between the brain and the body and how they control perception and cognition. In return, how we perceive and think

17. Hood et al., *Psychology of Religion*, 44–45.

18. Ibid., 46–47.

19. Ibid., 47–49.

20. Ibid., 49–52.

21. Glenberg et al., "From the Revolution."

about what happens in our environment can change the very brain itself. This interplay of cognition and the body is called embodied cognition, and it contradicts a major perspective on mind and body provided by the dualism of René Descartes, the seventeenth-century philosopher who proposed a clear and definite separation between the material body (including the brain) and the immaterial (and much more important) mind. What embodied cognition illustrates is that this dualistic view of the body/brain and the mind is incorrect.

Examples of how the body affects cognitive and perceptual processes abound. The perception of the size of a softball is altered by how well the player is hitting (the ball looks physically larger to a "hot" batter). Distances appear farther and hills appear steeper if the body is physically fatigued.[22] Imagining (mentalizing) an action, as might occur when you read a book where the main character is running from some kind of threat, produces neural activity in those brain areas involved in running. When imagining some action with one's dominant hand, right-handers will show neural activity in the premotor cortex of the left hemisphere (controlling the right hand), while left-handers will have activity in the right premotor cortex which controls the left hand. Even reading action verbs is sufficient to initiate these neural patterns. Right-handers also tend to associate good things with the right side of the body and bad things with the left. The opposite pattern is seen in left-handers.[23] Thinking about or creating a mental image of your loved one's face generates neural activity in the same brain area (fusiform face area) as looking at a picture of the person's face or looking at the person's actual face.[24] The mental act and the physical act overlap. The thought is embodied in the brain; it is not just the result of mental activity.

Religion can be considered as a kind of cognition (or at least religion has cognitive components). Might the cognitive components of religion be embodied like other cognitive processes seem to be? What is the relationship, if any, between religious cognition and the physicality of the body, including the brain? Chapter 4 will consider the relationship between religious experiences and the brain in greater detail, but for now we will note that the body (including the brain) can be considered the locus of

22. Ibid., 577–78.
23. Casasanto, "Different Bodies," 378–80.
24. O'Craven and Kanwisher, "Mental Imagery."

religiousness—religion is embodied as well as embedded in the environment around us.[25]

Many of us tend to imagine God with human-like characteristics. Even though we might understand intellectually that God is spirit and completely other than us, we still tend to anthropomorphize God, at least a little. Whether it is imagining God as an old man with a white beard when we are children, or thinking about God as a father-like figure, or treating God as a kind of best friend with whom we have a personal relationship, we often let human-like qualities shape how we conceptualize God. To a certain extent this is understandable. We can only really imagine God using the categories that are available to us. The biblical authors used images that meant something to them given their time and geographical place. God was like a mother hen, a rock, a light, and an eagle. Human qualities were also attributed to God by the biblical authors, so God was seen to be like a father, a king, a potter, a groom waiting for his bride, a shepherd, and a nursing mother, to mention just a few. Also, as humans we are made in the image of God, so perhaps being made in God's image influences how we tend to imagine God. While we, again, might intellectually state that the Judeo-Christian God is omnipotent and omniscient, the findings of Barrett indicate that we nevertheless tend to act as if God is limited, like humans are limited, to doing one thing at a time. We have cognitive biases that lead us to think in particular categories, and these biases are influenced, in part, by our physical embodiment.[26]

As mentioned above, when we read about another person performing a particular kind of action (e.g., opening a door or running on a beach), we generally engage in motor simulations of those actions, and we have corresponding activity in the appropriate brain regions that mediate those actions. What might happen when we think about God and God's actions? Do we also simulate those actions? If so, perhaps our thinking and conceptualizing about God is limited by our own embodiment.[27] In addition to simulating the behaviors of others, we also simulate other people's emotions. Mirror neurons are neurons that were initially found in the premotor cortex of monkeys, but are now known to exist in diverse areas of the brain and in a variety of species, including humans (see chapter 6). These neurons become active when a particular response is made by a subject (e.g.,

---

25. Soliman et al., "It's Not."

26. Barrett, "Theological Correctness," 329.

27. Soliman et al., "It's Not," 854.

making a fist), but are also active when the subject sees another individual making the same response.[28] Mirror neurons are thought to be involved in our ability to empathize with others and to take another person's perspective. When we watch a movie or attend a play, we might see one of the characters express happiness or sadness or anger. When we see this display of emotion on the screen or on the stage, we might find ourselves feeling happy, sad, or angry. To the extent that we do share these emotions with the actor, it is in part through the actions of these special neurons and the overlap in neural pathways in the actor and the observer. We might also get a sense of what God might be feeling or thinking. For many individuals, determining God's will (including what God wants for us or how God might feel about our behavior) is of utmost concern. Could a similar process involving mirror neuron circuits give us some insight into God's intent and will?[29]

Other evidence illustrating the role the body plays in religious cognition comes from research which suggests that when we read about God's authoritarian nature or about God's benevolent nature, we become more authoritarian or more cooperative and prosocial ourselves. These results are similar to those in a nonreligious context where people who frown take longer to process positive valence words than words with a negative valence. Smiling people, of course, take longer to process the negative words.[30] Also, priming a person with a God-related word (such as *divine*) produces an upward gaze in the individual's visual field while priming the person with a devil-related word causes the person to shift attention to the lower part of the visual field.[31] Not only is there an upward bias for God-related words; there is a right-side bias for moral and good beliefs for right-handers and a left-side bias for the moral and good in left-handers.[32] We show preferences for products and people on the right side if we are right-handed. We also move objects in the world more easily with our dominant hand, and acting in accord with this ease can lead to judgments of truth and safety. God, too, shows a preference for the right side. In Psalm 48:10 we read that the Lord's right hand is filled with victory, in Isaiah 48:13 God's right hand spreads out the heavens, in Eph 1:20 we read that Jesus sits at the right hand of God

28. Pellegrino et al., "Understanding Motor."

29. Soliman et al., "It's Not," 854.

30. Ibid., 855.

31. Chasteen et al., "Thinking about."

32. Casasanto, "Embodiment."

the Father, and in Matthew 25:33 Gods puts the righteous (the sheep) on the right side and the unrighteous (the goats) on the left.[33]

Our moral judgments are influenced by our physicality in other ways. We have moral intuitions that are grounded in our physical reactions and in our environment. This suggests that our morality is not just the result of an outside code. Brain imaging studies indicate an overlap in the brain pathways and regions mediating physical disgust (e.g., gustatory disgust) and moral disgust. Activating physical disgust (for example, thinking about a dirty toilet) can accentuate the harshness of judgments of moral transgressions, and the act of cleaning (e.g., using hand sanitizer) can ease these moral judgments as well as feelings of guilt in the "cleaner."[34]

Religious rituals often include coordinated behavior such as kneeling, standing, dancing, chanting, or singing among the participants of the ritual. These behaviors are good examples of how we use our physical bodies in the course of worship. Synchronized and coordinated behaviors in a group of people increase the bond among the individuals. When a group of people engage in coordinated or ritual behavior, there is greater trust, cooperation, and social cohesion among those who participate.[35] Subtle imitations of another person (behaving in synchrony with that person) increases positive evaluations of the person. Synchronous behavior also increases memory in the imitator of the person's face and what the person says. So, if I am imitating someone, I am more likely to feel positive about that person and more likely to remember the person's face and what they said. Perhaps religious singing, dancing, or praying in unison can have the same kind of effect, and there is some evidence that such synchrony can promote prosocial behaviors as well.[36] One wonders what kind of effects such coordinated and synchronous ritual behavior might have. Will churches that have more synchronous religious rituals have greater unity? Can religious conflicts be reduced through synchronized interfaith activities?[37] These are questions for future psychologists of religion to address.

A growing body of literature suggests that religious beliefs and practices affect the body and that the body can affect religious beliefs and

---

33. Soliman et al., "It's Not," 856.

34. Ibid., 857.

35. Watson-Jones and Legare, "Social Functions"; Wiltermuth and Health, "Synchrony and Cooperation."

36. Cohen et al., "Religion"; Reddish et al., "Does Synchrony."

37. Soliman et al., "It's Not," 858.

practices. Traditionally, churches have generally required a person interested in joining the church community (in becoming a member of the church) to affirm a specific set of beliefs and act in particular ways before being welcomed into the community. The process might be described as Believing—Behaving—Belonging, where the correct beliefs and behavior must come before the opportunity to belong. We might say that the cognitions (religious cognition in this case) drive the behavior and ultimately the social connectivity with others.

An alternative process emphasizes sociality and behavior driving the cognitions. In this case, belonging to a particular group encourages the individual to act in ways similar to others in the group, which ultimately leads to the adoption of similar beliefs (Belonging—Behaving—Believing). Embodied cognition suggests that the more traditional direction of requiring adoption of a set of propositions and behaving in a certain way before being invited into full membership of the church might not be the only possible path. Perhaps inviting people into the church community (belonging) will have an effect on how they behave and, ultimately, what they believe. The divide between the physical and the mental is closed. Beliefs affect the body, but the body (what we do with it and how we use it to interact socially with others) can affect beliefs as well.

RITUALS

Rituals can be thought of as conventions prescribed by a particular society or culture. While inherited from society and varying from culture to culture, rituals are mediated by underlying psychological processes, preparing humans to engage and respond to these social conventions.[38] Rituals increase coordinated and cooperative group behavior, they ensure commitment to the group and ingroup values, they provide a way of identifying group members, and they serve to increase social coalitions, even among nonkin. Rituals can also help address the so-called free-rider problem in groups. There are always going to be individuals in a group who wish to take advantage of the benefits of group membership (e.g., common defense or sharing in the food provided by the group hunt) but not to take part in any of the responsibilities or costs of group membership (such as providing for the common defense or participating in the hunt). Free riders are problematic because the number of such individuals tends to increase, making

38. Watson-Jones and Legare, "Social Functions," 42.

the group subject to collapse, and eventually threatening the very existence of the group itself. Many people would like to benefit from their group's efforts (e.g., a group project at work or at school) without actually putting in any time or effort on the project. Group rituals can serve to control the free-rider problem because rituals often include costly actions (such as circumcision or affirming a set of beliefs) that serve as hard-to-fake signals of group membership. If a person is willing to take part in these costly actions (pledging to a fraternity for example), then that person is welcomed into the group as a trusted member. Rituals serve many important functions that help to facilitate group (and the individuals that make up the group) survival. For all of these reasons, rituals can be considered adaptive.

Religion and religious ritual, from a general psychological and an evolutionary psychology perspective, serve to improve group living, cooperation, trust, and cohesion. Beliefs in gods or in God, particularly a God or gods that punish people for immoral acts, function, in part, to encourage moral behavior among group members and to discourage free riders. Doctrines or beliefs about the gods or God are important in developing a strong group identity so that members of the group will cooperate and trust one another and will behave prosocially toward each other. (It is important to emphasize that the question of whether God exists is not being considered here; that clearly is not a question that can be answered through psychological science. It is the belief that God exists that serves these functions, and it is the origin of the belief and the function the belief serves for the group that is of interest to psychologists.)

Robert McCauley and Thomas Lawson have studied rituals, including religious rituals, across many cultures and have developed a model to try to describe the pattern, frequency, and form of particular customs.[39] An important component of their approach is the assumption that one of the functions of ritual is to facilitate memory. What is being done or expressed in the ritual act is important and should be remembered. One way to increase memory is to perform the ritual repeatedly. Cognitive psychology supports the suggestion that frequent performance of an event (or act) increases memory for the event. Rituals typically involve collective and coordinated behavior and actions, which tend to increase trust and cooperation among those involved. Rituals that are performed frequently (e.g., communion, weekly worship services, and the like) generally involve little sensory stimulation or emotional arousal, according to McCauley and

---

39. McCauley and Lawson, *Bring Ritual*, 1–37.

Lawson. The relatively high frequency of the ritual itself is sufficient to help ensure that the information being carried in the ritual is remembered.

Other rituals tend to have a higher level of sensory stimulation and emotional arousal. These rituals are typically performed on rare occasions or only once in a person's life and often mark the act of a divine person or entity directed to a specific human being. In these rituals, the sensory stimulation and high levels of emotion serve to facilitate memory of the crucial event. The high emotional content and sensory stimulation is particularly noteworthy in the individuals on whom the divine person is acting. For example, ordination into the priesthood or ministry, baptism, marriages, and initiation into adulthood generally involve higher levels of emotion and sensory stimulation than more frequently occurring rituals. The participants in these rituals might wear distinctive clothing (worn only on that occasion), unique decorations or food are provided, and special words said or vows made. Research on flashbulb and firsthand memories in cognitive psychology investigates the ease with which highly personal and distinct emotional experiences can be remembered by the individual.[40] To the extent that infrequent rituals are remembered by the participant, it might be because the high level of emotion can serve as a type of "somatic marker" giving information to the person as to the importance of the event.

THE DIVERSITY AND COMMONALITY
OF RELIGIOUS BELIEF

A tremendous amount of diversity in biological life exists on earth. Underlying this vast biodiversity are fundamental biological regularities that serve to drive the variability. In a similar way, there are psychological regularities that underlie the diversity in religious beliefs across cultures. Certain practices, beliefs and traditions survive, they have "psychological sticking power," while others do not.[41]

Most of the research in the psychology of religion has been conducted using participants that are WEIRD—Western, Educated, Industrialized, Rich, and Democratic. Over the past twenty years or so, more research has investigated psychological and religious phenomena using other demographics. Such cross-cultural research illustrates the degree of diversity among religions (theodiversity), calls into question the notion that religion

40. Hirst and Phelps, "Flashbulb Memories."
41. Norenzayan, "Theodiversity," 467–68.

is *sui generis*, and supports the ascription account advocated in this chapter. This cross-cultural research, however, also suggests some principles that underlie the variability in religion and religious experience. What are the psychological processes that all humans possess that influence whether or not a particular experience is deemed religious?

To believe in a deity, a person must be able to form mental representations of agents, particularly supernatural agents, and related rituals and practices. The person must also be committed to the belief that these supernatural agents are real and that the agents and related rituals provide an important source of meaning, comfort, and control in the person's life. Finally, specific cultural information must be available to and accepted by the person, leading the individual to believe that some of these deities should be believed in and committed to more than others. The cognitive processes required for this kind of belief are part of our intuitive cognition. For example, human minds intuitively or naturally believe in mind-body dualism (which can lead to beliefs in disembodied agents), teleology (leading to belief in creation with a purpose), and in essentialism (which leads to belief that one kind of thing cannot become another kind of thing, precluding evolution).[42] Such natural beliefs suggest that children are intuitive theists, believing in a supernatural, disembodied, creator God. While such beliefs are intuitive in the human mind, the exact expression of the beliefs do vary cross-culturally. Nevertheless, the diversity of beliefs (at least on the surface) might mask more fundamental psychological processes at work, processes that are part of our mind's natural or Type 1 cognition (see chapter 3 for a discussion of Type 1 and Type 2 cognition). It is the case that the vast majority of humanity adheres to a few religious traditions—the major world religions—perhaps reflecting these underlying intuitive cognitive processes.[43]

We are also motivated to find meaning and purpose in the events that happen to us. For many, religion provides a coherent meaning system, especially when we are threatened with loss of control, predictability, social connection with others, and death. The human mind makes meaning of and evaluates events in the environment, and this meaning making can be done either consciously or nonconsciously, providing coherence, control, identity, reduction of uncertainty, and behavioral guidance.[44] Re-

42. Ibid., 469–70.
43. Ibid., 468.
44. Paloutzian and Park, "Recent Progress," 11–12.

ligion is a common basis for meaning making, as is science, because it is comprehensive covering a lot of different concerns, issues, and goals. These religious beliefs, to the extent they are salient and readily available to the individual, can be used to make attributions or ascriptions of experiences. They can be used as a type of schema to help a person decide whether a particular experience or event is religious or nonreligious.[45]

Part of the diversity in religious belief is the presence of atheism. If belief in a deity is a product of the human mind's natural cognitive processes, then what is the origin of lack of theistic belief? Some have argued that atheism arises only under certain conditions, conditions that are atypical throughout the course of human history. If belief in gods or in God arises out of the natural and intuitive processes of the mind, then those processes exist because they have facilitated human survival.

We will discuss evolutionary psychology in greater detail in chapter 2, but a basic premise of this relatively new perspective on psychology is that the human mind operates the way it does today because it has been shaped though a million-plus years of human evolution to deal with certain kinds of environmental problems. As it pertains to intuitive religious beliefs, the idea is that finding meaning and purpose to events was selected for; those individuals who had minds that found pattern and meaning in environmental events survived to reproduce at greater levels than those individuals who did not have minds that functioned in that way. Also, those individuals whose minds tended to naturally look for agents as causes of events that occurred in the environment and to attribute mental processes (e.g., theory of mind) to those agents were more likely to survive and pass their genes on to the next generation (including those genes involved in the shaping of how the mind works). Eventually, certain cognitive and perceptual processes became intuitive to how the mind works. These mental processes became the default processes for human minds, and some of these default processes are utilized for religious purposes. Our ability to detect agency was generalized to the detection of supernatural agents. Our tendency to intuit that other individuals have minds (including detected agents, natural and supernatural) was utilized for religious purposes as well. The mind, including the natural tendency to find supernatural agents and to attribute mind (intentions, desires, and so forth) to those agents, works the way it does because the mind has evolved over the millennia within environments

45. Park, "Religion and Meaning," 357–65.

that fostered that kind of cognition and those mental processes. Theism became natural.

If theism is natural, then it is atheism that needs to be explained because it seems to be contrary to the way the human mind operates. It has been suggested that atheism only develops in environments that are quite different from the ones humans have inhabited for the previous million-plus years. In foraging societies, which were typical for early humans, cooperation among the individuals making up a small group of hunters and gatherers was fairly easy to maintain. Food sharing, caring for children, defense, and other vital concerns were met through local moral norms. The scope of religion's moral involvement was minimal, and the gods of these foraging societies tended to be small, distant, and limited in knowledge and moral concern.[46]

As groups became larger and agriculture began to replace hunting and gathering, state-level societies became more prevalent. Greater individual anonymity was possible within the larger group because it became harder to keep track of all group members. For these larger groups, larger gods were required, gods that were more involved in moral concerns because the older norms, those norms that tended to control behavior in the smaller groups where anonymity was difficult or impossible, were no longer adequate. The demands of this kind of state-level society still required group cooperation, trust, and cohesion. Gods became more powerful, all-knowing, very concerned with moral issues, and more interested in punishment for moral failures because it was important for the good of the group for members to cooperate and trust each other, a development that furthered the spread of sociality among human communities.[47]

In both the smaller and larger societies, the human mind's evolved capabilities provided a natural or intuitive belief in supernatural agents (theism) that had minds and were interested, to a lesser or greater extent depending on the size of the society, in the moral behavior of the group members. One way to understand the rise of atheism today is to consider that we no longer live in foraging or even agricultural societies as the vast majority of our human ancestors did. Many people in the world today live in highly industrialized, educated, and urban societies (WEIRD) where the day-to-day concerns of getting along with other members of our group in order to survive are not quite so pressing. People in these societies are

---

46. Norenzayan, "Theodiversity," 473.
47. Purzycki et al., "Moralistic Gods."

privileged compared to many people in the less industrialized and educated parts of the world. They do not have to worry as much about the necessities of daily life, such as clean water, adequate food, safety from threats, and so forth. Most people in these modern industrialized societies are exposed to a variety of opinions and have an abundance of free time to contemplate these diverse ideas. In this new environment in human history, the pressing concerns that shaped the human mind and the way it works in the past no longer seem to apply. The natural beliefs that emerge from the evolved mind might no longer be seen as necessary. Other beliefs can be considered, beliefs that, perhaps, are contrary to the way the human mind naturally works.[48] Unnatural ways of thinking are now possible, ways of thinking that require nonnatural processes that are not intuitive or automatic and that require effort. An example of a nonnatural way of thinking is science (as compared to natural religion), which requires an entirely different way of using the mind and its faculties. To say that science represents an unnatural way that the mind works is not to say that it is wrong. It simply means that it is contrary to the intuitive and automatic thinking that emerges out of the more natural way that the mind interacts with the environment.[49]

RESEARCH METHODS IN PSYCHOLOGY AND THE PSYCHOLOGY OF RELIGION

If religion and religious experiences are grounded in the same kind of psychological mechanisms that underlie all of our experiences, then the methods of psychological science should be applicable to the study of religious thoughts, feelings, and behaviors. Psychology uses scientific methods to investigate its subject matter, human behavior and mental processes. When psychology was founded in the late nineteenth century, physics and physiology were the disciplines that were making a lot of advances in knowledge, so psychology tried to be like those natural sciences in its methodology. Psychology, however, is different from many sciences in that what psychologists are interested in measuring is often not readily observable. Researchers in psychology might be interested in studying personality, attitude, intelligence, gender, memory, anxiety, or beliefs, including religious beliefs. The difficulty is that these constructs are not publicly observable. In other words, my attitudes are not necessarily observable by another person. The

48. Barrett, *Why Would*, 115–18.
49. McCauley, *Why Religion*, 83–143.

same is true for my personality or my beliefs. While a physiologists might be able to directly determine the speed at which a neural impulse travels down an axon or measure the amount of neurotransmitter released at the synapse, psychologists have to find indirect ways to measure much of what interests them. (I do not mean to suggest these physiological measurements would not require a lot of work, just that what the physiologist is trying to measure is available for anyone with the right equipment to see.)

When doing research, psychologists typically try to determine the relationship between two or more variables. A variable is anything that has a quantity or quality that can vary. Anxiety, gender, attitude, and belief are all variables in that each can change in value: more or less anxiety, male or female gender, positive or negative attitude, and so forth. So, for example, a psychologist might want to know how gender is related to religious belief. Do males or females tend to have more religious belief? Other times, researchers might be interested in determining a more causal connection between variables. In order to establish a causal relationship between variables, the researcher needs to manipulate the values of one variable and measure the effects of that manipulation on the second variable. The variable that is selected to be manipulated is called the independent variable and the measured variable is called the dependent variable. (The value of the measured variable is said to depend upon the independent variable.) As a psychologist, one might be interested in assessing the causal relationship between being watched and good behavior. The independent variable is being watched, the dependent variable is good behavior. The manipulation might include a group of people who believe they are being watched and a second group of individuals who believe they are alone. The dependent variable, what is being measured, is good behavior. We might expect those individuals who are being watched to engage in more good behavior than those who are not being watched. By observing the behavior of the participants in the study, we would be able to answer that question.

As I mentioned above, a problem in psychology is that what we want to manipulate or measure often cannot be manipulated or measured directly. If religious belief is our dependent variable, for example, how do we measure that? How do we measure anxiety or memory or learning or intelligence or any number of variables that interest psychologists? How do we know if we are observing learning or intelligence or religious belief? We have to define what we mean by these constructs, and psychologists define constructs like these behaviorally. Intelligence is defined by deciding, for the purposes of the study, what behaviors are intelligent and what behaviors are not. On such a measure of intelligence, intelligent behavior might be knowing vocabulary words or performing well on mathematical reasoning questions. Definitions where constructs like intelligence, personality, or learning, for instance, are described according to behavior are called operational definitions. Psychologists use these operational definitions to specify exactly how they are going to measure the dependent variable, as well as exactly how they are going to manipulate the independent variable.

Because psychology is interested in measuring variables such as intelligence, personality, memory, self-esteem, and other such nonpublic constructs, it is necessary for researchers to demonstrate that the construct they think is being measured (e.g., religious orientation) is actually being measured. This is the important methodological principle of validity: Are you as the researcher measuring what you claim to be measuring? If I claim that the questionnaire I administered to the participants in my study is measuring religious orientation, the questionnaire cannot be measuring something else instead (either intentionally or more likely by mistake). Fortunately, there are statistical procedures that can be employed to support the researcher's claim that the questionnaire or survey being used is valid, measuring what it is supposed to be measuring.

The measurement of the dependent variable must also be reliable, meaning that it needs to yield consistent data or values. If the survey I am using to assess religiosity is reliable, then the scores on the religiosity survey must be similar every time I administer it to a particular individual. The survey must indicate that a person has a particular level of religiosity (within a given amount of deviation) each time the individual takes the survey. As is the case with validity, there are statistical procedures to determine the reliability of questionnaires and surveys.

When it comes to measuring religiosity, there are dozens of ways that can and have been used. From assessing church attendance, frequency of prayer and reading Scripture, to using sophisticated neural imaging techniques (see chapter 4), psychologists are open to a variety of ways to measure religious experience (emotions, beliefs, behaviors, and the like). In most cases, psychologist use self-report measures of religiosity where the person whose religiosity is being measured completes a questionnaire or survey. There are dozens of different kinds of questionnaires that a psychologist can use depending on if the researcher is interested in measuring religious beliefs, practices, attitudes, orientation, development, commitment, involvement, values, coping, mysticism, fundamentalism, forgiveness, or views of death and the afterlife. Peter Hill and Ralph Hood, two psychologists who have been measuring and studying the psychology of religion for many years, collected over 100 of these surveys and questionnaires, along with measures of validity and reliability for each one, in *Measures of Religiosity*.[50]

Much of the information about the psychology of religion covered in this book comes from research using the questionnaires provided in *Measures* or from techniques and approaches adopted from other areas of psychology, such as cognitive, physiological, and social psychology. The point is that, if the underlying psychological processes involved in mediating religious experiences (behavior, emotion, and belief) are similar to or the same as the psychological processes underlying nonreligious experiences, then the same kind of scientific methods that most psychologists use to investigate nonreligious experiences can be applied to the study of religious experiences as well. That is exactly what psychologists have been doing, at a growing pace, for the past forty years, and it is some of the findings from this research on the psychology of religion that is discussed in the chapters that follow.

50. Hill and Hood, *Measures of Religiosity*.

2

Evolution of Religion
Is God Finally Dead?

God is dead. God remains dead. And we have killed him.[1]

Grounds for dismissing the existence of God (or gods) must be stronger
than observing that God's existence cannot be scientifically proven or
disproven or that many of the phenomena explained by appealing to God in
the past now may be "explained" scientifically. Such criteria for dismissing
belief would destroy many core beliefs along with belief in God.[2]

The death of God has been proclaimed or predicted for many decades.
Part of the reason, it is thought, belief in God will fade away is that
science increasingly shows us that the functions of such a supernatural being (e.g., creation) can be explained using natural causes. As knowledge
of how the universe works increases, including the understanding of human behavior, we will no longer resort to wishful thinking and fairy-tale
beliefs that postulate an all-powerful divine being who rewards the good
and punishes the bad. No longer will we need to believe in an afterlife, in
some otherworldly realm where all our earthly concerns will be no more.

1. Nietzsche, *Gay Science*, section 125, 119–20.
2. Barrett, *Why Would*, 122–23.

No longer will we believe that God (or gods) control the events of this life from the weather to whom we will marry to whether we arrive home safely following a trip in a car or airplane.

These predictions about the upcoming death of God (and the corresponding decline of religion) have been made, at least, since the nineteenth century. Over the past ten years, however, empirical data suggest that, indeed, there is a noticeable change in religious beliefs and practices, and this change is not limited to Europe (where the decline in religiosity has been developing over a number of years) but is occurring in the United States as well. Several recent surveys of the religious environment in America involving tens of thousands of adults indicate a significant change in religiosity.[3] The most important and reported finding is an increase in the percentage of the adult population in the United States who indicate that they are either atheists or agnostics, or have no particular religion. These individuals make up a group generally referred to as the "nones" because of their lack of identification with any religious tradition. The percentage of the U.S. adult population that identifies as "none" has risen over the past five years from 15 percent to 20 percent (6 percent identify as atheists and 14 percent report no particular religion). The Christian share of the U.S. population is on the decline, but almost all religious traditions and all regions of the country are affected by the decline. The decline in religiosity is seen in both men and women; in whites, blacks, and Latinos; and in those with college degrees as well as those with high school diplomas. Decline is also occurring in all age groups but is particularly noteworthy in young adults and is driven by generational replacement of the older generation with the younger. Approximately 36 percent young millennials (adults between eighteen and twenty-four), 34 percent of older millennials (between twenty-five and thirty-three years of age), and about 25 percent of Generation Xers report that they are religiously unaffiliated while 15 percent of fifty to sixty-four-year-olds are unaffiliated.[4] Specific religious traditions report declines as well. Since 2007 there has been a 14.7 percent decline among mainstream Protestants, a 3.1 percent decline among Catholics, and a small 0.9 percent decline reported among evangelical Protestants, which

---

3. Pew Research Center, "America's Changing"; Pew Research Center, "Nones"; Pew Research Center, "U.S. Public."

4. Pew Research Center, "America's Changing."; Pew Research Center, "Nones."

is relatively stable due primarily to the significant growth in nondenominational congregations over the last few years.[5]

Most of these surveys are of American adults. Other industrialized countries in Europe are less religious than the United States (where about 80 percent of Americans say they believe in God). In fact, the continued high belief in God in the U.S. has been cited as a counterexample to the secularization thesis, which proposes that modernization within a country leads to decreases in religiosity and increases in secular views. The United States, however, does not seem to be a counterexample, as these recent surveys suggest, and the decline reported in these surveys has, some argue, been occurring for many decades in America. While the decline in religiosity has been slow (and perhaps masked as a result), it is nevertheless present and is due to the same generational patterns that are found in secularized European countries—each successive generational cohort is less religious that the previous one.[6]

These surveys definitely show declines in various measures of religiosity, and they also clearly indicate that one in five American adults report no affiliation with any religious tradition. Nevertheless, most of these "nones" still say they believe in God (68 percent), and most describe themselves as religious and/or spiritual. While they definitely attend church infrequently (or never) and may not practice their faith as their parents and grandparents did, religious faith is still important for many of them. More than half feel a deep connection with nature, and 21 percent report praying every day.[7] It is also important to recognize that these surveys and the declines in religiosity reported in Europe are questioning people about their religiosity who live in WEIRD (Western, Educated, Industrialized, Rich, Democratic) countries. People who live in less industrialized or rich countries, or who live in non-Western parts of the world, are seldom included in these kinds of surveys. Religious beliefs in many of these non-WEIRD countries is not on the decline. In fact, Christianity (and other religions as well) is growing in much of South America, Africa, and Asia.

What are we to make of the death of God argument? Will humans eventually lose their religious beliefs as they become more modern, industrialized, democratic, and rich? Are people changing their religious practices and no longer affiliating with traditional religious institutions because

5. Pew Research Center, "America's Changing."
6. Voas and Chaves, "Is the Unites States," 1548.
7. Pew Research Center, "Nones."

they no longer believe in God? While the surveys in WEIRD parts of the world might suggest this, the fact that many of the "nones" still believe in God and that religion seems strong and growing in many parts of the world suggests that God, and even religion, is not dead. Research in a variety of areas, including biology, psychology, neuroscience, and cognitive science, also suggests that religion and God (or god) beliefs are unlikely to go away because they serve an important survival function for human beings. The present chapter (along with chapters 3 and 4) reviews some of this literature indicating that there are biological, neurological, psychological, and cognitive mechanisms that support religious belief. In particular, this chapter will discuss the role an evolutionary perspective can provide to the understanding of religion, and how this evolutionary perspective can intersect with the understanding of religion/spirituality provided by psychology. This evolutionary account considers the fundamental role religion seems to play in helping to create and maintain human social connections and groups. With such close ties to our biological and psychological nature, religion/spirituality is unlikely to "go away."

EVOLUTIONARY THEORY AND EVOLUTIONARY PSYCHOLOGY

Many theories of evolution (change) have been proposed over the years, but the theory developed by Charles Darwin in 1859 is the one that is widely accepted today as the best explanation for the diversity of life forms we find on our planet. The central features of Darwin's theory of evolution are variation, heritability, and selection. Risking gross oversimplification, we might begin to understand how evolution occurs by noting that physical traits of individual organisms are determined, at least in part, by genes. (Genes and environment interact in determining many of an individual's traits.) Height, weight, skin color, speed, and wing length are just some of the physical traits a particular individual of a species has that are influenced by that individual's genes. This genetic information comes from the individual's parents, half from the father and half from the mother. When the genetic code for these traits is passed to the offspring, mutations can occur; that is to say, some of the genetic information is not perfectly passed on from the father or mother to the offspring. Many times these mutations are neutral, and there is no noticeable positive or negative effect on the offspring. Sometimes, however, the mutation can result in a change in some physical trait in the offspring (e.g., a larger than normal beak in a finch) that proves to be either beneficial or detrimental to the offspring as it competes with other members of the species. If the larger beak size results in the finch getting access to less food than finches with the standard-size beak, then that finch will be less likely to survive and reproduce. The genetic code for the larger beak will be lost in the population because the variation of the larger beak was maladaptive; it resulted in lower survival rates and diminished opportunity to reproduce. If, however, a larger than normal beak results in the finch gaining access to more food than the finches with smaller beaks, then that individual finch will be more likely to survive to mate and pass its genetic information on to its offspring. Included in that genetic information will be the genetic code for the larger-than-normal beak. Over enough generations, finches with the genetic variation for the larger beak will come to predominate in the overall population of finches in that area, and the larger beak will be the new normal beak size.

Overpopulation spurs competition (of finches, for example), and those finches with physical traits that provide an advantage for survival (finding food or avoiding predators, for instance) will be more likely to reproduce and to pass these traits to their offspring. The variation in physical traits is inherited from one generation to the next. "Natural selection" is the term Darwin gave to the mechanism whereby nature "selects" which traits will be passed on. In a similar way that speed is selected for by thoroughbred breeders or coat color is selected for by breeders of certain species of dogs, nature "selects" physical traits through mutation, variation, heritability, and competition.[8] Adaptation is defined in terms of differences in survival and reproduction within a population, in that a trait that facilitates survival and reproduction is said to be adaptive.

The traits that we think about when considering natural selection and the theory of evolution are typically physiological or anatomical: eye color, the length of a giraffe's neck, the speed of a gazelle, or the strength of a lion's jaw. Traits subject to variation and natural selection can also be behavioral, however. There are variations in the behavior of individual organisms within a population. Many of these behavioral variations are neutral as to the survival of the individual, but some can be beneficial or detrimental. Additionally, psychological or mental traits, if they affect behavior, which they generally do, can be subject to the mechanisms of evolutionary change. This position is basic to the approach to psychology known as evolutionary

8. Gould, *Structure*, 13–24.

psychology, which brings the fundamental principles of evolutionary theory to the understanding of human behavior and mental processing. Just as the physical trait of beak size can be seen as a "solution" to the problem of obtaining food for finches, psychological mechanisms can be understood to be solutions to particular survival problems our human ancestors faced in the evolutionary past. Our preferences for specific foods (e.g., salt) or our aversion to heights can be understood as adaptations in that our human ancestors with such preferences or aversions were likely to eat more (rare at the time) food with the necessary level of sodium to support life and to avoid situations that are dangerous. Both of these psychological mechanisms (preferences and aversions) are, according to evolutionary psychology, adaptations that increased the chances of survival of the individual, who then passed on the genes for those traits to their offspring.

While there is no controversy regarding the importance of evolutionary theory in understanding the diversity of species, there is some debate as to how evolutionary changes occur, i.e., how much weight to give to the various mechanisms and at what level natural selection and adaptation occur. For many years, most evolutionary theorists argued that natural selection occurs only at the level of the gene or at the level of the individual. More recently, however, the proposal that adaptation occurs at multiple levels has gained acceptance. Multilevel selection argues that natural selection and adaptation occur at the level of the gene, the individual, and the group. It is this group-level selection that was very controversial thirty years ago but is broadly accepted today.[9] The acceptance of group-level selection opens up the possibility of considering social behaviors and social psychological mechanisms as adaptations that promote human survival and success.

There are differences in populations of groups. For example, differences exist in the warning cries of flocks of birds and in standards of morality in tribes of humans. An evolutionary psychological approach suggests that these differences between groups can result in survival and reproduction variations between different groups. Those flocks of birds with more effective warning cries are more likely to survive (and reproduce to pass on the genes that code for those warning cries) than are flocks of birds that have less effective warning cries. Those tribes of humans with more effective standards of morality (i.e., standards that result in greater success for the group) are more likely to survive, and the individuals that make up

9. Wilson, *Darwin's Cathedral*, 7–25.

those groups are more likely to pass on the genetic code for the behaviors and psychological mechanisms that make up those standards of morality.[10]

What standards of morality might result in greater success? Humans are a social species. We evolved living in hunter-gathering groups. These groups (compared to individuals living alone) were more successful at finding food as well as at avoiding dangers derived from predation. These small, hunter-gatherer groups were communities that needed to get along, to cooperate, to be cohesive, and to trust one another. Those standards of conduct or morality that facilitated trust, cooperation, and cohesion let to greater group success compared to groups that lacked the standards that led to cohesion, trust, and cooperation. Over time, because the groups that were cooperative and trusting survived at a higher rate than the groups that were not, these traits were passed on to the subsequent generations and eventually became a natural part of the human condition. As a result, humans have a kind of intuitive morality that guides us in our interactions with others and encourages us to get along with the other members of our particular group. This intuitive psychology is the result of psychological mechanisms that evolved to foster group living. (Of course, it is the individuals with the traits that are reproducing and passing on the genetic information to their offspring. But it is at the level of the group where the adaptation is taking place.)[11]

From an evolutionary psychology point of view, religion has important functions in keeping groups of individual humans united, cohesive, cooperative, and trusting. Studying religion from this evolutionary standpoint need not mean that religion is nothing but the product of the evolutionary mechanisms of variation, heritability, and natural selection. Considering religion from this perspective does, however, open up additional avenues of understanding the function of religion and why religion seems to be universal. It also suggests mechanisms whereby a biology (as well as a psychology) of religion might be expected. If religion is like other experiences, behaviors, and emotions, and if we can study religion using the methodologies of psychological science (see chapter 1), then perhaps we can study religion from an evolutionary perspective, as we can other behavioral, psychological, social, and cultural practices. For religion (experiences, emotions) to be understood from an evolutionary psychology

10. Example found in Ibid., 8.

11. Ibid., 20–28.

perspective, it needs to have an effect on behaviors that, in turn, influence survival and reproduction.[12]

EVOLUTIONARY PERSPECTIVES ON RELIGION

Many of the beliefs and rituals that make up religion seem difficult to understand from an evolutionary perspective. What possible adaptive advantage does belief in a supernatural being who is concerned with the day-to-day activities of millions of people have? How would celibacy, tithing, giving up certain foods or drinks, or wearing particular clothes be selected for through the mechanisms of evolution? Why would such practices and beliefs develop? How can we make sense of them? For some people, it is enough that God tells us to do these things or that the Bible (or some other sacred book) says that we should believe certain things and act in specific ways. Setting aside issues of scriptural interpretation and how we decide what a passage in the text actually means, for a psychologist, it is not enough to appeal to scripture. There must be a functional reason for religious practices and beliefs, especially when some of the beliefs seem counterfactual (God knows everything I think or do) or the practices do not obviously benefit us personally (giving 10 percent of my money to a church). An evolutionary approach tries to explain these religious beliefs and practices through appeal to the evolutionary principles identified above.[13]

Evolutionary theory and evolutionary psychology emphasize the adaptability of physical, behavioral, and psychological traits. What about religion? According to multilevel selection theory, religion might be adaptive at the level of the individual, at the level of the group, or at both levels. It might also be the case that religion is not adaptive per se, but is a by-product of cognitive and psychological mechanisms that are adaptive. For example, this approach maintains that the religious ritual of circumcision is not adaptive in and of itself, but the practice of engaging in painful and costly behaviors to identify yourself as a member of a group is adaptive. The religious practice of circumcision is utilizing a mechanism that has been selected for a nonreligious function, but the specific ritual itself is not adaptive. The adaptation and by-product accounts of religion are widely held among those who are interested in the evolution of religion. Finally, religious beliefs and practices might be maladaptive; they are wasteful

12. Ibid., 226.
13. Atran, *In Gods*, 3–18.

and false and either serve no adaptive function at all or are, perhaps, even harmful to the individual.[14]

For a trait (e.g., a cognitive trait such as a belief) to be adaptive, it must first be universal across cultures. Also, the trait must be easily acquired. Finally, the trait in question must be supported and mediated by biological systems. Such a biological system would include brain structures, neurochemistry, and even a genetic component (heritability). Religion satisfies each of these requirements. Religion (expressed in different ways) is universal, it is found early in human development (see chapter 3), and there is a clear biological system that supports and mediates it (see chapter 4), providing support for the suggestion that religion is, in fact, adaptive or is a by-product of adaptive cognitive and psychological mechanisms.[15]

If religion is an adaptation or a by-product, it does not necessarily follow that it must be always be good for us or always result in personal flourishing. There can be negative side effects to an adaptation. (Consider our preferences for salty foods. The preference is an obvious adaptation in an environment where salt is in short supply, but in today's environment, where sodium is readily available, consuming too much salt results in physical problems such as high blood pressure.) This example illustrates another important idea that a trait might have evolved because it was adaptive in the past, even if it is not clearly adaptive now. Nevertheless, seeing religion as an adaptation or as a by-product does mean that there are advantages to religion that result in increased survival for the individual or group. What, from an evolutionary perspective, might those advantages be?

The evolutionary perspective on religion tends to focus on the social benefits religion has on the group. Humans are a highly social species. We cannot survive on our own, we need to form collaborations and to cooperate with others to survive. These social motives are what drive much of the understanding of the evolution of religion. Johnson and colleagues point out that these social motives serve to protect the individual from nature and other humans, help avoid diseases, help care for offspring, provide social status to the individual, assist in mate acquisition and retention, and help in the formation of coalitions.[16] Even though there are many social and individual variations in how religion is practiced, these motives help to organize these variations and provide a way of understanding the role

14. Ruse, "Biologically," 44–48.
15. Harris and McNamara, "Is Religiousness."
16. Johnson et al., "Fundamental," 197.

religion plays in a group and how religion might be an adaptation for group survival and for the survival of individuals that make up the group.

Consider, for example, disease avoidance. Religious rituals centering on burial, washing, and healing serve to promote health through avoidance of contamination. So too would practices centered on religious exclusivity (keeping outsiders away who might carry diseases to which the local group is not immune) and food taboos and laws dealing with food purity and preparation. Religious practices such as fertility rituals, marriage rituals, community structure (monogamy or polygamy), and moral codes (pre-marital abstinence and mating restrictions) are all variations that serve the social motive of mate acquisition and retention. Religious rituals such as circumcision, baptism, and initiations can be seen as cultural variations in the social motive of care for offspring and other kin.[17]

It is important to remember that just because something (a belief, for example) can be understood, even partially, using natural mechanisms does not mean the belief is necessarily false. Many psychologists of religion are interested in where beliefs come from, what is their origin. Understanding the origin of a belief says nothing about whether the belief is true or false. In the present context, there may or may not be a God, but why have so many people across all cultures and across all of human history believed (and still believe) that there is? What is the origin of that belief? If we developed an understanding of the origin of the belief that 2 x 2 is 4 and knew where in the brain this belief was located and how the neural circuits that represent that belief work, the truth of the belief would remain. Developing an understanding of a particular religious belief (or other aspects of religion) with similar detail would not mean that the belief was untrue. Including an evolutionary account of the origin of religious beliefs and practices also does not mean that the beliefs and practices are not true. Psychologists of religion are interested in developing such an understanding. In the process, some of these psychologists will themselves believe in the truth of the belief, others will not. Those are personal decisions made for a variety of reasons (many of which psychology can begin to explain), but they are independent of the mechanisms that give rise to the belief itself. It is the mechanism that psychology is interested in understanding and explaining.

17. Ibid., 199–200.

BIG GODS AND PUNISHMENT

Human beings are a very social species. We need others to survive. Early humans formed hunter-gatherer groups to make finding food easier and to help provide for mutual protection. These hunter-gatherer groups tended to be small in size, but even in these relatively small groups, cohesion and cooperation were important. Social cognition refers to the mental processes that enable and facilitate social interactions. Getting along with other people around us requires certain psychological skills or mental tools (e.g., theory of mind), and these abilities are mediated by brain areas in the frontal lobe. Nonhuman primates are also, to varying degrees, social and live in groups, and a positive correlation exists between the volume of the neocortex (the most recently evolved area of the brain that covers most of the surface of the cerebral hemispheres) in primates and the size of the social group.[18] The need to keep these social group bonds cohesive is met through psychological processes mediated in the neocortex. The larger the social group, the larger the neocortex needs to be. If the group becomes too large, it will lose its cohesiveness, and the bonds of the group will fail.

Part of the reason groups remain cohesive is that each person in the group is accountable to the other members. If one person in the group does a favor for another, it is understood that some kind of reciprocity will occur in the future. In addition, it is difficult to hide one's behavior in a small group. As a result, individuals tend to behave in accordance to group norms, the normative behavior that is thought to be necessary to keep the group together. Behavior that breaks the norms of the group is readily visible in a small group. Individuals who want to "do their own thing" cannot hide. Free riders, those who want to take advantage of group membership but do not want to behave in accordance to group norms, are easily identified. If the group becomes too large, however, it becomes increasingly difficult to keep track of the behavior of the individual members of the group, and free riders become a problem that can threaten the cohesiveness of the group itself. For humans, the optimal size of the social group is around 150 (known as Dunbar's number). Given the size of our neocortex, this represents the number of people that we can reasonably "keep track of" to maintain group cohesiveness, and the number of people from whom one could expect reciprocity.[19]

18. Dunbar, "Social Brain," 169.
19. Ibid., 172.

Obviously, humans no longer live in hunter-gatherer groups (although a few such people groups remain). The agricultural revolution about twelve thousand years ago led to bigger and bigger societies (tribes and nations). How can humans live in such large groups, given the size of our neocortex, and keep the groups cohesive and cooperative? The problem of free riders becomes especially crucial in such large groups. How can individual behavior be monitored to ensure that it follows the norms of the group, norms established to keep the members of the group cooperative and trusting of one another? One obvious way to deal with free riders is to exercise punishment for behavior that falls outside of what is acceptable by the group. Punishment can stabilize groups and keep individual behavior consistent with group expectations. There are, however, costs associated with punishment. Most people do not like to be the punisher. Imagine that you are taking an exam in college and notice another student cheating on the exam. This behavior is clearly contrary to group expectations. The student cheating is a free rider and is getting an unfair advantage over the other students who are following the rules of the group. Reporting the student to the professor, however, is not an easy task. Many students will ignore the cheating because they do not want to get involved. Some professors will also ignore cheating they observe in their own classrooms because the process of confronting the student and going through a potential academic integrity hearing is too much work, particularly at the end of the academic year when both students and professors just want the semester to end and summer break to begin. Punishing free riders involves a cost that many people do not want to pay. If there is no punishment, however, the number of free riders tends to increase. If no one gets punished for cheating on an exam or plagiarizing a paper, then more and more cheating and plagiarizing will occur.

One option is to outsource the punishment to a third party. Police forces are good examples of outsourcing punishment. As a citizen of my community, I do not have to personally confront norm violators (lawbreakers), I can rely on the police to do it for me. Without modern police forces, however, how did the early agricultural societies handle punishment of individuals who violated group norms and threatened the very existence of the group? There were no doubt police-like groups in these early societies who served as punishers or "keepers of the peace." But these early police-like groups, as is the case for modern police forces, could not be everywhere and could not monitor every person's behavior all the time. Some other mechanism was needed to keep track of individual behavior and to make sure that violators of group norms would be punished. Without such a mechanism, group cohesiveness is threatened and so too are the individuals that make up the group. Cohesive, cooperative, and trusting groups are more likely to survive than those that lack these traits.

According to psychologist Ara Norenzayan, a solution to this problem of behavior monitoring and punishment was the introduction of supernatural punishment, deities that will do the monitoring and punishment. Studies of contemporary hunter-gatherer societies (there are still some left), as well as what anthropologists have discovered about these kinds of societies that existed in the past, suggest that these small groups tend to have deities that are not particularly interested in moral issues. These groups tend to be more closely related genetically and are small enough that they can keep track of the behavior of the individuals in the group; social transgressions are difficult to hide.[20] As societies become bigger, as they did during the agricultural revolution, groups tend to be made up of nonkin, it becomes more difficult to keep track of the behavior of the individuals in the group, and more difficult to manage and to know about other people's reputations.[21] It is in these larger groups that the deities become more interested in morality. Norenzayan calls these deities Big Gods. Big Gods are omnipresent and omniscient. Big Gods monitor the behavior of the individuals in the group to keep track of who is behaving properly and who is not. Big Gods, according to Norenzayan have become much more prevalent during the past twelve thousand years.[22] "Belief in certain kinds of supernatural watchers—Big Gods—is an essential ingredient that, along with rituals and other interlocking sets of social commitment devices, glued together total strangers into ever larger moral communities as cultural evolution gained pace in the past twelve millennia."[23]

According to this perspective, these all-seeing and all-knowing deities watch behavior to make sure it is consistent with what the group expects. These Big Gods are the gods of prosocial religions (religions that promote behaviors that help the group) and "facilitated the rise of cooperation in large groups of anonymous strangers. In turn, these expanding groups took their prosocial religious beliefs and practices with them, further ratcheting

---

20. Norenzayan, *Big Gods*, 7.

21. Laurin et al., "Outsourcing."

22. Norenzayan, *Big Gods*, 7–8.

23. Ibid., 10.

up large-scale cooperation in a runaway process of cultural evolution."[24] Belief in these Big Gods made larger, cooperative, and cohesive social groups possible. As these successful, large groups replaced the less successful groups, the Big Gods and the associated religious beliefs went with them. Belief in Big Gods promotes prosocial behavior that makes larger, more successful groups. These more successful groups further the spread of the belief in Big Gods and the expansion of prosociality.[25]

So, belief in Big Gods fosters behavior that is good for the group, so-called prosocial behavior. Is there any evidence to support this perspective? Is there evidence that people are more prosocial if they believe God (or god) is watching them? A number of studies do suggest that people are more prosocial if they believe they are being watched. People give more money in economic games, they cheat less and volunteer more, and are less aggressive if they believe they are being watched. Even the presence of eyes (e.g., faces on a calendar) in the environment is sufficient to increase prosocial behavior.[26] The kind of God is important as well. People are less likely to cheat if they believe in a punitive God than if they believe in a nice God. Crime rates are lower in countries with a high belief in God, and countries with a higher number of citizens who believe in hell (a punishing God) have the lowest levels of crime.[27] In addition, people are more prosocial on Sundays than on other days of the week (e.g., more responsive to charity appeals), a phenomenon known as the Sunday Effect.[28] Regular churchgoers watch less porn on Sundays, but the amount of porn they watch on other days of the week is similar to that of nonchurchgoers.[29] Each of these studies suggest that reminders of a watchful God (e.g., going to church on Sunday) who is interested in moral behavior increases prosocial behavior in the individual.

PROSOCIALITY

The religions of the Abrahamic tradition (Judaism, Christianity, and Islam) are all Big God religions. These are also religions that promote prosociality.

24. Ibid., 8.

25. Purzycki, "Moralistic Gods," 327.

26. Gervais and Norenzayan, "Like a Camera"; Norenzayan, Big Gods, 14.

27. Ibid., 43–47; Shariff and Norenzayan, "Mean Gods."

28. Malhotra, "(When) Are Religious People."

29. Norenzayan, Big Gods, 37–41.

The parable of the Good Samaritan is an example of prosocial teaching and of expanding prosocial behavior to those beyond one particular group (the ingroup). According to this evolutionary perspective, a significant reason why religions exist is that they promote group cohesion, trust, cooperation, and prosocial behavior. Groups that are more cooperative and trusting will be more successful than those that are not. We do tend to trust people more if they believe in God, particularly a God who is watchful, who is monitoring behavior, and who is interested in moral issues. We are also more likely to cooperate with such a person, even if the God the person believes in is not the God of our particular religion.[30] This is a primary reason why atheists are so distrusted in society.[31] What do they believe? In laboratory investigations involving economic games, people are more likely to trust a person of another religion than an atheist.[32]

What does the literature suggest about the effects of religion on prosocial behavior? Priming is an experimental technique used in cognitive psychology where the presentation of one stimulus affects the processing of or response to another stimulus. Although a temporary effect, people are nevertheless typically unaware of any effect the priming stimulus is having on their behavior or thinking.[33] For example, a participant in a cognitive psychology experiment might be asked to unscramble a list of words and put the words into a sentence. One of the words might be *divine*, but when place into proper grammatical order, the sentence per se has no religious content. The newly created sentence simply has a word in it that has some religious connotation. After unscrambling these kinds of lists and creating sentences, the participant is then asked to perform a task that is thought to measure prosociality, behavior that benefits another. Often economic or trust games are used for this purpose where the person is given an opportunity in the game to show generosity (and trust) toward another player. Being generous to the other player is considered to be an example of prosociality (see chapter 6 for a discussion of economic or trust games). When tested in this manner, religious primes do increase prosocial behavior (increasing altruism, decreasing cheating, and the like).[34]

30. Ibid., 59–65.
31. Gervais et al., "Do You Believe."
32. Norenzayan, *Big Gods*, 66–71.
33. Shariff et al., "Religious Priming."
34. Ibid.; Norenzayan and Shariff, "Origin."

While there is a moderate effect of religious primes on prosocial behavior, there is a question in the literature about how broad the effect is. Does the effect occur in all people, or in only religious individuals? Does the prosociality extend to all people, or to only people in your particular group? Do religious primes encourage only prosociality, or can they also promote negative social behaviors? Do neutral primes also promote prosocial behavior, or is the effect limited to religious concepts? These questions remain unanswered, but the priming studies can be taken to support the idea that religion evolved at least in part as a means to promote social living in humans. If this is the case, priming the concept of religion should increase positive behaviors directed toward others such as cooperation, generosity, trust, and volunteerism, and both laboratory experiments as well as naturalistic studies support this proposition.[35]

A possible mechanism whereby religion might promote prosocial behavior is through ritual. Group living, a hallmark of humans, necessitates some way to identify who is a member of the group and who is an outsider. This identification is required to ensure group cohesion and cooperation. Ritual seems to be a behavioral trademark of our species and is psychologically prepared.[36] Rituals can also include hard-to-fake, costly signals that can differentiate group members (with whom we can and should cooperate) with free riders. A number of studies in the lab, as well as in natural settings, indicate that rituals do increase prosocial behaviors, including cooperation and trust among the group members. The key component of the ritual in encouraging prosociality seems to be synchrony—and perhaps degree of physical exertion—of the ritualistic behavior.[37] A study by Xygalatas and colleagues showed in a natural setting that rituals that are more severe in nature (e.g., rituals involving body piercings and carrying heavy loads, for instance) induce greater prosocial behavior—generosity in this case. Suffering and perceived pain increased prosociality among the participants of the ritual as well as among observers of the ritual.[38] This finding supports the suggestion from earlier studies that religious ingroups that have more costly rules for membership have members who are more committed, and is consistent with evidence that churches that are more

35. Apicella et al., "Social Networks"; Rand et al., "Religious Motivations."

36. Watson-Jones and Legare, "Social Functions," 42.

37. Cohen et al., "Religion"; Reddish et al., "Does Synchrony"; Valdesolo et al., "Rhythm"; Wiltermuth and Heath, "Synchrony and Cooperation."

38. Xygalatas et al., "Extreme Rituals."

demanding in doctrine and behavior seem to show more growth (or at least fewer declines) in membership compared to more "liberal" churches.[39]

RELIGION AND TRIBALISM

As members of a social species, humans need to live in groups, and religion can be seen as contributing to group formation and maintenance through its effects on prosocial behaviors such as cooperation, trust, and generosity. Either as a direct adaptation or as a by-product, the evolutionary perspective on religion suggests that religious beliefs and behaviors help (religion is not unique in this) to identify group membership and promote sociality among the ingroup members. There can be a dark side to group formation and identity, however, and that is the identification of and behavior directed toward members of the outgroup.

Groups can have different preferences for food, social mores and taboos, worship patterns, leisurely activities, music, and burial practices. Many of these specific preferences contribute to what makes one culture so different from another. These preferences can also, however, lead to conflicts between groups as one group might seek to impose its preferences onto another group. Sometimes, these preferences can be changed into what are called sacred values which is a way of thinking about a preference in a nonmaterial manner. In other words, a preference for a particular food is not merely a preference for a particular kind of nutrition to provide energy for the body; it becomes part of what the people in a given group see as defining who they are and what it means to be a member of the group. When preferences are turned into sacred values, intergroup conflicts can become difficult to resolve, and the more people participate in religious rituals, the more likely they are to make their group preferences into sacred values. This effect is increased if the group perceives itself as threatened by another group.[40]

Religious groups often perceive themselves as threatened by other groups, religious or not. As mentioned above, the belief that one's behavior is being watched (e.g., by an omnipresent and omnipotent God) tends to increase prosocial behaviors such as generosity and trust, and this belief also seems to mediate the dislike and distrust many people have toward

---

39. Norenzayan and Shariff, "Origin"; Pew Research Center, "America's Changing."
40. Sheikh et al., "Religion."

atheists.[41] Secular institutions can also be a source of behavioral monitoring, and priming people with reminders of secular authority can decrease the distrust of atheists but not, it seems, of other outgroups.[42] Neither religious or secular institutions, however, can eliminate the distrust and dislike, or even the hatred, one group can have for another. The Southern Poverty Law Center reports that the number of groups on the radical right (e.g., hate groups, antigovernment groups, the KKK, racist black separatists) grew by 14 percent from 2014 to 2015, and there are over 1900 of these kinds of groups, just on the "right" side of the political spectrum.[43] Tribalism (loyalty to one's tribe, group, or party) within Christianity has been linked to some of the polarization so prevalent within American politics today.[44] Nationalism, racism, birtherism, and xenophobia are all examples of us-versus-them thinking so antithetical to Christianity but too often a major part of how Christians, as well as people of other religious traditions, respond to individuals of the outgroup.

Religion and Prejudice

Tribalism sounds like a very broad term, one that might not apply to regular people going about their everyday lives. Most people are not members of right- (or left-) wing ideological groups such as the KKK or some other hate group. We have seen that religion tends to promote prosocial behaviors, certainly among the ingroup and perhaps extends to some outgroups as well. That is the positive message, but what about the other side of the equation? What does the literature have to say about the relationship between religion and more common forms of prejudice? There is a long history of research on the relationship between religiosity (variously defined) and prejudice. Depending on how one operationalizes religion or religiosity (intrinsic, extrinsic, quest, fundamentalist, authoritarian), positive associations or negative associations have been found. More recent research attempts to measure relationships between religion and particular kinds of behavior, such as that directed toward specific groups. These studies suggest that religion is not associated with a universal acceptance of others, but with a kind of selective intolerance toward specific groups, often leading

41. Gervais et al., "Do You Believe."
42. Gervais and Norenzayan, "Reminders."
43. Southern Poverty Law Center, "Year."
44. Gushee, "Donald Trump and the Travesty of Christian Tribalism."

41

the religious person to behave in a manner that is inconsistent with their religion's traditional teachings. For example, religion is associated with less accepting attitudes toward homosexuals, and strong ingroup religious identity is related to racial derogation.[45]

As alluded to above, there are a number of paradoxes in the priming literature. In the context of religion and prejudicial behavior, participants primed with Christian words showed more racial prejudice directed toward African Americans than did subjects primed with neutral words, suggesting that the activation of Christian concepts increases prejudice. In addition, religious primes not only increase prosociality, generosity, and cooperation (as discussed above); they can also increase aggression, revenge behavior, and support for terrorism.[46] Overall, while religious primes can have positive effects on behavior, they can also produce derogation of outgroups, and negative attitudes and prejudicial behavior toward people who make up the outgroup.[47]

SUMMARY

An evolutionary perspective on religion suggests that religious beliefs and behaviors play an important role in the formation and maintenance of social groups, increasing trust and cooperation among the members of the ingroup. Groups that are more cohesive, trusting, and cooperative will be more successful than those groups that are not. As a result, the individuals that make up these cohesive and cooperative groups will have more reproductive success than individuals that are members of the less cohesive group. Given enough time and through the process of group-level adaptation, those behavioral and psychological traits that are utilized in cooperation and trust within a group will become part of the behavioral and psychological makeup of the human species. This evolutionary examination of religion does not mean that religion is nothing more than a byproduct of adaptive traits, but does provide an additional way of thinking about how religion developed and why it looks the way it does. Of course, theological perspectives are also important and should be incorporated into a multilevel understanding of the complex concept of religion.

45. Hall et al., "Why Don't We"; Rowatt et al., "Associations."
46. Johnson et al., "Priming Christian."
47. Ibid.; Johnson et al., "Religiosity and Prejudice."

The evolutionary perspective on religion also predicts that there will be biological and psychological mechanisms involved in religious behaviors, beliefs, and experiences. The following two chapters examine in some detail literature from the cognitive sciences and neurosciences (and related disciplines) confirming that indeed cognitive and neurological mechanisms mediate religious experiences. These mechanisms are exactly what one would expect if there is any truth to an evolutionary account of religion. Again, religion is complex, and a full understanding of it requires multiple perspectives, multiple disciplines, and multiple methodologies. If biological and psychological mechanisms have evolved to support religion, however, it is not likely that belief in God or in gods will completely go away. As Mark Twain said about reports of his own death, so also the report of the death of God was an exaggeration.

3

Cognitive Science of Religion
What is the Origin of Religious Beliefs?

The history of mankind is the history of our misunderstandings with god,
for he doesn't understand us, and we don't understand him.[1]

The beliefs that motivate religious people to behave as they do in their own
minds (the manifest functions) often depart from the adaptive consequences that ultimately sustain the beliefs (the latent functions).[2]

M odern psychology developed in the late nineteenth and early twentieth centuries and is typically defined as the scientific study of human
behavior and mental processes. For many of the founders of psychology,
religious experience was an important subject of investigation. These leading psychologists took care to present the new discipline of psychology as a
practical tool for the understanding of religion.[3] William James's book *The
Varieties of Religious Experience* is probably the best example of the new
psychology being used to try to understand religious behavior. To James,
the analysis of the "religious propensities of man" must "be at least as in-

1. Saramago, *Cain*, 78.
2. Wilson, *Darwin's Cathedral*, 121.
3. Pickren, "Whisper of Salvation."

teresting as any other of the facts pertaining to his mental constitution."[4] In spite of this, for most of the twentieth century psychology, under the influence of Freud and Skinner, who espoused negative views of religion, avoided the study of religion and religious behavior. Few psychologists interested in achieving tenure or in developing a strong publication record investigated this seemingly universal human concern. During the last two decades of that century, however, there was a noticeable change with researchers from a variety of disciplines (psychology, sociology, anthropology, and medicine) investigating religion and religious experiences. Much of this renewed interest was motivated by increased interest in positive psychology as well as from studies indicating that religion and spirituality have a salubrious effect on both physical and mental health.[5]

The cognitive sciences consist of a group of disciplines (e.g., psychology, linguistics, computer science, artificial intelligence, philosophy, and neuroscience) interested in studying the mind, and religious experiences (beliefs and behaviors) are now included as subject matter in this approach. The current chapter will review how religion and religious experience are understood from the perspective of the cognitive sciences. Included in this review will be a discussion of two different modes or kinds of thinking, sometimes called natural and unnatural cognition, and how religion is understood as a type of natural cognition or thought. Therefore, religion seems to come easily and early (in development) to people, and this is considered important in understanding the apparent universality of religious beliefs and behaviors. (Of course, specific religious beliefs and behaviors vary somewhat from culture to culture; however, there is a surprising amount of overlap between cultures in their religious beliefs, and this, along with the fact that religion is found in all known societies, is taken as partial evidence for the "naturalness" of religion in human societies.) In religious thinking, mind and minds play a crucial role, so this chapter will also include a review of the literature considering the role minds (one's own as well as the minds of others) play in the development of religious thinking. Included will be a discussion of the "mental tools" or modules thought by cognitive scientists to be involved in religious beliefs and behaviors and how these modules are studied. Finally, brief mention will be made of the role of evolutionary theory in the study of religion and the basic compatibility of this scientific approach with theism (also see chapter 2).

4. James, *Varieties*, 4.

5. Koenig et al., *Handbook*; Seligman and Csikszentmihalyi, "Positive Psychology."

Before beginning the discussion of these issues, however, it is helpful to consider whether religious experiences are different from other experiences. Of all the various kinds of experiences we have as humans, to what extent are religious experiences unique or similar to these? As discussed in chapter 1, the *sui generis* approach suggests that religiousness is inherent in the experience itself. There is a common core of experiences that refer to the numinous and mystical; therefore, religious experience is a unique kind of experience that taps into this core. Certain experiences are, by definition, religious and are always understood as such. An alternative approach argues that there is no common core for religious experiences. Experiences are not inherently religious; instead, the person having the experience ascribes it as being religious. This ascription model suggests that different kinds of experiences can be deemed religious by the person having the experience and is similar to the view taken by James in *Varieties* where, talking about the role of emotion in religious experience, he argued that there is no elementary religious emotion, "but only a common storehouse of emotions upon which religious objects may draw."[6] For the cognitive scientist, one is either investigating the cognitive mechanisms involved in these inherently religious experiences or studying how these mental mechanisms are involved in making a given experience special or religious. Either way, mental mechanisms are investigated in the cognitive science of religion, and the advances made in the last ten to fifteen years in this field are reviewed in this chapter.

WHAT IS THE COGNITIVE SCIENCE OF RELIGION?

The cognitive science of religion (CSR) uses theories in the cognitive sciences to understand the basic structure of those human thoughts and actions that can be deemed religious. CSR is not typically concerned with trying to define religion; rather, it attempts to understand why thoughts and behaviors considered religious take the form they do, and why these forms of thought and behavior are so common and recurrent across cultures.[7] Like all beliefs, religious beliefs reflect the underlying structures of the mind.[8] These cognitive structures shape and bias the kinds of concepts we form and influence how we experience the world, including those as-

6. James, *Varieties*, 33; Taves, *Religious Experience*, 3–8.
7. Barrett, "Cognitive Science of Religion."
8. Barrett, "Is the Spell"; Boyer, *Religion Explained*, 2–4.

pects of the world considered to be religious. CSR does not necessarily assume that its understanding of religious thoughts and actions is exhaustive. The goal for some researchers (for example, Pascal Boyer) is a complete and reductionistic account of religion. While these scientists typically believe current findings in CSR present a problem for theism, others do not see evidence from CSR as a threat for theological versions of religious beliefs.[9] Seen through this lens, reality is multileveled and stratified and so can be investigated on a number of levels and from a variety of perspectives. Religion, therefore, can be approached from different levels, each with its own methods of investigation. While one could, at least theoretically, obtain an exhaustive account about some aspect of reality using methods appropriate for a given level of analysis, other types of analyses can always be applied to further understand that particular phenomenon. A cognitive science study of religion is, therefore, appropriate as long as one uses the perspective in a nonreductionistic manner. Religion and religious experience can always be known more completely by applying methods appropriate from other levels of reality. (Of course, CSR, or theology for that matter, cannot tell us the truth or falsity of any belief. Identifying, for example, what mental processes are involved when we express the belief that $2 \times 2 = 4$ tells us nothing about the truth of that belief.)

NATURAL AND UNNATURAL COGNITION

In cognitive psychology (that area of psychology interested in mental processes) it is common to talk about two systems of thinking at work in the human mind. While different terminology is used to describe these two systems (Type 1 and Type 2, Nonreflective and Reflective, Intuitive and Rational), they generally differ in the following ways. The first system of thought is fast, nonconscious, automatic, effortless, and intuitive and is often called "natural cognition." The second system of thought is "unnatural cognition" and is (relative to natural cognition) slow, conscious, controlled, effortful, and reflective.[10] Examples of unnatural cognition include the beliefs that 849 divided by 3 is 283; that Abraham Lincoln was the sixteenth president of the United States; that there are tens of billions of neurons in the human brain; that Jesus was both wholly human and wholly divine; and that there are three persons in the Godhead, Father, Son and Holy Spirit. Examples of

9. Peterson, "Are Evolutionary/Cognitive."
10. McCauley, *Why Religion*, 1–9.

natural cognition include the beliefs that two solid objects cannot occupy the same space at the same time, that when objects are dropped they fall, and that cats do not give birth to dogs. Natural forms of cognition appear early in development (e.g., in childhood), address an important and basic problem (e.g., stay away from high places; they can be dangerous), and are found in all societies (even though the exact expression of the idea might be informed by a specific culture). (The idea that there are two kinds of cognitive styles is known as dual-process theory, and the above depiction of these two types of thinking is simplified and can be criticized in a number of ways. While this criticism is beyond the scope of the present chapter and does not change the basic point of the argument being made, some authors do have questions and concerns about dual-process theories in general.)[11]

Ideas, concepts, and beliefs that are derived from natural (or Type 1) cognition are typically easier to use than those derived from reflection and conscious effort (Type 2 or unnatural cognition). As an example, while we reflectively know that the earth spins on its axis and rotates around the sun, when we want to determine where the sun will be at dusk, we do not use that Type 2 knowledge to calculate the sun's position. Instead, in such real-time situations, we pretend that it is the sun that is moving and calculate its future position based on this intuitive or Type 1 kind of reasoning.[12] When solving problems in real time (i.e., in everyday contexts), we typically utilize natural cognition concepts over those derived through nonnatural cognition. As long as the problem (e.g., where will the sun be at dusk tonight?) can be solved reasonably successfully using this "quick and easy" method, we will do so. Cognitive scientists propose that we are biased toward this faster form of thinking because, in part, it takes less cognitive energy than the more reflective and effortful Type 2 cognition.

Barrett uses the term "theological correctness" to identify religious concepts that are the result of Type 2, reflective thinking. These are concepts that are considered to be part of doctrine or theology, such as the human/divine nature of Jesus, the virgin birth, and the three-person nature of the Godhead.[13] Such concepts do not flow naturally or automatically; they are the result of much effortful, reflective, and conscious thinking. We also, however, have concepts of God that are not correct theologically but are the result of a more natural kind of cognition. Many people intuitively concep-

11. Evans and Stanovich, "Dual-Process Theories."
12. Barrett, "Theological Correctness."
13. Ibid.

tualize God as an old man living in the clouds (a particular location). When pressed to reflect on this idea of God, these people will acknowledge that it is not theologically correct but is, nevertheless, a conceptualization of God that they hold. Just like we know the earth rotates around a stationary sun, Christians (at least of the traditional, orthodox variety) know that Jesus was both human and divine and that (a genderless) God is omniscient, omnipotent and omnipresent. But how do we conceptualize God in real-time problem solving situations where we do not have the opportunity to reflect on the theologically correct characteristics of God that theologians have developed (such as omniscience)? Do we resort to utilizing the understanding of God that comes from our Type 1 cognition? Are we biased toward this kind of thinking in religion as we seem to be in nonreligious contexts? Do these biases hold for religious concepts? Research in CSR suggests they do.

Barrett and Keil studied adult subjects from several religious traditions in both the United States and in India.[14] These participants were given questionnaires (specific to their religious tradition) to assess their conceptualizations of the divine. When given time to reflect on these questions, the subjects typically gave theologically correct responses. That is to say, the participants knew the correct conceptualization about God provided by their particular religion (e.g., in the Christian tradition, God is omnipresent and omnipotent). After completing the questionnaires, the subjects were given various stories, such as the following, to read and remember.

> A boy was swimming alone in a swift and rocky river. The boy got his left leg caught between two large, gray rocks and couldn't get out. Branches of trees kept bumping into him as they hurried past. He thought he was going to drown and so he began to struggle and pray. Though God was answering another prayer in another part of the world when the boy started praying, before long God responded by pushing one of the rocks so the boy could get his leg out. The boy struggled to the river bank and fell over exhausted.[15]

The important point of these stories was that they were completely consistent with the theologically correct conceptualizations that the subjects affirmed on the questionnaires completed only a few minutes before the scenarios were presented. When asked to recount the story, however, subjects typically remembered the story in a way that was consistent with a more natural conceptualization of God, rather than the theologically

14. Barrett and Keil, "Conceptualizing."
15. Ibid., 224.

correct idea of God. For example, Christian subjects remembered that God had to finish answering the prayer in the other part of the world before God could answer the boy's prayer by freeing him from the rocks. This real-time response was made even though, on the questionnaires, the same subjects reported the more theologically correct understanding that God is omnipresent and omnipotent. Despite this correct reflective knowledge about divine powers, the subjects seemed to use the more natural conceptualization of God when processing the stories.[16] Anecdotal evidence also suggests that we use concepts derived from Type 1 natural cognition in real-time, everyday contexts even though we reflectively know what is correct theologically. For example, a strict Calvinist might believe (reflectively) that God predetermines all events before the beginning of time, but will nevertheless pray for God's intervention on behalf of a sick family member. When pressed to "solve a religious problem" in real time, we tend to drop our theologically correct conceptualizations and fall back on the concepts that are easy to hold and use, derived from our intuitive, automatic, Type 1 or natural thinking. We are biased, in other words, toward theological incorrectness.[17]

IS RELIGION NATURAL?

Some ideas just seem intuitively right to us. That, of course, does not mean that the ideas are true (consider the idea that the sun revolves around the earth); it does mean that the ideas come to us without any conscious reflection or effort. They are natural in that sense. An important question in CSR is whether religion is natural. To pose this question is not to suggest that religion or religious belief is innate. It is simply to ask whether (at least some) religious beliefs qualify as natural in that they are derived from natural cognition, that kind of thinking that is automatic, effortless, intuitive, emerging early in development.

Robert McCauley, Justin Barrett, and Paul Bloom, three leading researchers in CSR, argue that at least some religious beliefs are natural. Bloom presents evidence that the beliefs in mind-body dualism, as well as the belief in divine agents, come naturally to children during their pre-school years.[18] Young children from all societies understand that physical

16. Ibid., 219–47.

17. McCauley, *Why Religion*, 210–21.

18. Bloom, *Descartes' Baby*, 189–227; Bloom, "Religion," 147–51.

bodies obey the laws of physics, but that souls follow social rules distinct from physical laws.[19] From this early age we believe that the physical world is different from the social world in its causes and effects, and this belief produces an intuitive dualism view of persons. We naturally see bodies and minds as entities from two separate domains, autonomous and potentially separable from each other.[20]

For example, preschool children will say that while the brain is responsible for most physical acts, it is not needed for many mental acts such as pretending, which is done by people, not brains. These preschool children also understand that when a person dies, the brain no longer works, but the person's psychological or mental properties continue to function. So, a child who is told the story of a mouse that dies will report that the dead mouse can still have thoughts and desires, even though its body does not work. These mental or psychological acts require a soul, not a body.[21] Children also understand that bodies and minds operate from different sets of laws, physics for bodies and rules of social engagement and relationships for minds. Even infants have a basic understanding of how physical objects can and cannot interact with each other, which supports the notion that a distinction between the physical and the psychological is natural to human thinking. An infant knows, for example, that if an object is put on a table and the table is removed, the object will fall. How do psychologists doing research with infants know this? Infants will stare longer at an event that is surprising to them. When the table is removed and the object does not fall—because it is suspended by hidden wires—the infant will stare longer at this surprising event than if the object falls like it is supposed to when the table is removed.[22] Babies would find flying chairs and disappearing sofas surprising. That is not how those kinds of objects are supposed to act. As Bloom puts it in summarizing this line of research, "we are dualists who have two ways of looking at the world: in terms of bodies and in terms of souls. A direct consequence of this dualism is the idea that bodies and souls are separate. And from this follow certain notions that we hold dear, including the concepts of self, identity, and life after death."[23]

19. Ibid., 147–51.

20. Cohen and Barrett, "When Minds."

21. Bloom, "Religion."

22. Bloom, "Is God."

23. Bloom, *Descartes' Baby*, 191.

Not only do infants come prepared with a fundamental understanding of the behavior of objects, they also come ready to interact socially with other humans. This basic understanding of social entities is seen in the preference newborns have for faces and the sound of the human voice (especially the mother's). Infants recognize different emotions and can mimic these emotions at an early age. They also can readily identify goals toward which others are working and show preferences toward objects that act in prosocial ways, obeying the rules of social engagement.[24]

Children seem to have an intuitive dualism, but they also naturally see agency in the world around them. Kelemen uses the term "promiscuous teleology" to describe the tendency in infants and children to see purpose and design in events and objects in their world.[25] American children, during the preschool years, know the difference between artifacts, which are made by humans, and natural objects, which are not, but their knowledge of most natural objects is rather limited. The work of Kelemen and others suggests that children compensate for this lack of knowledge of nonliving, natural objects by using their understanding of intentional behavior. As noted above in the study by Kuhlmeier et al., children have a basic knowledge of intention, and they use that knowledge to try to understand the nonliving natural world as well as the biological world. Children from religious as well as nonreligious backgrounds will state that even if nonliving, natural objects such as clouds, rivers, and mountains are not made by humans; they are made by some other kind of intentional being (e.g., God) and exist for a purpose.[26] By the fourth grade, as the children begin to learn about natural explanations that come to replace the teleological ones, this promiscuous teleology is less robust, but it never ceases entirely; the predilection to see purpose, meaning, and design continues into adulthood. We can see this when people report seeing the face of Satan in the smoke rising from the fires at the World Trade Center on 9/11 or when the image of the Virgin Mary or Jesus is seen in toast, floor tiles, or clouds. This tendency toward purpose might also help explain the resistance to a Darwinian understanding of evolutionary theory, which postulates that the mechanisms of natural selection are entirely nondirectional and nondesigned.

In general it seems that children are "intuitive theists" in that they show a bias to see purpose for all objects and behaviors and are inclined to

24. Kuhlmeier et al., "Attribution."
"25. Kelemen, "Why Are Rocks."
26. Ibid.

see natural phenomena as created and designed by some kind of agent.[27] These attributions of purpose and design could be the by-products of a mind that is orientated toward social entities and biased to see intention in the behavior of others. This preference for intention spills over onto other situations as well, leading to the kind of early thinking style characteristic of religious ideas.

Justin Barrett also talks about how children are born believers.[28] By this Barrett means that children have "a naturally developing receptivity to many core religious beliefs, particularly beliefs about the existence of supernatural beings" and that given some encouragement through interaction with the environment will become believers in supernatural agency.[29] This form of natural religious belief is contrasted with theology, however. Children are not natural theologians; they are not born with a "receptivity" to any particular set of theological ideas or to any specific theological tradition.

Barrett argues that the tendency to see gods or supernatural agents around us is natural and is "a predictable expression of our biology's development in a normal environment."[30] Children, therefore, are predisposed toward believing in some kind of god because gods "occupy a sweet spot in their natural way of thinking."[31] To an infant, agents have certain traits, some of which are human-like (e.g., agents move on their own, agents act to attain goals), and some of which are different from humans (e.g., agents do not have to look like humans, agents can be invisible).

Just because there is overlap in the traits of humans and the gods does not mean that children cannot distinguish between them as agents or that children treat them in the same way. God concepts and human concepts have different developmental trajectories.[32] One view of how children come to understand the concept of God or god suggests that god concepts result from projecting humanness onto the god. In other words, children conceptualize god as they do humans; they first form a thorough conceptualization of what humanness is and then assign that concept to the god of their specific religious tradition. This approach is known as the anthropo-

27. Kelemen, "Are Children."
28. Barrett, *Born Believers*, 15–42.
29. Ibid., 150.
30. Ibid., 20.
31. Ibid., 20.
32. Barrett et al., "God's Beliefs versus Mother's."

morphism hypothesis and was favored by a number of early developmental psychologists, most notably Jean Piaget. In contrast, the preparedness hypothesis suggests that children's conceptualizations of god or God are not projections from those made for humans (such as the parents) but are the result of early developing mental tools used to form general conceptualizations about intentional agents and that, by default, this device assumes superhuman properties for these intentional agents. God concepts play on these default assumptions.[33]

Evidence supporting the preparedness hypothesis comes from the false-belief test used extensively in studying children and what they know and think about other minds. There are variations in the false-belief test, but the basic procedure tests a child's knowledge of what the child thinks another person knows. An example of the false-belief test follows. A child is shown a cracker box and is asked what the box contains. The child will reasonably answer that the box contains crackers, as labeled. The child is then shown the contents of the box and sees that the box actually contains rocks. The next step in the false-belief test is to ask the child what another child who enters the room and who has not looked into the box will say is in the box. A three-year-old child will answer by saying that the new child will say (and believe) that there are rocks in the box. A five-year-old child will report that the new child will say (and believe) that there are crackers in the box. This result is interpreted as indicating that between the ages of three and five the child who is being tested has developed a theory of mind (ToM) insofar that at three the child assumed that since she knew the contents of the box (rocks) so would the new child. By the age of five, however, the tested child now understands that the new child will have a false belief. The new child will believe that there are crackers in the box instead of the rocks. What is interesting for CSR researchers is what this tested child will say about what God knows is in the box and how that knowledge differs from the child's mother.

If the anthropomorphism hypothesis is correct, beliefs about what God knows should change and be similar to beliefs about what others (e.g., the mother) know. Because the beliefs of the mother (or other human) are projected onto God, the beliefs about what each can know will be similar. According to the anthropomorphism hypothesis, children should begin (at age three) by believing God's and mother's beliefs are infallible (they both know there are rocks in the box), but shift (by age five) to claiming that

33. Barrett and Richert, "Anthropomorphism."

both God's and mother's beliefs are fallible (both will believe that there are crackers in the box). The results of the false-belief test indicate, however, that when the child is asked about what God and mother would believe is in the box, while mother's beliefs move from being infallible to being fallible, God's beliefs remain infallible. At both three and five years of age, children report that God will say there are rocks in the box, appreciating that God would not be fooled by the box's appearance as mother is.[34] These results are consistent with the preparedness hypothesis. Children are prepared to conceptualize humans and God in different ways, reflecting, perhaps, how God occupies "a sweet spot in their natural way of thinking."[35]

McCauley makes the case that religion is natural and contrasts religion with science which, McCauley argues, is not natural from a cognitive standpoint.[36] Science (like theology) is unnatural in that it is the product of Type 2 thinking, which is effortful, conscious, and reflective. Scientific ideas do not just come to us intuitively or early in life. They are the product of long, difficult reflection on the problems of nature (or, in the case of theology, problems dealing with the nature of God). This is not to say that all of science is the result of unnatural cognition. It is simply to suggest that science is unnatural when compared to religion. The beliefs (models, theories) about the world that come from reflective, scientific thinking often vary significantly from the beliefs about the world that emerge from natural, unreflective thought. Part of why science is considered by McCauley to be unnatural is that many of the theories simply do not seem right to us. Scientific theories often seem contrary to how the world intuitively seems. Paul Bloom, speaking about the seeming unnaturalness of evolutionary theory, put it this way. "The theory of natural selection is an empirically supported account of our existence. But almost nobody believes it. We may intellectually grasp it, but it will never feel right. Our gut feeling is that design requires a designer."[37] The same can be said of many scientific (or theological) theories from atomic theory to evolutionary theory to the doctrine (theological theory) of hypostatic union—the divine/human nature of Jesus. The desk on which I write seems solid to me (intuitively), but it is actually (according to physics) full of air. Species cannot change (a dog cannot give birth to a cat), but over time and given genetic mutations (and

34. Ibid.
35. Barrett, *Born Believers*, 20.
36. McCauley, *Why Religion*, 87.
37. Bloom, "Is God," 112.

some other conditions according to biology), one species can evolve into another. How can Jesus be *both* one kind of thing (human) at the same time he is another kind of thing (divine)? The results of reflective, Type 2 thinking seem odd. These beliefs (whether scientific or theological) often violate what is obvious to us. They are unnatural.

One of the beliefs of science that is at odds with the more natural kind of thinking characterizing religion concerns the role of agents ("beings . . . that not merely respond to their environment but also initiate action on the basis of their own internal states, such as beliefs and desires").[38] Belief in agents comes naturally to us and is a product of Type 1 cognition. Over the last three centuries, however, science has systematically eliminated any role of agents from its theories. Science looks for natural causes (molecular, cellular, neural) to explain phenomena. Appealing to agents is not considered legitimate in science. Another challenge to the more natural kind of cognition comes in the form of reflective, disciplined criticism of theories.[39] We do not critically analyze the products of our Type 1 cognition. These beliefs are used as heuristics; they are typically "good enough" for solving most of the problems we face during the course of a typical day. Disciplined criticism of theories is necessary in science. Science progresses, in part, because of robust analysis of proposed theories. It takes training and effort to learn how to think critically. What constitutes relevant evidence? How should one go about collecting good data to assess a particular theory? Experiments in science can be considered created "situations in which humans' natural cognitive systems are uninformative and, thus, unhelpful."[40] In other words, the very heart of the scientific process consists of artificial (or unnatural) situations where our natural and intuitive cognitive processes will not help us.

We can see the difficulty inherent in Type 2 thinking by noting how people typically have difficulty with syllogistic reasoning problems. We have a hard time solving reasoning problems, particularly if conditionals are involved, when they are presented to us in abstract form. When the same problems are made more concrete (supposedly triggering Type 1 thinking), they becomes easier. For example, Wason presented subjects with the following problem.[41] Four cards were placed on a table in front of

38. Barrett, *Why Would*, 4.

39. McCauley, *Why Religion*, 119.

40. Ibid., 121.

41. Wason, "Reasoning."

the subjects. Each card had either a letter or a number on it. The subjects were given the following conditional statement: "If a card has a vowel on one side, then it has an even number on the other side." The subjects were then told: "assuming that each of these cards has a letter on one side and a number on the other, indicate only those cards that you definitely need to turn over in order to ascertain if this conditional is true." In one example, the cards were

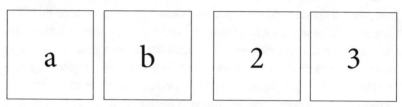

The correct answer in this abstract example is to turn over the "a" card (because *a* is a vowel) and the "3" card (because 3 is not an even number). Only about 5 percent of the subjects correctly identified the "a" and the "3" as the correct cards. This kind of problem requires Type 2 thinking. It takes conscious effort to come up with the answer. If, on the other hand, the same problem is made more concrete, nearly everyone can provide the correct answer. So, for example, if the following problem is presented, the answer "jumps out" to us. The problem requires Type 1 thinking and is easier. "If a person is drinking a beer, then he must be over twenty years of age. Assuming that each of these cards has information about what a person is drinking on one side and about his or her age on the other, indicate only those cards that you definitely need to turn over in order to ascertain if any of these people are breaking the law."

Drinking beer	Drinking Coke	24 years old	16 years old

When the problem is reformulated (as above) to detect cheaters in a social setting, almost everyone gets it right. Dealing with others in a social situation typically requires Type 1 thinking, and we are good at this. It is natural.[42]

42. McCauley, *Why Religion*, 56–57.

Humans also typically find statistical and probabilistic thinking difficult. We neglect to consider regression toward the mean, fail to take base rates into account, and do not consider sample sizes when determining the significance of a statistical test. Statistical reasoning requires Type 2, reflective cognition. We also show bias toward making judgments based on using shortcuts or heuristics, which often lead to the correct decisions in "the real world" of everyday living but can produce errors when the situation calls for a more deliberate and reflective kind of cognition. Kahneman describes a number of these biases and how they affect the decisions we make, including the availability heuristic.[43] Availability refers to the tendency we have to estimate probabilities according to how easily we can come up with an example. Many people are afraid to fly, in part, because it is so easy to remember a plane crash where hundreds of people were killed. The memory of this event can bias us to believe that it is more dangerous to fly than to drive, even though flying is (statistically) many times safer. In many day-to-day situations, it is helpful to make decisions based on how quickly a similar situation comes to mind. (I did A the last time I was in a situation like the one I am in now, so I will do A again.) It is in situations that require a more reflective form of decision-making and thinking that this bias can lead us to an error. It takes effort to counter the natural belief that being thirty thousand feet in the air in a confined metal space is dangerous.

The answer to the question, is religion natural? is yes. Religious (rather than theological) beliefs are the product of the kind of cognition that is intuitive, effortless, and automatic. Religious beliefs, such as dualism, creationism, and teleology, appear early in childhood and are difficult to eliminate (if one wanted to). This does not mean that religion is innate. It does mean that beliefs that most people consider to be religious in character are the product of natural mental mechanisms as are the other, nonreligious intuitive beliefs that we hold. Religious thought "rests on normal mental structures and processes."[44] Therefore, these beliefs do not need to be "explained away" as illusions or techniques of behavioral control.[45]

43. Kahneman, *Thinking*, 129–136.
44. Tremlin, *Minds and Gods*, 108.
45. Freud, *Future*; Skinner, *Science*, 350–58.

IMPORTANCE OF MINDS

CSR begins the study of religious belief and behavior by acknowledging that (1) because of common human biology and similar natural environments, minds develop, as far as basic intuitive and causal reasoning are concerned, in a similar fashion across cultures and societies; (2) human minds are highly specialized combinations of subsystems that solve particular kinds of problems: they are not general information processing machines; (3) minds do not passively receive information from the environment, but rather actively shape and color perception and cognition; (4) this shaping and coloring of the human mind affects patterns of thought and action, including religious thought and action; and (5) these religious thoughts and actions can be explained by reference to the basic conceptual structures of the human mind: some thoughts and actions are more likely to develop because of the way human minds naturally work—through natural cognition.[46]

An important example of natural cognition of interest to cognitive psychologists is the belief that other people have thoughts, emotions, and intentions, and that I can know what these other thoughts, emotions, and intentions are. This understanding about others (which develops around five years of age) is known as a theory of mind and is necessary in order for a person to have good social relationships with others. Additionally, humans "naturally" believe that there are agents in the world and that those agents cause things to happen.

Many of the beliefs about agents, bodies, minds, and souls can be considered religious by the person who holds them, and because they are natural products of the way our minds operate, they come easily to us at an early age and are difficult to eliminate. Beliefs that are a product of the slower, more reflective cognitive style are harder to come by and are less likely to last. Over the next few pages, some basic content of CSR will be examined. First, is a discussion of a "mental toolbox" followed by an examination of some of the tools that are in the box including a device that looks for agency and another concerned with what those agents think (i.e., what kind of minds do they have).

46. Barrett, "Is the Spell."

Mental Tools or Modules

A basic tenet of CSR is that to understand how religious beliefs develop, you need to understand how any kind of belief develops. The reason for this is that religious and nonreligious beliefs are products of the same mental tools. From this perspective, the mind is seen as a kind of mental workshop with all kinds of different, specialized tools available.[47] Just as a hammer or wrench is made for a particular kind of job, so, too, are mental tools used for particular reasons.

These tools of the mind tend to operate automatically. We do not consciously select the correct mental tool to accomplish the cognitive task at hand. With occasional exceptions, we access these tools nonconsciously, and once the tool is selected, the task or problem is solved rapidly and efficiently without the expenditure of a lot of mental effort. Some of the tools at our disposal are thought to be (1) an object-detection device (for recognizing a thing we encounter as an object), (2) an object describer (for providing the appropriate characteristics to the object; what it can and cannot do), (3) a living-thing describer (which provides important characteristics to objects identified as living things), and (4) an animal identifier (the object detected is an animal with certain characteristics that might overlap with living things but that are specific to animals as well). Again, these tools are accessed automatically. We do not have to reflect or think hard about the characteristics of a living thing when we encounter one. The identification and the knowledge of the appropriate characteristics of a living thing are intuitive.

We can think of these tools as consisting of three categories.[48] First are categorizers, which receive information from our senses and use that information to assess what kind of thing we have encountered. The most important categorizer for the purposes of this discussion is the agency-detection device. Other categorizers include the object-detection device, the animal identifier (mentioned above), the artifact identifier, and the face detector. Second are describers, which are tools that provide the necessary properties to a given object identified by a categorizer. The living-thing describer mentioned above would automatically generate the properties required for a living thing, including that (1) it requires nutrition, (2) it grows, (3) it can reproduce, and (4) it will eventually die. The agency-detection device

47. Barrett, *Why Would*, 3–6.
48. Ibid., 3–6.

categorizer mentioned above has a describer known as the Theory of Mind (ToM), which generates the properties we expect agents to possess. Additional describers include the object describer and the artifact describer. The third group of tools are facilitators, which function to coordinate social activity and other behaviors that depend on situational factors. For example, facilitators help people understand the behavior of others in particular situations that are more complex and that require more explaining than is provided by appeals to beliefs and desires (which is what ToM provides). While all of these tools operate nonconsciously and are present in all adults, they are not innate or hardwired into the brain. They do not necessarily inevitably develop, although they do generally appear early in a person's development (perhaps even in early infancy).

The Agency-Detection Device

One of the most important categorizers in CSR is the mental tool that detects agency. For example, if we are walking along a dark street at night and we hear a noise in an alley that we just passed, we naturally believe, at least initially, that an agent was the cause of that noise (perhaps a potential mugger). We might later discover that it was just the wind that blew over a garbage can, but the fast, nonconscious, automatic, effortless, and intuitive belief (the natural cognition) is in the existence of an agent as the cause. We are biased to have this belief because the predilection for this cognition has survival advantages. It is better (as far as survival during the course of human history is concerned) if we immediately assume or believe that the noise we just heard is a possible threat because we can then take appropriate action in response. While we may be wrong about the possibility of a threat to us (it was just the wind blowing over a garbage can), that false-positive is a small price to pay. It is better to believe it is a threat and turn out to be wrong than to believe that the noise is no threat and turn out to be wrong.

The ability to distinguish objects and agents in the environment is crucial for our survival, and because agents are so important our mind has a mental tool to quickly spot them, or to at least suspect their presence.[49] Our agency-detection system is hypersensitive; we see intention and agency even if, at times, none is there. Agents are the mind's natural, default explanation. Humans have a strong tendency to interpret ambiguous evidence as caused by an agent. There is a tradeoff between speed and

49. Tremlin, *Minds and Gods*, 5–11.

accuracy, with speed being the more important factor. This does lead to occasional mistakes, but the tradeoff is worth it for survival reasons. Justin Barrett refers to this heightened setting of the agency-detection device as the Hypersensitive Agent Detection Device (or HADD).[50] One important piece of evidence that triggers HADD is movement. Even dots moving around on a screen are enough to get HADD to see them as moving because of an agent. This automatic and nonconscious tendency to see agency in the environment (especially triggered by movement) is thought to have survival advantage for the reasons described above.

Theory of Mind (ToM)

Not all events in the environment are caused by an agent. Sometimes HADD automatically identifies an agent as the cause (the noise in the alley), but upon conscious reflection we determine that the noise was merely a garbage can lid that blew off due to the wind. There is still a cause, but there is no agent involved. Once HADD determines that an agent has produced some event in the environment, however, then other cognitive tools are utilized from the mental toolbox. Our knowledge of agents leads us to intuitively assume that the agent has a mind. Agents are beings that think, and agents are understood primarily in mentalistic terms.[51] The identification of an agent automatically elicits the use of the ToM tool. Agents move with a purpose in a goal-directed manner. Agents, therefore, have intentions and desires. In short, agents have minds.

These mental tools are important in our god beliefs. In the first place, gods are agents. In the second place, gods have minds. The importance of HADD and ToM is illustrated in a story related by Barrett in his book *Why Would Anyone Believe in God?* I include the story in full.[52]

> One day, Doug was working in a grain silo when leaked propane exploded. The first explosion rushed all around him and out the second-level windows high above him. Stunned by not being harmed by the blast, he tried to get out the door, only to discover that the explosion had jammed the doors. Knowing that a second, larger explosion was coming and he had no way out, Doug muttered hopelessly, "Take me home, Lord." He distinctly heard a

50. Barrett, *Why Would*, 31–44.
51. Tremlin, *Minds and Gods*, 75–80.
52. Barrett, *Why Would*, 34.

voice say, "Not yet," and then felt some invisible hands lift him a dozen feet in the air and out of a second-story window, then safely to the ground below. Once he had landed outside the silo, a safe distance away, the silo and attached barn exploded into rubble. He stumbled to the farm office, where coworkers took him to the hospital. At the hospital, Doug told the doctor that God sent angels to save him. The dumbfounded doctor reluctantly agreed it was a possibility given that the amount of propane gas in the man's lungs should have been fatal, yet he was not only alive but also conscious and talking. Doug, the doctor, and all staff of the farm believed this event to be caused by supernatural agency.

Of course, the described event could have been caused by angels sent by God to rescue Doug. At least many Christian theists are open to this possibility. The question for CSR is what is the origin of the belief? From where does it come? Even if God did it, why would we believe that? Doug, the doctor, and the staff of the farm seek a cause for this highly unlikely event. Finding no obvious mechanistic or biological cause, HADD finds an agent. Once the agent is found, ToM springs into action to provide mental traits. Barrett argues that this belief (and other kinds of religious beliefs) has its origin in the work of the HADD and ToM mental tools.[53]

God beliefs, then, are formed by the working of natural mental tools that operate to help us make quick assessments of events and objects in our environment. In this respect, beliefs about gods or God are no different, as far as their origin is concerned, than other intuitive beliefs that we hold.[54] Beliefs do spread from person to person, however. What accounts for the transmission of religious beliefs? Boyer and others make the case that particular religious beliefs spread because they violate certain features of categorizers and describers. This makes them, in the words of Justin Barrett, Minimally Counterintuitive (MCI).[55] MCI concepts meet most assumptions of the categorizers and describers, but they have just enough violations to make them interesting and memorable. In fact, concepts with a single violation are more successfully transmitted than those with many violations or those with no violations that are entirely consistent with the category-level expectations.[56] MCI concepts stand out just enough to make them special, but not too much to make them completely unbelievable. A

53. Ibid., 34–36.

54. Gervais, "Perceiving."

55. Barrett, *Why Would*, 21–30; Boyer, *Religion Explained*, 51–87.

56. Barrett and Nyhof, "Spreading."

talking cat violates the assumptions of the animal describer and is therefore MCI and likely to be remembered, but a cat that not only talks but also flies would be too unbelievable. Religious concepts are MCI; they are memorable enough to be passed on to others, to be transmitted and spread.[57]

THE INFLUENCE OF EVOLUTIONARY THEORY

A central issue in CSR is why people have religious beliefs in the first place. According to evolutionary psychology, the mind's structures or tools exist because they, like physical characteristics, confer a survival advantage. Are the specific mental constructs deemed religious adaptations providing survival advantage? One view is to say yes, religious concepts are the products of natural selection and serve to benefit the religious individual. Those individuals with mental concepts that bias them to see reality in religious terms will have a reproductive advantage over those individuals who lack these mental tools.[58] The adaptationist argument is supported, some suggest, by evidence of a salubrious effect of religion on physical and mental health. Among other findings, people who score high on measures of religiosity tend to live longer, have lower rates of disease, and have a higher satisfaction with life. If a religious person lives longer, so the argument goes, then religion is adaptive.

A version of this adaptation approach is to argue that selection occurs at the level of the group, and that it is the group, not the individual per se, that benefits from religious mental constructs. Group selection is controversial and was rejected as an evolutionary mechanism in the mid-twentieth century, but is now considered by many to be one way selection can occur. David Sloan Wilson refers to multilevel selection theory to express his view that selection can and does occur at more than one level of biology.[59] Those groups showing greater degrees of cohesion, trust, and cooperation (fostered by religious beliefs and practices) would be more likely to survive, and the individual members of those groups would pass these traits to their offspring.

Another perspective suggests that religion is not adaptive, per se, but is a by-product of adaptations that serve nonreligious practices. For example, a cognitive structure that promotes group solidarity and cooperation

---

57. Barrett, "Exploring"; Norenzayan, *Big Gods*, 29–32.
58. Sosis and Alcorta, "Signaling, Solidarity."
59. Wilson, *Darwin's Cathedral*, 10.

would be selected because it serves to make the group stronger (perhaps aiding in hunting for food and defense of the group). This cognitive tool could also, as a secondary benefit, foster religious beliefs, but it is not the religious beliefs that are selected; it is the tendency toward cooperation with members of one's group that is selected. Religion is, therefore, a by-product, not directly adaptive.

Sosis and Alcorta argue that selective pressures did, in fact, shape the human capacity for religion and that physical, psychological, and reproductive benefits result. These authors see these benefits developing because religious beliefs and practices promote group solidarity. Groups form in order to obtain resources, and this group activity requires coordinated action among many individuals. Moral systems (part of a group's religious practices) help regulate behavior needed for a coordinated and effective group (see chapter 6). To the extent that religion enhances cooperation among individuals and fosters coordinated group behavior, it provides a selective advantage over a competing group that is less coordinated and efficient.[60]

Whether seen as an adaptation or as a by-product, from an evolutionary perspective religious beliefs and behaviors provide a selection advantage over individuals or groups who do not possess these kinds of beliefs and behaviors. While there is some controversy over whether religion increases group cohesion, cooperation, and solidarity, the view of many in CSR is that it does increase prosociality, thus making those groups more successful than groups without those qualities.[61]

Humans are highly social and depend on others in the social group. Over the course of human history, group sizes have expanded from primarily kin-based groups to larger bands of individuals that are unrelated genetically. Such increases in social group size make relations among these unrelated and even anonymous individuals more difficult to monitor. It becomes harder to remember who is part of the group and who is not, and monitoring free riders becomes a concern as well. Free riders are those individuals who want to take advantage of group membership (e.g., for safety), but do not want to pay the price for belonging to the group (e.g., to take part of battles between groups for territory). Such cheating demonstrated by free riders threatens the group. As a result it is important for groups to know who is and who is not a reliable member of the group so that trust and cooperation among group members can increase.

60. Sosis and Alcorta, "Signaling, Solidarity."
61. Galen, "Does Religious"; Myers, "Reflections"; and Saroglou, "Is Religion."

What evidence from CSR supports the idea that religious beliefs and behaviors increase group cohesion, trust, and cooperation? In a review of this literature, Norenzayan and Shariff report that experimentally inducing religious thought (nonconsciously) reduces the rate of cheating and increases altruistic behavior in strangers. They also note the long-known finding that religious believers tend to be more altruistic, have higher rates of volunteerism, and give more to charities than their nonreligious counterparts. The authors suggest that competition between human social groups for resources favors large groups over small.[62] Until relatively recently in human history, however, large groups lacked institutional and social-monitoring systems and were thus susceptible to collapse due to the possibility of cheating and the presence of free riders. Consider, for example, the individual who repeatedly eats of the group's food but does not participate, in an active way, in the hunt itself. If one person is allowed to get away with being a free rider, why not a second person? Why not a third person? The potential for a free ride on the backs of others in the group must be reduced for any large-scale cooperative endeavor.

Religion comes into play insofar as religious beliefs and behaviors act to increase trust and cooperation among group members. Particular beliefs and behaviors (e.g., religious rituals) act, in part, to signal group membership, and because many of these beliefs and behaviors are costly emotionally, physically, or even monetarily, a person's willingness to accept the beliefs or perform the behaviors signals devotion and trustworthiness.[63] Rituals in nonhumans increase communication of social information and coordinate social behaviors, and synchronous behaviors in humans (e.g., music, dance, marching) increase subsequent cooperation with others, even when the cooperation requires personal sacrifice.[64] While potentially costly, beliefs and rituals are useful in that they provide signals of a person's intent vis-à-vis the group, readying the participants for social interaction. The person who is willing to accept particular beliefs (e.g., a virgin birth, resurrection of the body) and to perform certain rituals (e.g., circumcision, baptism, tithing) can be trusted because that person is more like the other members of the group in these important ways. A preference for people who share our attributes or personal tastes is seen in adults, but it is also

62. Norenzayan and Shariff, "Origin."

63. Ibid.; Bulbulia and Sosis, "Signaling Theory."

64. Alcorta and Sosis, "Ritual, Emotion"; Wiltermuth and Heath, "Synchrony and Cooperation."

seen in young children and even infants, suggesting that this preference for "ingroup" individuals is acquired at an early age.[65]

As social groups get larger and harder to monitor, one way of promoting cooperation and trust among group members, according to CSR, is the belief in an omniscient God, one who is directly interested in morality. The moral sense, an important part of human nature, also evolved to encourage cooperation, altruism, and virtue, and prosocial behavior is encouraged in groups through these moral judgments.[66] According to this view, early humans inherited social instincts that induced pleasure in the presence of other members of the group and feelings of sympathy for them. With the development of higher mental processes such as language, the proper way to treat others in the group could be effectively communicated, which developed into a sense of morality. These evolved mechanisms lead individuals to behave in prosocial ways that produce psychological states experienced as awe, righteousness, gratitude, love, forgiveness, empathy, loyalty, and so forth (the social emotions).[67] Some behaviors are deemed acceptable to the group, others not acceptable. The primatologist Frans de Waal sees the social emotions, especially empathy, as important in promoting group cohesion. Empathy evolved as the primary mechanism for altruism, which is directed toward those with whom one has a positive or close relationship. Altruism is withheld from strangers or defectors from the group.[68]

Cross-cultural studies suggest that the larger the social group, the more likely the group is to show beliefs in strong deities that are directly concerned with personal morality of group members and that are also willing to punish violators of group norms.[69] It seems that belief in supernatural monitoring and punishment (as well as belief in an afterlife) are important to promoting prosocial behavior among groups and increasing trust and cooperation.[70] Graham and Haidt argue that shared beliefs in supernatural agents as moralizing gods solve many commitment and cooperation problems in large groups by helping to promote ingroup loyalty and suppressing selfishness and free riding.[71]

65. Hamlin et al., "Not Like Me."
66. Krebs, "Morality"; Norenzayan, *Big Gods*, 23–29
67. Krebs, "Morality."
68. De Waal, "Putting."
69. Atran and Henrich, Evolution of Religion."
70. Atkinson and Bourrat, "Beliefs"; Shariff and Norenzayan, "Mean Gods."
71. Graham and Haidt, "Beyond Beliefs."

IS CSR COMPATIBLE WITH THEISM?

CSR leads to the conclusion that many of our religious beliefs arise from mental mechanisms or tools that evolved over time to serve other, non-religious purposes. Agency-detection devices, theory of mind mechanisms, and other tools evolved to solve problems associated with survival, both physical and social. Some people are troubled by this notion because it suggests that these religious ideas are spurious and might be unreliable. If a belief in God is merely a by-product of a mental tool that evolved to help us solve problems with physical survival, then how can we be sure that the belief in God is justifiable? If the mental tool does not exist specifically to give us the true belief that God exists, how can we know if we can trust the belief?

Just because religious beliefs, from a CSR account, might be by-products of mental mechanisms that have evolved over time to serve other, non-religious purposes does not necessarily make the beliefs suspicious. Many of our nonreligious beliefs are also by-products of mental mechanisms that evolved for other purposes. For example, there is no obvious selection advantage to knowing calculus or in knowing about quantum physics, and the beliefs or propositions produced by these fields can be viewed as by-products. This does not mean, however, that the beliefs about calculus or quantum physics are necessarily false.

Most researchers in CSR seem in their writings to be neutral in their views about the relevance of this work to the truth of religious beliefs. While the producers of CSR research may be ambiguous about this issue, many consumers of this research are less so and often interpret CSR research as supporting their atheistic worldviews. These individuals typically hold (1) that the methods of science are the only way to accurately study the physical world (methodological naturalism), and (2) that only the physical or material world exists (ontological naturalism). Belief in methodological naturalism does not necessitate belief in ontological naturalism, but for many, ontological naturalism is the starting point. If ontological naturalism is true, then methodological naturalism is not merely the only way to acquire true knowledge of the physical world, it is the only way to acquire true knowledge at all. No distinction is made between methodological and ontological naturalism in that belief in one entails belief in the other. If one assumes only a physical world, then a nonphysical God cannot exist. If one assumes that only the methods of science can give us truth, then the claims of religion cannot be true. Of course, one can hold that the best way to study the physical world is through methodological naturalism without believing that only the physical world exists. One can, and should, make a distinction between methodological and ontological naturalism.

Leech and Visala distinguish between two subsets of propositions that can make up a religious worldview.[72] Subset A are propositions that are essential for the survival of the worldview (e.g., there is a God). Subset B consists of propositions that are not essential but could be modified or even rejected without threatening the continuing existence of the worldview. An example of a subset B proposition might be, God created the world in six twenty-four-hour days about ten thousand years ago. The findings from CSR do not seem to threaten any subset A propositions. CSR is (or certainly can be) agnostic to the truth or falsity of religious claims. CSR is interested in the origin of the beliefs, not in whether they are true or false. Learning about the mental mechanisms that result in religious beliefs does not challenge the justification for accepting those beliefs.[73] Having an account (even a complete account if that was possible) of why humans nearly universally believe that other people have minds does not mean that we should stop believing that others have minds. Belief in minds and belief in gods are both the result of an intuitive, Type 1 or natural type of cognition. There is no empirical evidence that other minds exist, just as there is no empirical evidence that gods or God exists. Neither belief is weakened by scientific evidence clarifying how those beliefs develop out of the normal, natural workings of the human mind.[74]

Another worry some people have is that CSR (or science in general) is trying to develop a complete and reductionistic account of religious belief and behavior. On the contrary, CSR is interested in a partial account of some aspects of religion. Perhaps some in the field have a goal (or desire) to reduce religious belief to "nothing but" mental modules (and their correlated neural mechanisms), but CSR can certainly be viewed, as most researchers in the field do view it, more modestly. While CSR might uncover natural mental mechanism for belief in God, one can also incorporate other, nonnatural causes into the complete account as well. Perhaps a personal God who desires a relationship with creation implanted religious beliefs in human minds in the way described by CSR. While that is certainly not

72. Leech and Visala, "Cognitive Science."

73. Murray, "Scientific"; Murray and Goldberg, "Evolutionary."

74. Barrett, "Cognitive Science, Religion and Theology."

a question that can be answered by CSR, it is a position that is compatible with CSR theory.

Let us give Justin Barrett, a leading figure in CSR, the final word when it comes to what CSR can and cannot tell us and about the naturalness of religious belief. Barrett writes in his book *Why Would Anyone Believe in God?*

> Widespread belief in God arises from the operation of natural processes of the human mind in ordinary human environments. Belief in God does not amount to anything strange or peculiar; on the contrary, such belief is nearly inevitable . . . Even if this natural tendency toward belief in God can be conclusively demonstrated to be the work of evolved capacities, Christians need not be deterred. God may have fine-tuned the cosmos to allow for life and for evolution and then orchestrated mutations and selection to produce the sort of organisms we are—evolution through 'supernatural selection.'[75]

75. Barrett, *Why Would*, 122–23.

4

Neuroscience of Religion
Is My Brain Involved in My Experience of God?

So of all our raptures and our drynesses, our longings and pantings,
our questions and beliefs. They are equally organically founded, be they
religious or of non-religious content. To plead the organic causation of a
religious state of mind, then, in refutation of its claim to possess superior
spiritual value, is quite illogical and arbitrary . . . Otherwise none of our
thoughts and feelings, not even our scientific doctrines, not even our
dis-beliefs, could retain any value as revelations of the truth, for every one
of them without exception flows from the state of its possessor's body at the
time.[1]

Religious melancholy, whatever peculiarities it may have *qua* religious, is
at any rate melancholy. Religious happiness is happiness. Religious trance
is trance. And the moment we renounce the absurd notion that a thing is
exploded away as soon as it is classed with others, or its origin is shown;
the moment we agree to stand by experimental results and inner quality,
in judging of values—who does not see that we are likely to ascertain
the distinctive significance of religious melancholy and happiness, or of
religious trances, far better by comparing them as conscientiously as we can

1. James, *Varieties*, 17–18.

with other varieties of melancholy, happiness, and trance, than by refusing
to consider their place in any more general series, and treating them as if
they were outside of nature's order altogether?[2]

*N*euroscience is an umbrella term that refers to disciplines that are interested in the study of the brain and the nervous system. Specific disciplines, such as physiology, biology, chemistry, psychology, and cognitive
science, among others, have subareas within the disciplines that come under the umbrella of neuroscience. For example, there are physiologists who
are interested in investigating the physiology of neurons (neurophysiol-
ogy), psychologists who study the role of the brain in behavior (behavioral
neuroscientists), and cognitive scientists who research the involvement of
the brain in higher-level mental processes such as memory and decision-
making (cognitive neuroscientists). Some of these neuroscientists (whether
from psychology, biology, cognitive science or one of the other disciplines)
are interested in learning about how the brain is involved in experiences
that are deemed religious. Whether these religious experiences are fundamentally behaviors, emotions, cognitions, or some mixture, these scientists
are interested in understanding the neuroscience of religion—the role of
the brain in religious experience.

Sometimes this field of investigation is called *neurotheology*, a term
first used by Aldous Huxley in his 1962 novel *Island*. Today, the word is intended to describe the examination of how the brain is involved in religious
experience. In some respects the term is unfortunate insofar as it implies
that something is being learned about God or that the "neurotheologian"
is studying about and making statements about the nature of God. Psychologists have been interested in the psychological processes underlying
religion for over one hundred years, but the study of experiences deemed
religious from a neuroscientific perspective only dates back to the 1980s.
Neuroscience of religion is a more appropriate phrase to denote the work of
individuals who research how the brain is involved in religious experience,
and this terminology matches the much older and more established discipline of the psychology of religion, the subject of the current book.

To simply say that neuroscience is interested in how the brain and
nervous system works ignores the important fact that explanations in the

2. Ibid., 28–29.

neurosciences span multiple levels, describe many kinds of mechanisms, and utilize information from a variety of fields.[3] A good neuroscience explanation involves understanding behaviors, brain systems underlying those behaviors, functions and properties of brain systems and regions, electrical and physiological characteristics of neurons, and structures and changes in molecules that compose the cells and chemicals that make up the brain areas.[4] The nervous system is perhaps the most complex entity in the universe, and successful attempts to understand how it works require transdisciplinary research investigating multiple levels—behavioral, system, cellular, and molecular. No one level is more vital or important than another, and explanations at one level do not rule out the need for explanations at other, equally valuable levels. A strong explanation in the neurosciences is able to integrate across these various levels. Even though higher-level phenomena typically depend upon the lower-level mechanisms for their existence, it is not necessarily the case that every instance or element of the higher-level phenomenon must be reducible to or identical to some element at the lower level.[5] Therefore, explanations in the neurosciences are not good or bad: they are discovered and described facts. This is true for explanations in the neuroscience of religion as well. Whatever explanations are proposed for a particular religious experience (hopefully explanations that incorporate multiple levels), the explanation, if true, is an objective feature of the way the nervous system works.[6]

Methodologically, neuroscientists typically look for correlations between some behavioral or cognitive task (or some religious experience in the case of the neuroscience of religion) and activity in a particular region of the brain. Finding such an association does not mean that the brain activity causes or explains the particular behavior or cognition. It does not necessarily mean that the particular brain region is even involved in the specific task, because the region might instead be involved in some other phenomenon that cannot be separated from the task under investigation.[7] But you have to start somewhere, and neuroscientists who study religious experience (as well as those who read the research in the neuroscience of religion) must keep in mind the multilevel perspective and transdisciplinary

---

3. Craver, *Explaining*, 1.

4. Ibid., 2.

5. Ibid., 257–67.

6. Ibid., 22–28.

7. Ibid., 60.

approach fundamental to the neuroscientific study of any experience, including those deemed religious.

Technological developments over the past thirty years have changed the way neuroscientists study the brain's involvement in behavior. Prior to the latter part of the twentieth century, brain scientists typically investigated how the brain affected behavior by using methods such as staining nerve cells and examining the cells under a microscope. This procedure enabled scientists to map connections between different brain regions. Other procedures included stimulation or ablation studies where thin electrodes were implanted in the brain to deliver electrical current to a particular group of cells. By introducing mild electrical current to the electrode, the researcher could stimulate the cells to see what effect such stimulation had on the behavior of the organism (often a laboratory rat). Stronger current applied to the electrode would destroy the neural cells, and the impact of removing that brain area could be assessed. Various methods of damaging neural tissue (e.g., through the injection of chemicals) and observing the subsequent effect on behavior were developed and became standard practice in neuroscience laboratories for much of the twentieth century.

In the latter part of that century and into the twenty-first century, newer strategies were developed that enabled researchers to look at brain tissue, first its structure and then its function, without the necessity of performing surgeries on lab animals to implant electrodes for stimulation or ablation. These newer technologies were even applicable to use on human as well as animal subjects. While stimulation and ablations are still used, these brain imaging technologies are invaluable in ascertaining the role the brain plays in various behavioral, emotional, and cognitive functions. One of the earliest of these newer technologies is computed tomography or CT scan. This brain imaging technique is a painless and fast way to produce a picture of the brain (or other organ of the body) to determine if any injury or damage has occurred. While this technology is useful for the neurologist who is doing a medical assessment on a patient to try to diagnose the cause of a particular set of symptoms, the CT scan does not have a lot of appeal to the neuroscience researcher because it provides a static picture of the brain. Another type of scan that provides a clearer and more detailed picture of the brain is magnetic resonance imaging (MRI), but this procedure too is more helpful to the neurologist than to the researcher in neuroscience.

Much more useful procedures for the neuroscientist are those technologies that result in a dynamic image of the brain, an image of the brain in action. The neuroscientist is often interested in determining what area or region of the brain is active when a particular behavior is performed, a specific emotion felt, or a certain cognition experienced. These functional brain imaging procedures are in many respects the gold standard in neuroscience research because they are thought to reveal, in a more concrete way, which brain regions mediate which experiences. One of the first of these functional imaging procedures was positron emission tomography (PET), which involves the injection of a radioactive isotope (e.g., radio-labeled glucose which has a short half-life) into the subject's bloodstream. Glucose is the only source of energy that the brain can utilize, so the glucose is taken up by the brain, and the radioactive traces are concentrated in the more active brain tissue. As the tracer decays, positrons are emitted which collide with electrons producing particles. These particles are detected by the PET scanner and transformed into a color-coded pattern of brain activity with the brighter colors of the PET image representing the more active brain regions.

Another brain imaging procedure that is standard in neuroscience research is fMRI (functional magnetic resonance imaging), which measures changes in blood oxygen level that occur in brain tissue. Again, the rationale behind this technology is that the more active brain tissue will require more glucose and oxygen, both of which are carried in the blood. In the case of fMRI, it is the oxygen level changes in the blood (called BOLD for blood-oxygen-level dependence) that are measured and used to create the image of the active brain. The earlier fMRI scanners did not provide particularly good resolution, but more recent versions of the technology have produced excellent resolution across time and space. Additional technologies are single photon emission computed tomography (SPECT), which is similar to fMRI but involves the use of radionuclides and photon emission to generate a three-dimensional colored map of tissue activity, and the non-invasive quantitative electroencephalography (EEG) in which, using electrodes placed on the surface of the scalp, EEG activity is transformed into colorful images showing electrical activity over the surface of the brain.[8]

8. McNamara and Butler, "Neuropsychology," 217–19.

OVERVIEW OF THE ROLE THE BRAIN PLAYS IN RELIGIOUS EXPERIENCE

Initial investigations into the brain's involvement in religious experience focused on the area of the brain called the temporal lobe. Each of the two hemispheres of the brain is divided into four basic sections or lobes: the frontal lobe, the parietal lobe, the occipital lobe, and the temporal lobe. Each lobe has certain brain circuitry that carries out particular functions so, for example, the frontal lobe has an area (called the motor cortex) that is involved in motor movement. The parietal lobe has a region devoted to bodily sensations such as touch (the somatosensory cortex), and the occipital lobe is primarily responsible for the processing of visual stimuli. The temporal lobe, along the side of the brain roughly behind the ear, has areas devoted to the perception of auditory stimuli (the auditory cortex) as well as sections involved in the processing of language. The reason why early researchers in the neuroscience of religion focused their attention on the temporal lobe was because some people with temporal lobe epilepsy (seizures that originate in the temporal lobe) report heightened religiosity and ecstatic experiences preceding, during, or after the seizures themselves.

This association between religion and epilepsy was noted as early as 400 BCE. At that time, some saw the seizures as a curse from the gods while others believed that those with the seizures had prophetic powers. Although Hippocrates discounted any connection between the seizures and religion, the association nevertheless remained. In the Middle Ages, epilepsy was associated with witchcraft, possession, and magic, and the visions and religious experiences of the Apostle Paul and Joan of Arc were thought by many to be due to epilepsy.[9] More recently, Fyodor Dostoyevsky had epilepsy and likened the experiences surrounding the seizures to ultimate joy and truth. Dostoyevsky described his epilepsy to a friend using religious language when he said that "The air was filled with a big noise and I tried to move. I felt the heaven was going down upon the earth, and that it had engulfed me. I have really touched God. He came into me myself; yes, God exists, I cried, You all, healthy people, have no idea what joy that joy is which we epileptics experience the second before a seizure. Mahomet, in his Koran, said he had seen Paradise and had gone into it. All these stupid clever men are quite sure that he was a liar and a charlatan. But no, he did not lie, he really had been in Paradise during an attack of epilepsy; he was

9. Devinsky, "Religious," 76–77.

a victim of this disease as I am. I do not know whether this joy lasts for seconds or hours or months, but believe me, I would not exchange it for all the delights of this world."[10] The actual prevalence of religious experience associated with epilepsy is between .4 and 3.9 percent, depending on if the experiences occur before, during, or after the seizures, and can consist of premonitory auras or actual conversions.[11] It was these actual or presumed associations between epilepsy and religiosity that motivated early researchers to begin their study of the neuroscience of religion by examining the temporal lobes.

One of these early investigators was Michael Persinger, who began his work in this area in the 1980s. Persinger found that he could invoke a feeling of sensed presence in his laboratory subjects by applying a pulsed magnetic field over the temporoparietal region (the junction of the temporal and parietal lobes), a feeling that Persinger considered religious in nature.[12] In fact, Persinger concluded that religion is reducible to what he called temporal lobe transients, brief electrical events centered in the temporal lobe. These temporal lobe events are what produce religious experiences.[13] Other researchers, however, did not find that application of a magnetic pulse would generate any experiences as described by Persinger, but that various personality characteristics indicative of suggestibility were associated with the generation of these sensory experiences in both religious and nonreligious participants.[14] Methodological problems with Persinger's work call into question his conclusions. For example, it is not clear that Persinger used double-blind procedures, leaving open the possibility of experimenter bias in the studies. Also, while Persinger claimed that application of the magnetic pulse produced transient temporal lobe electrical events, he provided no brain imaging data to demonstrate that the magnetic pulses produced any changes in the brain at all, let alone the kind of neural events he said were necessary and sufficient for religious experiences.

While Persinger and some others limited their study of the neuroscience of religion to examining the temporal lobe, many researchers recognize that religion, like most human experiences, is complex and multidimensional and is likely to involve a variety of distributed brain regions

10. Ibid., 76.

11. Devinsky and Lai, "Spirituality."

12. Persinger and Healey, "Experimental."

13. Persinger, "Religious."

14. Granqvist et al., "Sensed Presence."

and structures. While there has been some talk, particularly in the popular media, of a so-called God spot that is responsible for religious experience, in fact almost all researchers examining the neuroscience of religion acknowledge that multiple structures and networks distributed across the entirety of the brain are involved in the mediation of religious experience. This is, of course, exactly what one would expect when an experience involves such a diversity of behaviors, emotions, cognitions, and the like. Once the networks are identified, it then becomes possible to ask important questions such as, whether these networks are also involved in other forms of behavior, emotion, or cognition, such as agency detection and theory of mind (see chapter 3); whether the networks utilize specific neurotransmitters; whether the networks become active in any noticeable developmental pattern that would reflect the pattern of religious development across the life span; and whether lesions in these brain structures and networks affect religiosity.[15] The research reviewed below indicates that there are neural systems and networks activated when a person has a religious experience or performs a religious act. These systems involve parts of all four lobes of the brain, many different interconnecting networks, and several different neurotransmitter systems.

Religious experiences are associated not only with temporal lobe epilepsy; they are also linked to various psychopathologies such as bipolar disorder, schizophrenia, and obsessive-compulsive disorder. There are even correlations between religiosity and autism spectrum disorders with decreased religiosity associated with higher scores on measures of autism.[16] In addition, various psychotropic drugs such as phencyclidine and ketamine that act on the glutamate system, amphetamines that act on dopamine circuits, and mescaline and psilocybin that act at serotonergic synapses, are known to produce religious experiences. Glutamate is involved in consciousness, cognition, learning, and memory; dopamine is involved in reinforcement, motivation, memory, attention, and mood; and serotonin is involved in arousal and mood regulation. The complex phenomenon of religion certainly includes elements of motivation, reinforcement, cognition, learning, mood, and consciousness. The findings that various neurotransmitter systems and diverse psychopathologies are implicated in religious experiences is further support for the idea that a complex experience such as religion would be mediated via multiple systems in the brain.

15. McNamara and Butler, "Neuropsychology," 216–17.
16. Caldwell-Harris et al., "Religious," 3362.

Frontal Lobes

Studies in the neuroscience of religion have found that various brain areas in the frontal lobes are involved in religious experiences. Specific cortical areas in the frontal lobe include the medial orbitofrontal cortex (MOFC) and the prefrontal cortex (PFC). The MOFC is implicated in the subjective experiences of music and smell and in ethical, social, and emotionally related behaviors that are seen in social affiliation, judgment, and self-awareness. The PFC consists of several regions, many of which are associated with various aspects of religious experience. For example, the lateral PFC is involved in higher-level cognitive functions such as decision-making and controlling behavior. The medial and ventral PFC is implicated in moral judgment tasks, moral reasoning, and regulation of moral emotions, and is active during self-referential judgments. The medial PFC is also involved in theory of mind and thinking about one's own emotional state.[17]

Temporal Lobes

The temporal lobes are involved in religious experience, but not in the simplistic way proposed by Persinger. There are many interconnections between the various lobes and structures of the brain, and temporal lobe structures are implicated in a variety of experiences that can be deemed religious. Temporal lobe structures are implicated in moral decision-making, self-image, autobiographical memories, learning and memory, the connection of objects and motivations toward those objects, spatial awareness, language processing, and the integration of external sensory experience and internal somatic state, each of which can be part of religious behaviors, cognitions, and emotions. Included in the temporal lobes are a number of brain structures that collectively make up the limbic system, and these structures are also implicated in a variety of experiences that can be considered religious by the person having them. The anterior cingulate cortex (ACC) monitors action consequences and participates in the regulation of autonomic physiological processes, while the posterior cingulate cortex (PCC) helps to mediate moral judgment and monitors conflicts between moral goals. The amygdala also mediates moral judgment; is involved in the processing of emotionally negative situations; and is involved in the processing of reward, punishment, and avoidance. A final structure that

---

17. Fingelkurts and Fingelkurts, "Is Our Brain," 305–7.

makes up the limbic system is the hippocampus, which is crucial for the acquisition and retrieval of many kinds of learning, including spatial learning and memory.[18]

Parietal Lobes

Areas of the parietal lobe important in religious experience include the temporoparietal junction (TPJ—implicated in false-belief attributions, semantic processing, and theory of mind processing), the parietal cortex (involved in spatial relations), and the posterior superior parietal lobule (responsible for orientation of the self in space and a sense of boundary between the self and the rest of the world). Also involved are the inferior parietal lobule (which generates abstract concepts and processes self/other distinctions) and the angular gyrus (which is activated in moral judgment tasks and helps generate a first-person representation of one's behavior). Both hemispheres of the brain are involved in religious experiences (although not necessarily in the exact same manner).[19] It is important to keep in mind that none of these brain areas, neural systems, or neurotransmitters is uniquely involved in mediating religious experiences. As mentioned above, these brain areas mediate a variety of behaviors, cognitions, and emotions some of which might be deemed religious in context.[20] As an example of the overlap between the mediation of these structures in both religious and nonreligious experiences, the medial PFC and the TPJ are active during personal prayer; these same areas are also involved in social cognition and when we are interacting with other humans. This type of prayer also activates reward circuitry in the brain—it is pleasurable and reinforcing. The implication of this finding is that talking to God during personal prayer (as opposed to in a more formal prayer such as the Lord's Prayer) is similar neurologically to talking to a "real" person. God to the Christians who were participating in this study is seen as a person rather than as an abstract entity.[21] This finding suggests that we generally use Type 1 cognition over the more abstract Type 2 cognition when thinking of God (see chapter 3). We tend to see God in more human terms, even though

18. Ibid., 305–7.
19. Ibid., 305–7.
20. Azari et al., "Neural"; Kapogiannis et al., "Cognitive."
21. Schjoedt, "Religious Brain."

the theologically correct view conceives of God in a more abstract way (as omnipresent, omnipotent, and so forth).

Other studies of prayer also show this overlap with brain areas involved in social cognition and relationships. The results of these brain imaging studies suggest that when people pray to a God they believe to be real and capable of answering the prayer, areas of the brain that mediate interpersonal relationships (e.g., TPJ) become active, implying that the person is treating the prayer as a conversation with a loved one. These kinds of improvised or conversational prayers represent an intersubjective experience comparable to normal interpersonal interaction. These prayers also, like interactions with loved ones, activate dopaminergic centers in the brain making the prayers rewarding and pleasurable.[22]

VARIATIONS IN BELIEF AND UNBELIEF

Religion is sometimes dismissed by nonreligious individuals as no more than a security blanket or pacifier for those who need comfort and protection against the harsh reality of everyday life. Figures such as the nineteenth-century philosophers Ludwig Feuerbach and Karl Marx as well as the physician/neurologist Sigmund Freud (who was heavily influenced by Feuerbach's writings) saw religion as a projection, the opium of the people, or an illusion born of wishful thinking. Terror management theory in psychology proposes that threats of death are relieved through the use of some form of meaning-making system, such as religion, which can provide a perspective through which one can understand and respond to immediate existential concerns. Indeed, religion does offer many believers comfort in difficult times of stress, illness, and death. How might religion have such a comforting effect, one that research shows can even have positive benefits to mental and physical health? How can religious behaviors, emotions, and cognitions influence how one thinks about and responds to life's challenges?

Belief systems, such as religious belief systems, influence how we perceive and think about the world, affecting our motivations, our emotions, our attitudes, and our cognitions. Belief systems also often have symbols connected to them. Do symbols have an effect on how we think, and if so, do they have this effect because of associations the symbols have with certain ideas and beliefs or do they affect the brain more directly? Do visual symbols, such as a cross or a circle, influence us through their effects on

22. Neubauer, "Prayer"; Schjoedt et al., "Highly Religious," 199–201.

cognitive processes, or can they affect the early stages of visual processing itself? What is the mechanism by which religious symbols might impact how we think about the world and even our perception of the world? Kyle Johnson and colleagues investigated how religious symbols might affect brain functioning, hypothesizing that such religious symbols do interact with the brain on a primary level. The authors also proposed that religiosity can affect how positive and negative visual symbols interact with neural function.[23]

Johnson and colleagues used BOLD (blood-oxygen-level dependence) imaging on volunteers from a variety of religious backgrounds, including atheists. The participants in the study viewed various emotional symbols, some with religious content and some without, some with positive valence and some with a negative valence. Those symbols with positive religious content included a cross and a heart; those with a negative religious valence included various satanic symbols. Positive nonreligious symbols included a smiley face and a dollar sign; an example of a negative nonreligious symbol was a swastika. Finally, neutral symbols such as a square and a diamond were used as controls.

The participants in the study also completed the Beliefs About God Assessment Form (BAGAF), which measures adaptive or maladaptive emotional responses toward God, and the Quest Scale (Q), which provides an indication of the degree to which religion is seen as involving an open-ended search for meaning in life and a dialogue with the existential questions life raises. The scores on these religious measures were correlated with brain responses to the various types of symbols presented to the participants.

If symbols affect not only cognition but sensory processing itself, then perhaps religious and nonreligious symbols will produce different brain activity in the primary visual processing area of the brain. The authors hypothesized that the religious symbols would produce a more robust form of activity in the primary visual cortex (V1) compared to the nonreligious symbols. The results of the study revealed that the negative religious symbols, but not the positive symbols, were associated with decreased V1 activity. Positive religious symbols correlated with greater V1 activity compared with nonreligious symbols. On the religiosity measures, the authors found

23. Johnson et al., "Pilot Study."

that higher religiousness scores (Q) were associated with reduced V1 processing of the negative symbols.[24]

The results of the Johnson et al. study suggest that the emotional nature of the religious symbol (whether it is a positive or a negative symbol) affects brain activity in the primary visual cortex. The authors also showed that people with a more negative view of God (as measured on the BAGAF) were more likely to activate the insula and the amygdala when processing symbols, brain structures known to be involved in negative emotional responding. Overall, these results indicate that religiosity is correlated with decreased activation of V1 to negative symbols, and that stronger negative emotional beliefs alter the way the brain perceives emotional symbols. The authors conclude that religiosity (a type belief system) might modulate early visual processing in response to emotional symbols thereby changing how we think about the world and even our perception of the world by reducing cognitive bias or prejudice.[25]

How we think about and perceive the world, our emotions, and our motivations can also influence overall health. Many studies indicate that religiosity is associated with improved mental and physical health.[26] Creating meaning is a basic human need, and religion, as a meaning-making system, creates meaning by providing goals, order, control, and coherence between beliefs. Conflict, expectancy violation, error, and uncertainty are associated with anxiety, and they also activate the anterior cingulate cortex (ACC). The ACC, in turn, is linked to error-related negativity (ERN) which is a pattern of neural activity that occurs between 50 and 100 ms after people make errors. ERN is larger in people diagnosed with anxiety disorders and is reduced with anti-anxiety medications as well as with alcohol (which also reduces anxiety). The ACC, then, is considered a type of distress detector, signally when vigilance and control are needed.

If religion's palliative effects on health involve the creation of meaning, then perhaps that effect might be detected neurologically through the ACC. Studies by Inzlicht et al. found that religion correlated with decreased activity in the ACC. Stronger religious zeal and greater belief in God associated with decreased ACC activity in response to error. Religion might have an effect on health via this reduced anxiety-related activity in the ACC,

24. Ibid.

25. Ibid.

26. Cobb et al., *Oxford Textbook*; Koenig et al., *Handbook*; Seybold, "Physiological Mechanisms."

which would alleviate distress. There is a clear connection between stress and illness, so the authors propose that the order, certainty, and meaning provided by religion decrease stress and influence overall health.[27]

If the brain is involved in religious experiences (behaviors, emotions, cognitions), what happens if the brain is damaged due to injury or stroke, or is impaired due to some developmental disorder? If the brain is involved in religious experiences, are the brains of nonbelievers noticeably different? Given the premise of this book and much of the psychology of religion literature, if religion is not *sui generis*, one would not expect there to be dramatic differences in the brains of religious and nonreligious individuals. The cognitive mechanisms underlying religious and nonreligious experiences are, from the ascription perspective (see chapter 1), the same. One would anticipate that the underlying neurobiological systems and mechanisms are similar as well.

Some studies have shown differences in structure and function in certain brain regions between individuals scoring high on various measures of religiosity and those scoring lower on these measures. Greater hippocampal atrophy (cell loss) was observed for those individuals reporting a life-changing religious experience compared to those who did not report such an experience.[28] Associations between religious activity and atrophy in the orbitofrontal cortex (OFC), particularly in the left hemisphere, have also been reported. Less atrophy was observed in participants who had a life-changing religious or spiritual experience during the course of the study, which lasted up to eight years, or who reported being born again at the beginning of the study.[29] Other differences between individuals who score high on religiosity and those who score low include variations in temporal cortex and precuneus, suggesting that important aspects of religiosity are correlated with volume modifications in some brain areas.[30]

Some religions, for example Christianity, emphasize a change in how one views the self. Christians are called upon to follow the example set by Christ and to deny themselves in order to live a more spiritual life. Christians are also encouraged to try to evaluate themselves from God's perspective. What would God think of us and our behavior? Are we being good disciples of Christ and modeling ourselves after Jesus? Han and colleagues

27. Inzlicht et al., "Need to Believe"; Inzlicht et al., "Neural Markers."
28. Owen et al., "Religious Factors."
29. Hayward et al., "Associations."
30. Kapogiannis et al., "Neuroanatomical."

used functional brain imaging techniques to determine if there were differences in functional anatomy in brain areas involved in social cognition between Christian and nonreligious subjects. The ventromedial prefrontal cortex (VMPFC) is involved in self-related processing of stimuli (how does this stimulus relate to my own self), while the dorsomedial prefrontal cortex (DMPFC) is implicated in reappraisal and evaluation of the self. These differences are especially noted for individuals in Western and individualistic cultures more so than in people from Eastern and collectivist societies. Compared to nonreligious participants, Christians showed stronger activity in the DMPFC (when asked to evaluate the self from God's perspective) relative to the VMPFC, suggesting that people with religious and nonreligious beliefs utilized different brain substrates for self-referencing.[31] The VMPFC also shows greater activity in both Christians and nonbelievers when the participant accepts truth claims, whether the truth claims are religious or not. In other words, belief (religious belief and nonreligious belief) is correlated with activity in the VMPFC. Disbelief and uncertainty regarding truth are mediated by medial PFC, parts of the insula, and the superior parietal lobe.[32]

These results are not particularly impressive, but they do indicate that there are some functional and even structural differences between the brains of religious (variously defined) and nonreligious people. It needs to be remembered, however, that the environment and the kinds of experiences we have can affect brain function and structure, so reporting differences between religious and nonreligious brains does not mean that the neural differences existed prior to the religious preferences.[33] The results of these studies also suggest that it is the content of the truth claims that results in the activation of different brain regions, not differences in the individuals (religious or not) themselves.

Are there changes in religious/spiritual experiences associated with changes in brain structure or function due to injury or disease? Mention has already been made of the association between temporal lobe epilepsy and increases in religiosity in some individuals. Reports also indicate that decreases in religiosity/spirituality are found in some people with Parkinson's disease, a disorder attributed to loss of brain cells that use dopamine

31. Han et al., "Neural Consequences."
32. Harris et al., "Functional"; Harris et al., "Neural Correlates."
33. Hayward et al., "Associations."

as a neurotransmitter.[34] Autism, a disorder linked to deficiencies in theory of mind and social cognition, is also linked to decreases in religiosity. Studies show that autistic individuals are only 11 percent as likely to believe in God.[35] If relationship to God is a kind of interpersonal relationship that involves areas of the brain that mediate social cognition and theory of mind, perhaps individuals with difficulties with cognitive processes involved in relating to others and reading other minds would have decreased experiences of relationship with God.[36]

MEDITATION/MYSTICAL EXPERIENCE

The early work of Persinger and others focused on the temporal lobe as a potential site for the brain's mediation of religious experience. The observation that some patients with temporal lobe epilepsy reported religious experiences before, during, or after the seizures was part of the rationale for examining the temporal lobe by these researchers. Sometimes the experiences the patients reported were of a mystical nature, a feeling of ineffability and timelessness, a sense of being lost in something bigger than oneself, an experience of spacelessness. These observations led some to consider whether a model of mystical experience in particular, in addition to religious experience more generally, might not involve the temporal lobes including the related limbic system structures. This temporolimbic model of mystical experience, however, seems to be inadequate for explaining the complexity of mystical experiences (just as limiting general religious experience to temporal lobe events was an insufficient explanation). Studies of epileptic patients indicate that while some mystical experiences occur among these individuals, such as ineffability, timelessness, and a loss of a sense of space, others do not (e.g., inner subjectivity, sacredness, and unity with something larger than oneself). These data suggest that the temporal lobe is not uniquely involved in the generation of mystical experiences, and that the temporal lobe model might be inadequate for understanding the brain's involvement in these kinds of religious experiences.[37]

Mystical experience is complex and seems better explained, from a neurological perspective, by examining activity in a variety of brain areas

34. McNamara et al., "Chemistry of Religiosity."
35. Neubauer, "Prayer," 99.
36. Caldwell-Harris et al., "Religious," 3362.
37. Bradford, "Emotion"; Greyson et al., "Mystical."

in the parietal and frontal lobes. Andrew Newberg and his colleagues used Franciscan nuns in contemplative prayer and Buddhist monks during meditation to see what brain areas are involved when these religious practitioners had what they described as peak religious experience, a sense of absorption into something beyond themselves and a loss of a sense of space and time. Using SPECT imaging, Newberg found a variety of brain areas involved, including several in the frontal and parietal lobes. In particular, the results showed increased activity in the frontal lobes, perhaps reflecting the increased attention required for prayer and meditation, and decreased activity in the posterior superior parietal cortex which is believed to be involved in generating a map of the self in relation to the rest of the world. Inhibition in this area is hypothesized to produce the reported experience of unity with God (for the Catholic nuns) or unity with the world or higher order of reality (for the Buddhist monks) that is part of the peak religious experience.[38]

These findings are consistent with those from the laboratory of Mario Beauregard, who used fMRI to identify neural correlates of mystical experiences in Carmelite nuns. These findings also showed activity in a variety of brain areas that are associated with mystical experience, including brain regions involved in visual perception (occipital, temporal, and parietal lobes), representation of the self (parietal lobe), and emotions (limbic system, frontal, parietal lobes).[39] Additional evidence for the involvement of frontal and parietal lobes in the mystical experiences of selflessness or self-transcendence come from studies of patients with brain damage. Selective damage to posterior parietal regions produce an increase of self-transcendence, supporting the suggestion that the parietal lobe is involved with defining and perceiving the self and with self-related cognition (such as autobiographical memory). The parietal cortex, particularly in the right hemisphere, seems to be critical in differentiating the self from the nonself, and damage to this area results in various disorders of the self (e.g., impairments in self-awareness and difficulty identifying the self in space). These results with brain damaged individuals support the findings of Newberg and others hypothesizing that inhibition of these areas during contemplative prayer or meditation might be the neural mechanism for the peak religious experiences of a sense of self-absorption into something

---

38. Newberg and D'Aquili, *Why God*, 113–27; Newberg et al., "Measurement."
39. Beauregard and Paquette, "Neural Correlates."

beyond oneself and loss of the sense of time and space.[40] Meditation and prayer can also produce great pleasure in practitioners because these activities stimulate the same reward pathways that produce the rewarding and pleasurable effects of natural reinforcers such as food and water, as well as for any substance or activity that can become addictive.[41]

CRITIQUE OF THE NEUROSCIENCE PERSPECTIVE

A great deal of attention is directed toward experiences that seem to defy current psychological models of mind and physical models of reality. Near-death experiences (NDEs) are reported in upwards of 18 percent of cardiac arrest survivors, and the descriptions of the experience seems to call into question the prevailing models of mind/brain relationship. How can current psychology (or physics for that matter) explain this kind of complex conscious experience that typically includes feelings of peace and joy, a sense of being out of one's body, encountering other beings, a life review, seeing another realm of reality, confronting a barrier to that realm, and then returning to one's body? Can a materialist and reductionistic psychology that patterned itself after nineteenth-century physics ever explain such experiences?[42] While a variety of hypotheses have been proposed (e.g., altered blood gases, anoxia, neurotoxins, neuroanatomical malfunctions), the phenomenon itself seems incredible and generates great excitement among those who read the many books published on the subject.

Part of the near-death-experience often includes a sense of being outside of one's body. These out-of-body experiences (OBEs) also present some potential problems for contemporary scientific theories of how the body and brain are related. While some argue that both NDE and OBE represent challenges for neuroscience and psychology and demand new models of consciousness based on quantum physics, others suggest that adequate explanations for NDE and OBE either already exist or are being experimentally developed using current scientific theories.[43] Indeed, OBEs are already being induced experimentally in the lab.[44]

---

40. Johnstone et al., "Right Parietal"; Urgesi et al., "Spiritual Brain."
41. Sharp, "Meditation-Induced Bliss."
42. Greyson, "Implications."
43. Ibid.; Agrillo, "Near-Death Experience"; Lynn et al., "Near-Death Experiences."
44. Braithwaite et al., "Cognitive Correlates."

NDE and OBE are often used to challenge the neuroscience perspective on brain/mind relationships, but there are other reasons to question the neuroscientific approach to the kinds of experiences discussed in this chapter. What is the purpose of investigating religious experiences using the tools of neuroscience? Is the neuroscience of religion a useful approach to take if we want to understand religious and spiritual experiences? Some researchers, even though they use the methods of neuroscience and believe that these methods are necessary to ultimately understand the brain's involvement in human experience (religious or otherwise), do recognize the limitations of these methods and try to use caution in their conclusions.

While brain imaging is the gold standard for understanding which brain areas are involved in a particular behavioral or cognitive task, these technologies do have methodological limitations, and the images that result are interpreted based on important assumptions. Generally, brain imaging techniques (e.g., fMRI, SPECT, PET) do not measure neural signals directly; they instead measure changes in the metabolic demands of brain tissue. How much glucose or oxygen is utilized by the tissue? How much blood flow is going to certain brain areas? The assumption is that the more active the brain area is, the more glucose and oxygen it will require. The more activity in a particular brain site, the more blood will flow to that site delivering the necessary glucose and oxygen those active brain cells demand. This is a reasonable assumption, but the relationship between the metabolic signals and the electrical signals of the brain cells is not well understood. Also, spatial resolution of the images (although getting better all the time) is not yet adequate to get an exact reading on the precise brain areas activated during a particular task. In addition, there are timing issues. What is the difference in time between when a task is performed and when the brain "lights up" indicating a change in neural activity thought to be mediating that task? Both time and spatial concerns are embedded in the brain imaging process.[45]

To study brain activity associated with an experience (the target task), it is necessary to find an appropriate comparison or control condition, a task that is as close to the target task as possible, and compare brain activity patterns during the two tasks. The control task cannot be too similar to the target, or there will be no contrast; on the other hand, the control cannot be too dissimilar, or comparisons will be meaningless. Once these target and control tasks are identified, they are repeated many times across many

---

45. Spezio et al., "Religion."

individuals, and the brain activity associated with these tasks are averaged within and between the participants in the study using sophisticated statistical analyses. The colorful maps that are generated are actually statistical maps of the probability of where signals are based on the averaging across many individuals and many trials, not precise maps of brain signals per se.[46] So, when we see images of brain activity corresponding to particular religious or spiritual or mystical experiences, we need to keep in mind just how these images are created, what they actually are mapping, and the assumptions that underlie the methodology. These caveats do not invalidate the usefulness of imaging data. They simply remind us that human experience, including religious experience, cannot be reduced to nothing but neural activity. Reality is multileveled. Additional perspectives are needed.

HUMANISTS AND NEUROSCIENTISTS

The humanities consist of a set of disciplines that use literature, languages, history, the arts, religion, and philosophy to try to understand human experience. These approaches are often contrasted with the empirical methods of the sciences. A feud of sorts exists between those who work in the humanities and those who work in the sciences as to how complete a scientific description and understanding of humans and human experience can be. The biological scientist E. O. Wilson argued that all human knowledge, including economics, religion, sociology, and the arts, can be unified under a small set of natural laws (a process he calls consilience) that can be discovered using scientific methods.[47] Humanists critical of the idea that all human knowledge can be fully understood by following scientific methodology often cite scientists such as Francis Crick, Richard Dawkins, and Sam Harris as examples of, in their view, science claiming and promising more that it can or should. Francis Crick, along with his colleague James Watson, won the Nobel Prize in physiology or medicine for his discovery in 1953 of the structure of DNA. Crick, who died in 2004, began a scientific program later in his career investigating the neurological correlates of consciousness and famously (or infamously) said of humans that we are "nothing but a pack of neurons," by which he meant that all that characterizes human beings can be reduced to brain cells and neural

46. Schjoedt, "Religious Brain," 313–15.

47. Wilson, *Consilience*, 8–14.

chemicals.[48] Dawkins, the evolutionary biologist who has angered scientists as well as nonscientists by some of his statements, said in one of his books, "In a universe of blind physical forces and genetic replication, some people are going to get hurt, other people are going to get lucky, and you won't find any rhyme or reason in it, nor any justice. The universe that we observe has precisely the properties we should expect if there is, at bottom, no design, no purpose, no evil and no good, nothing but blind pitiless indifference."[49] Meanwhile, the neuroscientist Sam Harris wrote,

> The self that does not survive scrutiny is the *subject* of experi-ence in each present moment—the feeling of being a thinker of thoughts *inside* one's head, the sense of being an owner or inhabit-ant of a physical body, which this false self seems to appropriate as a kind of vehicle. Even if you don't believe such a homunculus ex-ists—perhaps because you believe, on the basis of science, that you are identical to your body and brain rather than a ghostly resident therein—you almost certainly *feel* like an internal self in almost every waking moment. And yet, however one looks for it, this self is nowhere to be found. It cannot be seen amid the particulars of experience, and it cannot be seen when experience itself is viewed as a totality. However, its *absence* can be found—and when it is, the feeling of being a self disappears.[50]

Each of these scientists has a completely negative view of religion (Dawkins and Harris are part of a group known as the New Atheists), but the principal reason they are criticized by humanists is because of their total commitment to science as the only way to knowledge. Only science with its use of empirical methods can lead to any truth. All human enterprise and experience can be understood scientifically, leaving nothing left for litera-ture, philosophy, religion, history, or any other perspective. Not only does Wilson have faith in the ultimate success of science to unify knowledge, the philosopher Patricia Churchland in her book *Neurophilosophy* maintains that brain science will ultimately lead to a full understanding of human behavior and cognition, leaving nothing for philosophy (or any of the other humanities) to tell us.[51] Indeed, it was Churchland's book published over

---

48. Crick, *Astonishing*, 3.
49. Dawkins, *River*, 133.
50. Harris, *Waking Up*, 92.
51. Churchland, *Neurophilosophy*, 1–10.

thirty years ago that is seen by many humanists as the impetus for the current feud that exists between humanists and neuroscientists.

Among the criticisms the humanists level against the neuroscientists is that the brain scientists are promising more than they can deliver. Neuroscientists will sometimes claim that even though current knowledge of how the brain produces consciousness (for example) is incomplete, the continued scientific pursuit of how the brain works will eventually lead to a complete understanding of brain function, including of free will, consciousness, mind, and so forth. Nothing will be left unknown when it comes to who we are as human beings. The scientific study of the brain will explain all.

Another point of tension between humanists and neuroscientists concerns how the brain and mind are related and the extent to which human beings are strictly determined in our behavior, thoughts, and emotions. The humanities tend to study the products of a human mind (literature, religion, and art) that are considered free and unconstrained by the brain, whereas the brain sciences investigate how the brain produces all human products through the workings of deterministic natural laws.[52] Despite findings from fields such as quantum physics suggesting that much of the natural world is indeterminate and unpredictable, neuroscientists stubbornly continue to insist that all human behavior and cognition is strictly determined. This difference in approach leads to quite a gap between the humanists and the neuroscientists. Additionally, the extent to which reductionism and quantification are used is also a point of contention. Scientists tend to believe that the best way to study a particular natural phenomenon is to reduce it to its component parts and use hypotheses, controlled experiments, and quantitative models to develop an understanding of it. Those in the humanities, however, tend to prefer a more holistic approach, believing that reducing a phenomenon to its parts often ends up eliminating the phenomenon entirely. Humanists also tend to be suspicious of too much quantification and hypothesis testing because these methods are part of a scientific worldview that includes a lot of philosophical assumptions that scientists tend to not recognize.[53]

Many humanists have called neuroscientists to task over these issues and others.[54] According to these humanist critics, human consciousness, personhood, culture, and the like cannot be reduced to brain cells firing

52. Slingerland and Collard, "Introduction," 10.

53. Ibid., 14–22.

54. Scruton, *Soul*, 51–75.

and neurochemicals being released. To reduce complex human experience to mere brain anatomy and physiology does not do justice to human nature. One critic, although one who also understands and respects the advances neuroscience has brought to our understanding of who we are as human persons, puts it this way. "The gist of neuroscience is that the adverbs 'simply' and 'merely' can exorcise the mystifications that have always surrounded the operations of the mind/brain, exposing the machinery that in fact produces emotions, behavior, and all the rest . . . If this could be true, if this most intricate and vital object could be translated into an effective simplicity for which the living world seems to provide no analogy, this indeed would be one of nature's wonders."[55]

As I view this battle between humanists and neuroscientists I see some merit in the humanist's case. Many neuroscientists do make philosophical assumptions that they refuse to acknowledge. Many neuroscientists do explain away complex human experiences as "nothing but" brain activity. Many neuroscientists do have a strong reductionist and materialistic worldview that they bring to their practice as scientists. Having said that, however, I also believe that the criticisms the humanists make are overdrawn and excessive. While many brain scientists do make such claims, others recognize these errors and are more cautious in what they proclaim and promise. Many neuroscientists (including some whose work is reported in this chapter) admit that science can only take us so far in our understanding the complexities of human nature and recognize a role for other approaches (including those represented by the humanities). Reality can be investigated using a number of different methods and approaches. A thorough analysis of the biological bases of religious experience can be useful in our understanding of this important human phenomenon. Perhaps someday a complete biological and chemical account of religious experiences will be obtained. Because reality is complex and multileveled, however, a complete account at the biological and chemical level will not rule out the need for an analysis of religious experience from psychological, sociological, anthropological, and theological perspectives (among others).

There is also a necessary distinction that needs to be made between reductionism (or naturalism) as a method and reductionism (or naturalism) as a philosophy. As discussed above, science in general and neuroscience in particular are often criticized for being reductionistic. Indeed, science is reductionistic in its methodology. Scientists working in the

55. Robinson, *Givenness*, 6.

laboratory typically do need to reduce that part of the natural world they are investigating into smaller parts in order to understand how those parts work. The idea is to then "reassemble" the parts into a whole, hoping that a better understanding of how the whole works will be known. This form of reductionism is called methodological reductionism and is how science operates. Scientists need to be methodological reductionists (at least at times) in order to investigate phenomena in the natural world. Scientists also are methodological naturalists in that they come to the study of nature assuming that, using empirical procedures, the natural mechanisms or causes of some particular phenomenon will be identified. The assumption of the methodological naturalist is that natural (as opposed to nonnatural or supernatural) causes are present and can be identified and known. Science has approached its subject matter in this reductive and naturalistic way for over three hundred years, and it has proven to be a highly successful approach. Natural mechanisms have indeed been identified that explain much of the workings of the natural world. Reductionism and naturalism as methods work and are thus part of the very definition of science.

Philosophical (or ontological) reductionism and naturalism, on the other hand, are not required for science. This form of reductionism holds that once you have reduced some phenomenon to its simpler parts and understood how those parts work, you have obtained a complete understanding of the phenomenon because the whole of the phenomenon is nothing more than the sum of the parts. Philosophical naturalism is the position that there is only the natural or material world. No other level of reality exists. We might say that methodological reductionism and naturalism describe the nature of science, while ontological reductionism and naturalism are views about the nature of reality itself. If philosophical or ontological (which pertains to the nature of things) reductionism and naturalism are true, then science would be the only path to knowledge because science is the method used to study the natural world. While I believe that methodological reductionism and naturalism are necessary to science, the philosophical versions are not. They may be held by a scientist, but they do not need to be. A scientist can be a reductionist and a naturalist in the lab without holding these as philosophical positions. A scientist does need to act, in the lab, as a naturalist. The scientist, in the lab, does need to act as if there are natural mechanisms or causes for the phenomenon being studied and believe that the methods used (e.g., reductionism) will reveal what those natural mechanisms and causes are. There may be nonnatural or supernatural causes for some phenomenon as well (e.g., some aspect of religious or spiritual experience), but if those supernatural causes exist, the scientist will not find them because science is limited to the search for natural mechanisms.

SUMMARY

What do we make of the research reported in this chapter? The brain is involved in all of our experiences: sensory, behavioral, cognitive, and emotional. If religion is solely dealing with supernatural events and has no physical representation, then the brain is probably not going to be involved in religious experiences. Christianity, however, places high importance on physicality. God created the physical world. God became part of that physical world in the person of Jesus. Jesus was physically resurrected. The Eucharist (for some Christians) involves the actual body and blood of Christ. There is a profound physicality to Christianity (and to many other religious traditions as well). We use our physical bodies to worship. Our physical bodies are part of our religious experiences, and the brain should be involved in those experiences as well.[56] The results of the studies reviewed in this chapter should come as no surprise. The chapters in this book point out ways the brain is implicated in thinking, decision-making, judgment, will, emotions, and morality. The brain is involved in our relationship to God as well. None of this proves or disproves the existence of God. God's existence is not a question that can be answered by any study discussed in this chapter or any other chapter of this book. These studies do not tell us where God is located in the brain (although some have made this claim in the past). The studies do suggest, however, what might be occurring physiologically when one reports having a religious experience. As mentioned in chapter 1, according to the ascription model, there does not seem to be anything psychologically unique about religious experiences. Similar psychological mechanisms are involved in experiences deemed to be religious as are involved in experiences not deemed to be religious. The same seems to be true for physiological mechanisms as well. Religious experiences utilize similar neural systems to those involved in nonreligious experiences.

We are made in the image of God. We are made for relationships, with others and with God, and the brain is the organ that mediates these relationships. Complex neural activity occurs in distributed areas of the

56. Seybold, "God and the Brain."

brain during various kinds of religious experiences. This diversity of activity reflects the multifaceted nature of religion and experiences associated with religion. There is no "God Spot"; many brain areas are involved. If the reality in which we find ourselves is accurately represented in the neural activity of the brain, then we should not be surprised or troubled by the fact that we experience God, who is part of the reality for Christians and other religious believers, by using our brains. "If we as embodied creatures are made for a relationship with God, would not God have made it possible to experience him through our embodied natures?"[57]

57. Seybold, "Biology of Spirituality," 94.

5

The Soul

Do We Have a Soul? Do We Need a Soul?

She had no certain notion what a soul is. She supposed it was not a mind or
a self. Whatever they are. She supposed it was what the Lord saw when His
regard fell upon any of us. But what can we know about that? Say we love
and forgive, and enjoy the beauty of another life, however elusive it might
be. Then, presumably, we have some idea of the soul we have encountered.[1]

One of the important ideas of the Judeo-Christian religious tradition
is that human beings are made in the image of God. Genesis 1:26
has God say, "Let us make man in our image, in our likeness" and verse
27 goes on to declare, "So God created man in his own image, in the image of God he created him; male and female he created them." But what
does being made in the divine image mean? Many of the characteristics
thought to be unique to humans have been proposed as part of the image
of God (*Imago Dei*), including reason, volition, consciousness, and morality. These qualities might also be subsumed under the title of soul. We are
made in the image of God in that we have a soul that connects us to God
in a way that other parts of God's creation are not connected. It is this soul,
then, that enables the qualities of reason, consciousness, volition, morality,

1. Robinson, *Home*, 110.

and so forth, which humans possess. Furthermore, this soul is thought by many to be something that is added to the human body. It is a nonmaterial thing that makes us (our body and soul) separate from the rest of creation. The problem with thinking of the image of God or the soul in terms of unique human capacities, however, is that many of these abilities are found in other animals.[2] Reasoning, volitional choice, consciousness, and at least rudimentary morality are seen in other primates and in some nonprimates as well. As the philosopher Alasdair MacIntyre put it, "Much that is intelligent animal in us is not specifically human."[3] A similar statement might be made about choice, consciousness and morality as well.

The picture of human nature painted by contemporary psychology, cognitive science, and neuroscience is one that some think is contrary to the image offered by the Judeo-Christian tradition. Some psychologists, neuroscientists, and philosophers have stated that today's science tells us that humans are nothing more than our biology, our bodies, or our brains. Francis Crick, a leading biological researcher and codiscoverer of the structure of the DNA molecule, maintained a materialistic perspective of human nature, reducing everything about us to brain cells and neural chemistry. More specifically, Crick, who died in 2004, said "You, your joys and your sorrows, your memories and your ambitions, your sense of personal identity and free will, are in fact no more than the behavior of a vast assembly of nerve cells and their associated molecules . . . You're nothing but a pack of neurons."[4] Crick went on to say "The idea that man has a disembodied soul is as unnecessary as the old idea that there was a Life Force. This is in head-on contradiction to the religious beliefs of billions of human beings alive today. How will such a radical challenge be received?"[5] Philosopher Thomas Metzinger put it this way, "There is a new image of man emerging, an image that will dramatically contradict almost all traditional images man has made of himself in the course of his cultural history . . . it will be strictly incompatible with the Christian image of man, as well as with many metaphysical conceptions developed in non-Western religions."[6] While this reductionistic view offered by contemporary science has been criticized,

2. Jeeves, "Introduction," 1–9.
3. MacIntyre, *Dependent*, 40.
4. Crick, *Astonishing*, 3.
5. Ibid., 261.
6. Metzinger, "Introduction," 6.

many Christians no doubt agree with Crick and Metzinger.[7] These believers might also think that the scientific view of human nature is incompatible with their religious beliefs and traditions. Those who want to have a view of human nature that is consistent with Christian tradition seem to be presented with a choice between holding a view that is true to religious beliefs or seeing human nature through the eyes of science. Perhaps, however, the choice presented by these scientists and philosophers is a false one.

This chapter begins with a discussion of what the soul is supposed to do. What functions does it serve? Why do we need a soul? Included in this discussion will be a review of some recent research findings in psychology, cognitive science, and neuroscience that suggest the very functions we attribute to the soul are closely linked to the functioning of the brain. In fact, we might even say (as some do) that this connection with the brain obviates the need for a soul at all. Why postulate the existence of a soul if we can explain the functions of the soul by appealing to what the brain does? Following this examination of the literature is a review of the important ways that thinkers (philosophers primarily) have understood what the soul is and how it might relate to the body. What is apparent is that there have been (and are now) various approaches to this so-called mind(soul)/body problem: some argue for a kind of dualism, others for a type of monism (or physicalism), and still other for something in between. The chapter will conclude by speculating on the implications of a physicalist account of the soul and discussing contemporary thoughts on the need for a soul.

WHAT DOES THE SOUL DO?

Throughout history, souls have been seen as one of the ways that humans and other animals differ. Humans have souls, animals do not. While this distinction between humans and animals has not been and is not now universally held, even among Christian philosophers and theologians, it is nevertheless a common view. Souls enable, according to this perspective, certain characteristics and capabilities in humans that are not seen in animals. Even if one believes that nonhuman animals possess souls (a view held by many theologians throughout church history such as Augustine and Aquinas), human souls nevertheless enable abilities that help to define us as a species. Some of these abilities are thought to be free will (or volition), a moral sense, judgment, rational decision-making, and enabling

7. Scruton, *Soul*, 51–75.

social relationships (including a relationship with the divine). For some people, the soul is that thing given to us by God that makes us in God's image; being made in the image of God means having a soul. As we will see below, however, research from a variety of disciplines, including psychology, cognitive science, and neuroscience challenges the notion that these abilities are uniquely human and that they are the result of the action of a thing called a soul.

Free Will

Free will, as it is commonly understood, is the ability human beings have to select how they will behave. The belief in free will is very compelling. We all have the sense that our actions are under our own control. We recognize that some of our actions are automatic and are done without much or any conscious thought, but we nevertheless believe that most of our behavior is, and certainly our important actions are, performed because we make a decision. We decide to perform behavior A and could choose to not perform behavior A or to perform another behavior if we wanted to. The belief that our behavior is under our own control is foundational for any view that holds people responsible for their actions. One of the reasons the behaviorism of the mid-twentieth century was resisted by so many was because it viewed human behavior as entirely dependent upon environmental stimuli. Ultimately, according to the behaviorist theory of B. F. Skinner, we cannot be held accountable for our actions because our behaviors are not selected by us; they are selected by contingencies found in the environment.[8] The nature of free will is an important topic of discussion and debate among religiously inclined philosophers as well as theologians. Scientists have also recently begun to investigate the extent to which people are free in their behavior, and their findings are seen by some as a challenge to the traditional view that humans consciously choose what their behavior will be and when they will act.

There is a substantial body of research in psychology suggesting that much of our everyday behavior is under the influence of nonconscious processes. While we do consciously and intentionally select some of our behavior, the majority of our moment-to-moment behavior is actually determined by stimuli and events that are beyond our conscious awareness. If this is the case, it is difficult to see how these behaviors are made in any

8. Skinner, *Science*, 6–8.

free manner if by "free" we mean through a conscious decision to perform behavior A instead of behavior B. For example, background music influences a person's choice of wine: more expensive wine is selected when the music is classical as opposed to top-forty.[9] Nonconscious or implicit factors can also affect other consumer behaviors such as how long we take to eat a meal or how long we spend walking the aisles in a store.[10] We adopt the physical behavior of others, such as walking speed, without intending to or being aware that we are doing so, and we like more those people whose behavior we (nonconsciously) adopt.[11] Smells and other stimuli affect our behavior without our conscious awareness or choice. Exposure to a citrus smell that has been associated with cleanliness, for example, makes it more likely we will clean up after ourselves.[12] This research suggests that there is a perceptual-behavioral link that engages our actions and produces behavior in us similar to the behavior we see in others. This connection, along with nonconscious guidance systems for motivation and evaluation, serves to affect our moods, goals, attitudes, and judgments, which influence how we interact with others.[13]

Other studies suggest that our behavior is determined before we are consciously aware of a decision to act. The best known of these studies is that of Libet, who took the position, based on his experimental research, that while free will does not initiate a voluntary act, it could still control the performance of the act through a type of neural "veto."[14] Libet recorded the electrical activity of the brain while his subjects performed a simple act: flicking the wrist or pressing a button whenever the subject "wanted" to do so. He also had subjects provide a subjective report of when the decision to flick the wrist or push the button was made. Libet found brain activity approximately five hundred miliseconds before the initiation of the act. This finding, of course, makes sense and is not surprising. Because muscular movement is initiated by electrical impulses generated by the motor cortex in the brain, there should be an electrical discharge in the brain before the movement actually occurs. What was surprising, however, was the measurement of electrical activity in the brain approximately three hundred

9. Areni and Kim, "Influence."

10. Dijksterhuis et al., "Unconscious Consumer."

11. Bargh et al., "Automaticity"; Chartrand and Bargh, "Chameleon Effect."

12. Hirsch, "Effects of Ambient"; Holland et al., "Smells."

13. Bargh and Chartrand, "Unbearable"; Bargh and Morsella, "Unconscious Mind."

14. Libet, "Unconscious Cerebral"; Libet, "Do We."

miliseconds before the subject reported a conscious decision to perform the action. This electrical response that preceded the reported intention of the subject to move was termed the readiness potential.[15] This finding (for some) questioned the idea of freedom entailed in voluntary action (e.g., the wrist flick or the button push in this experiment) because the reported awareness of intent to move came after the brain process correlated with the intent. It seems that consciousness "catches up" with an action after it has been processed by the brain; the conscious decision to perform the act is an illusion.[16] This early work was extended by Soon, Brass, Heinze, and Haynes, who used fMRI to show that brain activity in regions in the frontal and parietal cortex (activity encoding the decision to act) preceded the conscious awareness of the decision to act by up to ten seconds.[17] Both the Libet research and the subsequent study by Soon et al. (along with studies by other researchers in various labs) question the belief we all have that we consciously decide when to act. The implication of this research is that the behaviors are initiated nonconsciously before we are aware of any desire to perform them.[18] Where does this leave volition or free will? Libet argues that there still might be a role for conscious free will, even though conscious awareness occurs after the initiation of the act, in that the conscious will can affect the outcome by blocking or vetoing the process "so that no act occurs."[19]

These studies are not without their critics, who question the conclusions derived from the research.[20] Among the criticisms are those that focus on experimental methodology. Imagine that you are a subject in one of Libet's experiments. You are sitting in a laboratory and all you have to do is make a response (move a finger, flick your wrist, push a button) when you want to. Attached to your scalp are electrodes to record the electrical activity of various regions of the brain. Donald suggests that in this situation, the decision to move becomes the subject's "sole focus of attention . . . as a result, there is much subjective anticipation of each decision to move."[21] This kind of anticipation is very general and is not specific to the

15. Libet, "Unconscious Cerebral."
16. Donald, "Consciousness."
17. Soon et al., "Unconscious Determinants," 543–45.
18. Gazzaniga, *Who's in Charge?*, 129.
19. Libet, "Do We," 52.
20. Maoz et al., "On Reporting."
21. Donald, "Consciousness," 12.

response (e.g., a flick of the wrist) itself. The readiness potential, therefore, is a sign of a "general state of anticipation" to move, not as Libet suggested an unconscious decision to make the movement itself. This interpretation of the readiness potential and its appearance several seconds before the behavior is consistent with "the conclusion drawn in most studies of this effect prior to Libet's unusual claim, and by most investigators afterward."[22] In other words, there is no real threat to free will from these kinds of research results.

A leading figure in psychological research on free will is Roy Baumeister at Florida State University. Baumeister and his colleagues conceptualize free will as "an advanced form of agency and action control that permits people to resist acting in natural, animal ways . . . and to pursue enlightened self-interest in the context of a cultural environment." Baumeister goes on to suggest that "free will developed in evolution as an adaptation to the escalating demands and opportunities intrinsic to human social life and to facilitate the new kinds of social life that were emerging, notably human culture" and that "some actions are freer than others, and that the difference between them is demonstrably important in terms of inner processes, subjective perceptions, and social consequences."[23] Free will incorporates four main types of action control for Baumeister. The first form is *self-control*, the capacity to stop one's response and do something else. Responses in this context include overt behavior as well as thoughts and emotions. The second form of free will is *rational choice*, determining what response is the best in a given situation and doing it. *Planful behavior* is the third form of free will, the ability to make and follow plans, and the fourth form of free will is *initiative* which might, Baumeister suggests, be the first form to have evolved and is thus the foundation for the other three.[24]

Free will defined in this manner is a vital capacity that evolved in order to facilitate living in a social environment. In other words, free will has survival advantages. It evolved by utilizing some of the body's energy to support the psychological processes enabling action control. Given that there is a restricted supply of energy available for the body to use for all of its biological and psychological functions, only a limited amount of this energy can be used for free-will purposes, and evidence to support this contention comes from studies of self-control, the first of the forms of free

22. Ibid., 12.
23. Baumeister et al., "Choice, Free Will," 69.
24. Ibid., 67–82.

will listed above.[25] Performing a task that requires self-control impairs the execution of an immediately subsequent task that also requires self-control, a finding consistent with the hypothesis that self-control uses a limited energy source.[26] Exerting self-control consumes what we might call "self-control strength" which reduces the amount of strength available for subsequent tasks.[27]

Baumeister, Bratslavsky, Muraven, and Tice, over a series of four experiments, found that choice, active response, and self-regulation all utilize a common resource that leads to what the authors term ego depletion.[28] The authors found, for example, that choosing to eat one food over another or choosing to perform a personally meaningful attitude-relevant behavior (e.g., college students choosing to give either a pro- or antituition increase speech) resulted in decrements in persistence on subsequent performances (e.g., time spent trying to solve "unsolvable" puzzles). The authors also found that inhibiting emotion while watching a movie (e.g., suppressing laughter during a comedy) produced a decrease in performance on subsequent puzzles, and that a task requiring a high amount of self-regulation and concentration resulted in heightened passivity (i.e., decreased willingness to take action). The results of these experiments were interpreted by the authors to support the hypothesis that the self's capacity for active volition is limited, and that a number of seemingly unrelated acts result in ego depletion.[29]

Additional support for the limited-resource model of the self was found by Vohs et al., who found that making choices (among consumer goods or college courses for instance) reduced subsequent self-control (e.g., resulted in less physical stamina, reduced persistence in face of failure, and led to poorer quality in arithmetic calculations).[30] The authors also found that choosing is more debilitating on subsequent self-control than is merely deliberating and forming preferences about behavioral options or implementing choices made by someone else. Intellectual performance on logic and reasoning tasks (the second form of controlled action) is impaired by

25. Ibid.

26. Muraven et al., "Self-Control."

27. Muraven and Baumeister, "Self-Regulation."

28. Baumeister et al., "Ego Depletion."

29. Baumeister et al., "Free Will: Belief," 56–59.

30. Schooler et al., "Measuring and Manipulating," 77–90; Vohs et al., "Making Choices."

the previous exercise of attentional and emotional resources, which utilized self-control.[31]

What is the nature of this resource that gets depleted following the exercise of self-control? One possible answer to this question involves glucose. Blood glucose levels drop following the exercise of self-control, and low levels of glucose are correlated with poor performance on self-control tasks. Additionally, while acts of self-control impair performance on subsequent self-control tasks, consuming glucose (e.g., drinking lemonade sweetened with glucose) eliminates those impairments.[32] The mechanism whereby glucose improves self-control is uncertain, however. Sanders, Shirk, Burgin, and Martin found that merely gargling with a glucose solution (lemonade) can also improve performance on self-control tasks.[33] Given that the subjects in this study did not absorb any glucose, it is unlikely that the glucose increased energy levels in the subjects; this suggests a possible nonmetabolic alternative mechanism whereby glucose works by activating brain areas involved in reward.

The perspective on free will provided by Baumeister and colleagues has practical implications as well. If free will is dependent on an energy resource, then that resource can be conserved and replenished. Learning to "read" the level of this limited resource can help a person hold back on exertion of effort as the level runs low until the supply of energy can be renewed. Perhaps the analogy of an athlete conserving energy can be applied to the exercise of free will. Continuing with this analogy, one might be able, through practice, to strengthen this resource just as an athlete, through practice and exercise, can increase his or her abilities.[34] Indeed, studies do suggest that the capacity for self-control can be strengthened through exercise.[35]

Free will (self-control) in the model reviewed above is linked to our biology and is shaped by evolution; it has been selected because it has survival value for the organism. Humans are social animals and depend upon others (the social group) for survival. Any behavior that promotes the formation and maintenance of groups should be subject to natural selection. One of the benefits of free will from this perspective is that it promotes

31. Schmeichel et al., "Intellectual Performance."
32. Gailliot et al., "Self-Control Relies."
33. Sanders et al., "Gargle Effect."
34. Baumeister et al., "Choice, Free Will."
35. Muraven et al., "Longitudinal Improvement."

socialization and group formation and cohesion. A number of studies suggest that belief in free will does indeed promote prosocial behavior. For example, subjects induced to disbelieve in free will were less likely to help others and more likely to engage in aggressive behaviors.[36] In addition, encouraging a belief in free will decreases cheating behavior.[37] Less aggression, more helping, and less cheating are all behaviors that promote group cohesion, and individuals who are members of a strong social group are more likely to survive than those individuals who belong to less cohesive, weaker groups. Natural selection, therefore, would favor any psychological process (e.g., belief in free will) that results in behaviors (e.g., self-control) that promote socialization. As Baumeister puts it, "to succeed and live harmoniously in a cultural group, the animal is best served by being able to inhibit its impulses and desires. Perhaps ironically, free will is necessary to enable people to follow rules."[38]

Support for a biological basis for free will also comes from studies of control indicating that perception of control is adaptive and desirable and that the loss of control is aversive. Seeing control as desirable and the loss of control as aversive suggests that the psychological processes of emotion and motivation are involved. If so, the exercise of control should activate brain areas involved in emotion and motivation, and brain imaging research indicates that the prefrontal cortex (PFC) and striatum, regions associated with emotion, motivation, and reward, are indeed activated during behaviors involving control.[39] In addition, high self-control is correlated with less pathology and greater interpersonal success, which also supports the suggestion that control is important biologically and subject to natural selection.[40]

The work of Baumeister and his colleagues has been influential in shaping a scientific study of free will. His perspective on self-control, however, is not the only approach to an empirical understanding of freedom of choice. Another proposal suggests that diminished self-control is the result of a shift in motivational orientation and attentional focus. Specifically, using self-control at Time 1 causes the person to be more motivated to act in ways that are enjoyable and rewarding at Time 2. In addition to the change

36. Baumeister et al., "Prosocial Benefits."
37. Vohs and Schooler, "Value of Believing."
38. Baumeister, "Free Will," 16.
39. Leotti et al., "Born to Choose."
40. Tangney et al., "High Self-Control."

in motivation following self-control acts, there is a change in attention following self-control away from cues that signal the need to control and toward cues that signal gratification. These two processes, shifts in motivation and changes in attention following self-control acts at Time 1, lead the person to be less likely to utilize self-control in their behavior at Time 2.[41]

Other researchers are investigating the role of desire and temptation in self-control and the relationship between beliefs in free will and how people process both conscious and nonconscious information about self-agency.[42] The results of these studies indicate that decreasing a person's belief in free will through experimental manipulation results in antisocial behavior and also affects brain processes associated with intentional action, illustrating the effect that high-level cognitive beliefs can have on motor processes.[43]

Additional research on free will and self-control examines the role of the brain in these processes. Dozens of neuroimaging studies on agency have been conducted.[44] As an example of this research, Brass and Haggard investigated to see what neural mechanisms were involved in the inhibition (as a type of self-control) of intentional action.[45] The authors found that this inhibition of the intention to act involves areas in the frontomedian cortex, an area distinct and upstream from neural regions activated during intentional action or in the selection between alternative behaviors. This finding supports a top-down neural control mechanism that links intention to act with the act itself and is considered by the authors as a neural correlate for Libet's veto process of the conscious mind.

Some psychologists and neuroscientists argue that research such as Libet's suggests that belief in free will is an illusion. Behavior is strictly determined by neural events, which are, in turn, determined by chemical events, which are, ultimately, determined by events describable by physics. Other scientists, however, argue that belief in free will is still an option for those who want to hold to the belief, and there may be good reasons why a belief in free will should continue to be held.[46] As we have seen, a decrease in belief in free will has a negative effect on prosocial behavior as measured

41. Inzlicht and Schmeichel, "What Is."
42. Aarts and van den Bos, "On the Foundations"; Hofmann and van Dillen, "Desire."
43. Rigoni et al., "Inducing Disbelief"; Vohs and Schooler, "Value of Believing."
44. David, "New Frontiers."
45. Brass and Haggard, "To Do."
46. Schooler, "What Science."

by a decrease in helping behavior, an increase in aggression, and an increase in cheating.[47] Neuroscientist Michael Gazzaniga, who has in his research elucidated much of what we know about how the two hemispheres of the brain function, suggests that while belief in free will is "a powerful and overwhelming illusion that is almost impossible to shake," there is really little or no reason to try to eliminate the belief because it serves us well.[48] What about the supposed problem of responsibility? How can we hold a person responsible for his or her actions if there really is no such thing as free will, if it is only an illusion? Gazzaniga argues that, whether or not we are free, there is no scientific reason not to hold a person responsible. To justify this comment, Gazzaniga argues that mental states emerge out of the physical brain and that these mental states can and do constrain the brain processes that give rise to them. (Emergence is the process whereby lower-level complex systems self-organize to generate new properties that previously did not exist and that cannot be totally known by study of the lower-level system.) He also argues that the concept of personal responsibility must be considered in the context of the social group of which we all are a part. Responsibility is not to be found "in the brain" but is dependent on social interactions.

Determinists make four foundational claims about the relationship between the mind and the brain.[49] First, the brain (a physical entity) enables the mind. Second, the physical world is determined, so our brains are determined. Third, because our brains are determined and the brain is a necessary and sufficient organ that enables the mind, the mental events that arise from mind are also determined. Fourth, the mental event we call belief in free will is an illusion. Gazzaniga argues that while the first position above is essentially universally held by neuroscientists, the second position is under attack. The development of quantum physics in the early twentieth century has caused many physicists to question whether the physical world is completely determined. If position 2 is challenged, then so is position 3 that mental events are determined. Philosopher Mark Balaguer argues that the issue of complete physical (e.g., neural) determinism is unsettled at this point. Neither belief in determinism nor denial of determinism has been demonstrated by the empirical evidence, so the existence of free will

47. Baumeister et al., "Prosocial Benefits"; Vohs and Schooler, "Value of Believing."
48. Gazzaniga, *Who's in Charge?*, 75.
49. Ibid., 129.

is an open scientific question.[50] Free will and self-control, as mental properties, are emergent from the brain and depend on the physical events taking
place in the brain, but being emergent is not the same as being nonexistent.
There is still much we do not know about the fundamental nature of reality,
including the human mind and its influence on behavior. To categorically
deny the possibility of free will seems, to many, a claim that is not justified
given current knowledge. As Jonathan Schooler, a leading researcher in free
will and control put it,

> If science is not yet in a position to give people a definitive answer
> on the question of free will, what then should we tell them? My
> view is that scientists should inform the public of the facts but en-
> courage them to make up their own minds. Let's face it: ultimately,
> the question of free will boils down to metaphysical questions
> about the nature of the human spirit and its potential to transcend
> the limits of physical reality.[51]

In other words, some questions can be addressed by empirical science, but
not completely answered. The question of free will is one of those questions, but not, as discussed next, the only one.

Moral Sense

In addition to giving us freedom of action, the soul is often thought to enable us to know right from wrong and to behave in a morally acceptable
manner. This function of the soul is related to free will discussed above in
that behaving morally is, in part, possible because one has the freedom to act
in an amoral manner. Scientists from a variety of disciplines have recently
begun an empirical investigation into human morality. Psychologists study
the cognitive, emotional, developmental, and social mechanisms involved
in behaviors that are thought to define morality. In addition, primatologists
investigate the great apes, humans' closest relatives, to detect similarities
and differences between human moral behavior and the actions of the nonhuman primates that many would consider relevant to an understanding
of morality. One of the goals of this kind of comparative research is to try
to answer the question of the phylogenetic origin of morality.[52] Are there

50. Balaguer, *Free Will*, 21–24.
51. Schooler, "What Science," 213.
52. Tomasello and Vaish, "Origins."

premoral behaviors in the great apes (gorillas, bonobos, chimpanzees, and orangutans) that might have evolved into the kinds of behaviors in humans we recognize as moral acts?

Observations of the nonhuman great apes reveal behaviors of helping, sharing, and collaboration with others for mutual benefit. Chimpanzees, for example, will help other chimpanzees (and in some cases humans) by opening gates, delivering food, sharing tools for gathering food, and handing out-of-reach objects to others. The helping and sharing among chimpanzees most often involves reciprocity, but not always. Many times the behavior seems indicative of altruism in which the helping individual has positive affect toward the other. On the negative side, a chimpanzee will often retaliate against another when wronged, even if no material reward (like food) is obtained, which appears to have the effect of punishing the individual so that the transgression is less likely to occur in the future. Collaboration is also common in the great apes (chimpanzees have been studied the most), including forming alliances (even among nonkin) for group defense and for obtaining food.[53]

To note that cooperative social relationships exist in nonhuman primate species is not to say that those species behave in "human-like" moral ways. It is simply to acknowledge that human morality might have a biological basis to it. This is the approach to the study of morality taken by psychologists and primatologists who use comparative studies of animals to look for signs of empathy and altruism.

Empathy can be defined as the ability to feel what others are feeling and is a basic component of our social and emotional lives.[54] Examples of empathy and altruism are seen in animals from rats to birds to primates (human and nonhuman), and neurobiological mechanisms involved in empathy support the perspective of the biological origins of empathy and, by extension, perhaps of morality as well. Imaging studies using animals as well as humans show that empathy is broadly represented in the brain and uses a number of cortical and subcortical regions as well as the autonomic nervous system, endocrine system, and the hypothalamic-pituitary-adrenal axis.[55] The direction, therefore, is from emotion (empathy) to behavior (altruism) to morality. This research will be discussed in greater detail in chapter 6, but for the purposes of this chapter, it seems a soul (certainly an

53. Ibid.
54. Bernhardt and Singer, "Neural Basis."
55. Decety, "Neuroevolution."

immaterial one) is not required for at least some minimal level of moral behavior to be seen.

Judgment and Decision-Making

Another function attributed to the soul is the ability to make decisions and pass sound judgments. These decisions and judgments are thought to follow a rational reasoning process that involves the soul. Some of these judgments and decision, of course, deal with moral issues, and decision-making (both moral decisions and decisions that do not involve any moral question) is another area where research in psychology, cognitive science, and neuroscience can provide helpful insights.

It must first be said that most of the decisions and judgments we make are made without any conscious awareness on our part. We make thousands of decisions during a typical day automatically and effortlessly. These decisions and judgments involve movements we make, feeling we have, attitudes we develop, and thoughts about other people. A few research studies will illustrate this point. In a well-known and often cited study, individuals who were primed with particular constructs behaved in ways consistent with that construct. For example, in one study subjects were given sentences to read in which were embedded words (such as "Florida" and "gray") intended to prime the concept of elderly. The subjects primed in this way took longer to walk down the hall of the laboratory following the experiment than those subjects who read similar sentences without the "elderly" words.[56] In another study, subjects were working alongside an individual who was (unbeknownst to the subject) actually a confederate, that is to say was part of the experimental team of researchers. This confederate behaved in various ways (e.g., rubbed his face or shook her foot), and it was found that the subject acted in a way that mimicked the confederate. If the confederate rubbed his face, the subject was more likely to rub his face; if the confederate shook her foot, then the subject was more likely to shake her foot.[57] It is important to note that in none of these experiments did the subjects know that their behavior was mimicking the confederate or that their behavior was influenced by words they had read suggesting the concept of elderly. Their "decisions" to rub the face, shake their foot, or walk at a slow pace down the hall were made without conscious awareness;

56. Bargh et al., "Automaticity."
57. Chartrand and Bargh, "Chameleon Effect."

the decisions were automatic and nonconscious. Hundreds of other studies could be cited to support this basic point: automatic and nonconscious processes influence much of our behavior, our emotions, and our thoughts.

Two different types of thinking are found in humans, and researchers use various terms to distinguish the two modes: for example Type 1 and Type 2, Natural and Unnatural, or Intuitive and Rational.[58] While different terms are used, the distinctions between the types are similar. One is slow, conscious, reflective, effortful, and rational (Type 2, Unnatural, Rational) while the other is (relatively) fast, automatic, effortless, and intuitive (Type 1, Natural, Intuitive). Most of our decisions and judgments are the product of Type 1, Natural, Intuitive thought. In addition, there are sometimes conflicts or inconsistencies between a thought that is the product of the slow, reflective cognitive process and a thought that is the product of the fast, automatic, and intuitive cognitive process. Research from Banaji and her colleagues on implicit attitudes indicates that what one says about his or her attitude on an explicit test (e.g., a questionnaire that measures conscious, reflective attitudes on some topic) is often very different from what an implicit (nonconscious, automatic) measure of that person's attitude reveals.[59]

Some of the judgments and decisions we make involve moral issues, and while many of these moral decisions and judgments are the result of the slow, reflective, and conscious cognitive process, more are the result of the fast, nonconscious, automatic thinking mode. Making quick, intuitive, and emotionally based moral decisions, for "seeing" what is right and what is wrong, is important in maintaining the complex interactions that characterize human social life, and we have evolved mechanisms to accomplish this task.[60] Emotion is particularly important for these quick and automatic moral decisions. We often know that a particular behavior is wrong even if we cannot come up with a good rational reason for the decision, and various brain regions (i.e., prefrontal and frontal areas, amygdala, cingulate cortex) have been identified as being correlated with particular kinds of moral decisions—for example personal versus impersonal moral judgments.[61] In the study of moral decision-making, moral dilemmas are used to see the extent to which emotions are important in the nature of

58. Haidt, "Emotional Dog"; Kahneman, *Thinking*, 19–30; McCauley, *Why Religion*, 3–9.

59. Greenwald and Banaji, "Implicit Social."

60. Greene, "From Neural."

61. Greene and Haidt, "How"; Haidt, "Emotional Dog."

the moral decision. One dilemma used is known as the trolley dilemma in which a trolley is traveling down the tracks toward five people. The people will be killed unless you (the subject in the research study) pull a switch diverting the trolley onto another set of tracks where it will strike and kill one person. Pulling the switch saves five people but kills one. Should you pull the switch? The vast majority of people say yes, pulling the switch is morally acceptable in this circumstance. The second dilemma (footbridge) is similar to the first in that a trolley is heading toward five people. In this case, however, you are standing on a bridge over the tracks alongside a large person. The trolley will strike and kill the five people unless you push this large person off the bridge and onto the tracks where he will be struck and killed by the trolley, but the trolley will be stopped saving the other five people. Again, five people saved at the cost of one person's life. While the numbers are the same in the two dilemmas, the decisions most people make are quite different. As mentioned before, the vast majority of people say it is morally permissible to pull the lever to divert the train, but the majority of participants given the footbridge dilemma say that it is morally wrong to push the person off the bridge to stop the trolley. Most people say they would not push the person off the bridge. What is the difference between these two dilemmas that produces such dramatically different moral decisions? In a variety of studies, Greene and his research associates have suggested that the principal difference between these two conditions is the role of emotion.[62] The first, trolley dilemma is thought to be impersonal in that only a switch needs to be pulled. The second, footbridge dilemma is more personal in that a human being must be physically touched and pushed off the bridge onto the tracks. Neuroimaging studies show that the personal dilemma (and other dilemmas where a more personal act is required) activates areas in the brain (medial prefrontal cortex and the amygdala) involved in the processing of emotion, whereas the impersonal dilemmas do not. This initial emotional response of "No, this is wrong" to the harmful action in the footbridge dilemma is modulated by brain regions (perhaps the ventral medial prefrontal cortex) in the trolley dilemma, placing the behavior into situational context and resulting in an "all-things-considered" moral judgment that it is permissible to throw the switch killing one person to save five.[63]

62. Greene et al., "fMRI Investigation."
63. Cushman and Greene, "Finding Faults."

In addition to the more personal and physical nature of the footbridge dilemma, the footbridge case is understood by the subject as a "harm performed as a means to an end" situation whereas in the trolley dilemma, the harm is seen as a by-product or side effect of saving the others.[64] Together, the combination of the physical/personal and the means-to-an-end / by-product nature of the dilemmas helps produce different moral decisions in the two situations. Perhaps this underlies the ethical distinction between permitting an outcome to happen (i.e., passive euthanasia, in which death is understood as a kind of side effect of withholding treatment) and inflicting an outcome (i.e., active euthanasia, in which death is the desired end of a particular act).

Are moral decisions and judgments affected by the two different kinds of thinking discussed above? Is there a fast, intuitive, and emotional component as well as a slower, more reflective aspect to our moral decisions? One way of teasing apart these two thinking processes is to impose a cognitively demanding task on subject while a decision is being made. The rationale for this is as follows: If a decision is made on the basis of the fast, automatic, and nonconscious cognitive system (Type 1) alone, then adding a task that requires a lot of conscious, reflective thought (Type 2) would not affect the decision itself. Type 1 is doing all the work as far as making the decision is concerned. If, however, the decision task requires both Type 1 and Type 2 cognitive processing, then adding a second task that demands controlled, conscious, reflective cognition (increasing what's called cognitive load) should tax Type 2 processing and have an overall effect on the decision itself. Studies indicate that imposing cognitive load does slow down the decision-making process; this suggests that moral judgments and decisions utilized these two kinds of thinking.[65]

This approach should serve to remind us that while we tend to think of decisions and judgments as rational processes, an underlying layer of emotion is at work as well. In addition, we need to remember that decision-making and judgment are embodied. Damasio introduced the somatic-marker hypothesis to emphasize the role the body plays in providing important information we use to make decisions.[66] When we are confronted with a particular situation and we need to make a decision on what to do (e.g., to approach and pursue the situation or to escape and avoid the situation),

64. Ibid.
65. Ibid.
66. Damasio, *Descartes' Error*, 165–201.

we utilize real-time feedback from our bodies to help us decide. The body gets this information (the somatic-marker) from biological predispositions (acquired through human evolutionary history—members of our species have been in similar situations in the past) as well as from our individual histories. There is also, within the brain itself, neural activity that represents the judgment and decision-making process.[67] Some of the neural activity represents option A (throw the switch and divert the trolley), and different activity might represent option B (do not throw the switch because the trolley will still kill another human being) and so on for all the possible decision options available. This neural activity represents the reasons for and against certain options. We are still making our decision for particular reasons, but the decision-making process is clearly embodied.[68]

Image of God

There are actually several interpretations found in the Christian tradition of what it means to be made in the image of God.[69] One perspective is that the *Imago Dei* is the human capacity for reason. As alluded to above, the capacity for reason is no longer thought to be unique to humans in that research suggests it is seen in primates and perhaps other animals as well. If reason is the defining feature of the image of God (and a trait or capability of the soul), then humans share that image with other animals, and these other animals also possess a soul. (This last statement, that non-human animals possess a soul, is not that controversial in that it has been and is held by many Christian philosophers. These philosophers would generally not agree that animals are made in God's image.) Another view sees the human capacity for morality as an indicator of being made in God's image. Once again, however, if this is part of what it means to be made in the divine image, then we need to recognize that nonhuman animals, especially primates, have shown behaviors that when seen in humans are thought to be indicative of at least the beginnings of morality. For example, the primatologist Frans de Waal has documented altruistic behavior in a variety of species.[70] While we cannot automatically assume that the same psychological experience underlies similar behaviors in two species, it does

67. Forbes and Grafman, "Role."
68. Roskies, "Freedom."
69. Jeeves, "Neuroscience"; Thiselton, "Image."
70. De Waal, "Putting."

suggest that we need to be careful in attributing moral behavior to a soul or to the result of being made in the image of God.

Still another way of conceptualizing what it means to be made in God's image is to understand it in terms of relationships. A Trinitarian God can be understood as Father, Son, and Holy Spirit in relationship. Being made in that image is to be made for relationship. In this regard as well there is evidence from the study of nonhuman animals that can be incorporated into this perspective. Certainly animals have the capacity for relationships as do humans. Von Economo neurons are large brain cells found in humans, the great apes, and some monkeys that are thought to be involved in social cognition, self-awareness, and social relationships.[71] These neurons are also found in other highly social species such as dolphins and elephants. In humans (where the neurons are most prevalent), these neurons are rare at birth but increase in number during the first eight months of life.[72] They are found in the frontoinsular and anterior cingulate cortex and are more numerous in the right hemisphere than the left (the right hemisphere is thought to be more involved in social relationships than the left hemisphere). We might conceptualize the soul as those cognitive processes that enable us to have relationships, with ourselves (self-awareness), with others (social relationships), and with God.[73] The von Economo neurons, along with mirror neurons and other neural mechanisms discussed in the preceding pages, offer a possible biological mechanism whereby these "soulish" properties might be instantiated. This is not to reduce relationships (or soul) to "nothing but" these neural mechanisms, but to simply provide a mechanism for the embodiment of soul.

None of this is to suggest that there are not real and significant distinctions between humans and nonhuman animals in their experiences. It is simply to recognize that any claim that the soul or the image of God incorporates these kinds of abilities is to create the need to explain how these abilities, because they are also found to one degree or another in animals, are important for humans to carry the divine image or to have a soul.

Walton summarizes what the image of God means by saying that the *Imago Dei* conveys divine qualities and attributes. As such, the image (1) serves a functional capacity for humans (What are we to do? We are to do God's work on earth.), (2) provides a title or identity for humans that

71. Evrard et al., "Von Economo Neurons."

72. Allman et al., "Von Economo Neurons."

73. Brown, "Cognitive Contributions."

other animals do not have, and (3) stands in for the Creator. According to Walton, "In the biblical view, people in the image of God embody God's qualities and do God's work. They are symbols of God's presence and act on God's behalf as God's representatives."[74] Walton's remarks emphasize the importance of relationships in conveying these divine qualities and attributes.

APPROACHES TO SOUL

Most people as they read this chapter will probably come to the issue of what we are as human beings from a perspective called dualism. This view has a long and important history in western thought, and it is a perspective that is easy and natural to believe. We might even be intuitive dualists as we contemplate who we are as human persons. Research in developmental psychology suggests that dualism comes naturally to children because they have two distinct cognitive systems, one dealing with material objects and one for social entities.[75] Even as children, we seem to have the understanding that material objects operate according to physical laws while minds obey different kinds of rules involving social engagement. These differing sets of causes and effects in the social and physical worlds lead to a dualistic picture of persons; minds and bodies are different kinds of things operating according to different types of causes.[76] A study of adults, however, indicated that a simple dualistic perspective of persons is not necessarily the default option. Richert and Harris found that the adults in their study made a distinction between not only the body and soul, but also the soul and mind.[77] The mind was conceptualized as a cognitive organ responsible for decision-making, thinking, memory, and so forth. As such, the mind is connected to the life cycle of the biological body, affected by growth and development. The soul, on the other hand, was conceptualized in a more spiritual manner, disconnected from the body, and does not play a significant role in any cognitive processes.

While there are various types of dualisms (more on this below), we can generally say that, in regard to what constitutes human nature, dualism postulates the existence of two different kinds of entities, a material entity

74. Walton, "Human Origins," 883.

75. Bloom, *Descartes' Baby*, 198–208; Bloom, "Religion."

76. Cohen and Barrett, "When Minds."

77. Richert and Harris, "Dualism Revisited."

(e.g., body) and an immaterial entity (e.g., mind, soul, spirit). These two different entities might be called substances by some dualists or properties by other dualists; one entity might emerge from the other or be created specifically out of nothing (*ex nihilo*); and the two entities could be completely independent of each other or, more likely, could have some form of interaction or interdependence.

Substance Dualism

The oldest form of dualism comes from Greek philosophy, specifically the philosophy of Plato. Plato believed in a very real immaterial world (the World of Forms) that constitutes actual, ultimate truth. The material world, of which humans are a part, is but a shadow of this true world as Plato famously indicated in his well-known Parable of the Cave. Therefore, Plato was not interested in studying or in obtaining knowledge of this material world. He was interested in the immaterial World of the Forms, ultimate Truth. For Plato, there is a fundamental dualism in existence: this material world (which is essentially unimportant for a person interested in knowledge) and the ultimate immaterial world from which all knowledge and truth comes. Another important dualism for Plato, however, was the dualism that constitutes human nature. Humans are composed of a material or physical body, but more importantly humans also have an immaterial soul, and it is this immaterial entity that is the basis of consciousness or personhood. Plato also believed that the soul was eternal. Each person's immaterial soul exists in the World of the Forms before being "imprisoned" in the mortal, physical body. Just as the immaterial world is more important than the material world, so too the immaterial soul is more vital for humans than the physical body.

This form of dualism was very influential in Western thinking and philosophy, and it has been important in Western Christianity as well. It is probably safe to say that the majority of theologians in the West, up until the twentieth century anyway, were dualists in their anthropology. While this is likely true, it is important to note that it is not the case that Scripture itself explicitly teaches a dualistic anthropology.[78] Many Christians today get their understanding of the soul from this Platonic philosophy, even though they erroneously think it is a view of human nature clearly presented in both the Old and New Testaments. Many biblical scholars and

78. Goetz, "Substance Dualism."

theologians maintain that the Old and New Testaments do not present any particular anthropology. That is to say, the biblical authors do not seem to be interested in this philosophical question of what humans are made of and what the relationship is between the body and the soul. When the Bible does speak on these topics, the image of humanity we get is a holistic one. We are both bodies and souls, or we are embodied souls.[79] The biblical picture of humanity, again to the extent that the Bible is even concerned with this topic, certainly is not a picture consistent with Platonism and its view of a disembodied soul "imprisoned" in an earthly, physical body.

A similar kind of dualism was developed in the seventeenth century by the French philosopher René Descartes, and is known as Cartesian dualism. This brand of dualism posits that human nature is composed of two independent *substances*: a material body and an immaterial soul. The noun *substance* is important as a means of distinguishing Descartes's dualism from other types. The body, to Descartes, is material and as such operates according to fairly well-known physical and mechanical laws. As a mechanical substance, the body operates according to these laws, and its behavior is determined by physical causes and is, therefore, predictable. These physical and mechanical laws were being worked out at the time by natural philosophers of the day such as Robert Boyle, Thomas Willis and, later and most notably, Isaac Newton. Animals are entirely mechanical creatures that can be studied and understood using the newly revealed laws of nature. Humans, on the other hand, not only have this mechanical and determined body; they also have another substance: an immaterial soul. This immaterial substance cannot be described or understood according to physical and mechanical laws. As an immaterial substance, the soul must be known through alternative methods. There is, therefore, a clear distinction between the body and the soul (or mind). The soul is a different kind of thing or substance. Significantly, for Descartes the soul was more important than the body. Descartes famously said that human identity is demonstrable by the fact that humans can think. We are, fundamentally to Descartes, thinking things or substances (Descartes's first principle is, "I think, therefore, I am").

Although we have these two independent substances, it is clear that the mind can affect the body. If so, there must be some form of interaction between these two substances. Descartes developed a theory of mind/body interaction that, most agree, is completely untenable. Nevertheless, it

79. Green, "Humanity"; Stone, "Soul."

is this form of dualism, substance dualism (specifically Cartesian substance dualism) that is likely thought of when dualism is mentioned, and it is this form of dualism that is typically rejected by most neuroscientists and psychologists, and many philosophers. It is important to remember, however, that there are different types of dualisms, and the dualisms of Plato and Descartes are of just one kind.

To say that substance dualism has fallen out of favor among many contemporary philosophers is not to say that substance dualism has been completely rejected by all philosophers today. For these philosophers, the commonsense notion held by most people that we do, in fact, have a soul is important evidence for the existence of the soul. By soul, these philosophers often mean a substance that is immaterial, but "which has or exemplifies essential properties or characteristics that it cannot lose without ceasing to exist."[80] The soul is a simple, immaterial substance with certain psychological properties such as pleasure, desire, thinking, and others.

Problems with Dualism

There are a number of problems with traditional forms of dualism (such as substance dualism), which are recognized by dualists as well as those who offer alternative views. One problem is to determine which organisms have souls and which do not. While there is no necessary connection between dualism and theism, many dualists also believe in a divine being who gives organisms a soul. Opinions on when this individual soul is given to the organism varies among dualists and need not concern us here. What does concern us for this discussion is the problem of which organisms are given a soul and which ones are not. (This problem is potentially an issue for all theories of mind/soul but is seen to be particularly problematic for substance dualism.) If the soul is given by God and enables thought, feeling, and the like, which animals do we believe have these mental qualities? Saying that no animal (or only the very "highest" among the animal species) has a soul can and has led to a mistreatment of animals (they cannot feel pain, so it does not matter what we do to them).

Another problem for traditional dualisms is the growing evidence indicating an extremely close connection between these mental abilities and the activity of the physical brain (as described earlier in this chapter). If the soul is an immaterial entity, why should there be such a vital connection

80. Goetz, "Substance Dualism," 36.

between the functions of the soul and the functioning of the brain? More on this connection between the mental and the physical is described below. For a traditional dualist (e.g., following Cartesian dualism), this connection must be explained, and a number of versions of dualism (e.g., the emergent dualism of Hasker) have been proposed to do just that. Related to this problem is how to integrate the evidence for continuity of species and common descent with the idea that God creates each individual soul. Do animals with more complex neural circuitry get more advanced kinds of souls? Does the soul assist in the evolutionary development of the nervous system itself? Given the overwhelming evidence for a role of natural selection (and perhaps other mechanisms) in the evolution of humans, dualism needs to incorporate this evidence into an account of the connection between soul and body (or brain). Ignoring the evidence is not an option for a viable theory of mind.[81]

Emergent Dualisms

In addition to the dualisms that propose a separate and independent substance (along with the body), there are various forms of dualisms that postulate the existence of an entity that while not the body itself, is, nevertheless closely tied to the body. One of the better-known examples of emergent dualism is that of William Hasker, who argues for an immaterial entity that emerges out of the physical structure of the brain.[82] An emergent is something that, although entirely new, nevertheless comes out of elements that already exist. This new emergent is not something that is dropped in from the outside, nor is it predictable from knowledge of the elements themselves.[83] In the case of mind and its relation to the body, emergent dualism maintains that the mind emerges out of the physical elements of the brain. When the physical elements that make up the brain (neurons, neurochemicals, and so forth) are in a particular state of complexity and organization, new laws and systems of interaction emerge. These laws play a significant role in mental activity (i.e., consciousness, thought). These mental laws are not part of the underlying physical laws that govern the physical elements themselves; they are not reducible to the physical elements. The emerging laws are new. With these new laws in existence, there is also now a new

81. Hasker, "Souls."

82. Hasker, *Emergent Self*, 188–203

83. Hasker, "Souls."

form of causality. The emergent mind can exercise a direct causal effect on the underlying physical elements themselves. This emergent mind is not independent of the brain, nor is it entirely predictable based on what we know of how the brain works. It does, however, have an effect on the workings of the physical brain. This emerging entity for Hasker is the individual person or self.

Hasker gives the example of a magnetic field to illustrate what he means by an emergent property.[84] A magnetic field is generated by the arrangement of an assembly of iron molecules in a complex pattern. In such a state of physical complexity, a new entity (the magnetic field) is generated or emerges. Nothing in the iron molecules themselves would predict the generation of this new property of magnetism. It is a new kind of thing, although dependent on the iron molecules for its generation. In a similar manner, Hasker suggests, an assembly of neurons arranged in a particular, complex way allows for the generation of a new entity, the personal self.

The person is constituted by the mind and body for Hasker, but the mind is not composed of underlying physical components because the mind (consciousness, mental activity) is unified, which requires a unity (or "simple substance" in philosophical language). Because the body is composed of parts, it cannot be the source of mental experience. How can a thing made of parts explain unity of consciousness? Which part (of the brain for example) causes the unity? A self is needed to account for the unity of consciousness. Hasker's position differs from the substance dualism described above in that, with Hasker, the individual (or self) is dependent on the brain. Without a functioning brain, there is no emergent individual or self. Given a certain level of organization and complexity of the brain and nervous system, a conscious state emerges. This state is immaterial for Hasker, even though it emerges out of the material brain. The necessity of an immaterial entity (the emergent self) is required for philosophical reasons (i.e., unity of consciousness), but Hasker is interested in bringing his philosophical position (as much as he sees is possible) in line with contemporary brain science. This emergent self does exercise control over the brain. The mind can control the brain and its physical properties. (It should be noted here that the terms "soul," "self," and "individual" are used more or less interchangeably in this literature. The important point is not so much the term, but the proposal that some entity—called by various

---

84. Hasker, *Emergent Self*, 190–91.

names—emerges out of the material brain and is clearly distinct from the material itself.)

The emergent dualism of Hasker has the advantage over substance dualism of avoiding some of the problems with dualism listed above. If the mind is an emergent of the brain, then the close connection seen between physical brain events and mental events is expected. Also, the evidence of evolutionary theory fits in well with emergent dualism. More complex, highly developed brains produce more complex and sophisticated states of mental activity. These states of mental activity, in turn, have a direct effect on behavior, which can be shaped by natural selection.[85]

Like Hasker, philosopher Eric LaRock modifies traditional dualism to suggest that what emerges out of the complex, organized brain is a conscious subject which can causally influence the structure and function of the brain.[86] Arguing that a neuroscientific view of the person is insufficient, postulating an emergent conscious subject provides explanatory advantages over traditional forms of dualism as well as purely scientific accounts. The advantages emergent dualism has over traditional dualism, LaRock suggests, include its closer connection to the findings of modern neuroscience and psychology and its insistence that the emergent subject is spatial (which, it is claimed, makes emergent dualism safe from the problem of how an immaterial, nonspatial soul could affect a physical, spatial body), and includes areas of the PFC.

We might think of the emergent subject, to use language from psychology, as a kind of hypothetical construct. Hypothetical constructs are explanatory variables that are not directly observable. Examples in psychology included intelligence, personality, and motivation These constructs are used to explain phenomena and are thought to have certain properties that, while not necessarily demonstrated by empirical investigations, can guide future research. They are a type of shorthand explanation for the observed data. How can discreet areas of the brain involved in the processing of a particular stimulus set (e.g., a visual/auditory stimuli), produce a unified, phenomenal experience? The visual stimuli of the experience will be processed in various brain areas involved in vision. Part of the visual experience will be processed in cortical areas used for color, while other aspects of the visual experienced will be processed in cortical areas detecting visual movement, and so on. The auditory components of the experience will be

85. Hasker, "Souls."
86. LaRock, "From Biological."

processed in still different brain areas. Despite the distribution of process-ing areas, the phenomenal experience is unified. Visual and auditory com-ponents come together into a singular phenomenal event. There is no good neuroscientific explanation for how this unified experience, called binding, occurs.[87] The self can be proposed (as a kind of hypothetical construct like intelligence, learning, motivation, personality, attitude) to try to explain the binding problem. It is the self that binds the disparate neural processing together. Psychology is used to this kind of move when it proposes that learning occurs to account for behavioral change between Time 1 and Time 2 or that a person performs well on mathematical or verbal tasks because of a construct called intelligence. In addition, hypothetical constructs pro-vide, and should provide, possibilities for empirical testing of the construct. If the self does exist and is doing a particular kind of work, then we should expect to observe particular kinds of outcomes in our psychological (or neuroscientific) work that are different from the outcomes predicted from a different proposition (e.g., from the proposition that there is nothing but neural activity in the different cortical areas to account for binding).

Materialism

Perhaps the most common view of human personhood held by philoso-phers and scientists today is known as materialism. Typically contrasted with dualisms of various sorts, materialism (in its most extreme and re-ductive form) sees humans as composed of only one kind of thing, mat-ter. For a materialist, the only substance that exists in reality is matter, so it is only matter that can compose humans as well. Because humans are physical things, all that can be known about humans can be described and explained according to materialist principles and laws. The implication for psychology is that all of the experiences we understand to be mental are actually explained and determined by physical causes. This assumption is the basis for Francis Crick's quotation in the opening paragraphs of this chapter, that all of our joys, desires, beliefs, and so forth are nothing more than neurons and brain chemicals. A further implication is that human behavior is ultimately determined by these same physical events, so choice, decisions, judgments, and morality are strictly determined actions. All behavior has physical causes; there is no room for mental causation. This

87. LaRock, "Disambiguation."

notion is known in philosophy as causal closure of the physical and is a central feature of materialism.

Problems with Materialism

The problem with materialism, at least of the variety held by scholars such as Crick, is that a strictly reductionistic account of mind cannot, according to dualists, explain the phenomena of inner experience. The term used by philosophers of mind for these phenomena is *qualia*. Examples of qualia include the taste of an orange, the color of an apple, the smell of a flower, and the pain of a bee sting. Each of us has these experiences (called first-person or subjective experiences), and we operate on a day-to-day basis on the assumption that my experience of the color red as I look at an apple is the same experience that you have as you look at the same red apple. In addition, my experience of the red apple today is the same experience of red that I had when I looked at that apple yesterday. If, as the reductive materialist insists, these conscious experiences are nothing but physical activity in the underlying system (i.e., the brain), how can these subjective experiences be explained? Why should there be inner experience at all in a physical system, and how can the firing of brain cells and the release of neural chemicals produce these experiences? This "hard problem of consciousness" is a significant limitation of a purely materialistic understanding of the mind.[88]

Another problem for a materialist account, critics argue, is that it cannot explain how reason occurs.[89] If all human experience (including mental experience) is due to material mechanisms (the principle of causal closure of the physical), there is no role for subjective consciousness (e.g., thoughts, plans, desires, and so forth). The materialist has not been able to (and Hasker speculates cannot) develop an account of how physical events, that have physical causes, can produce nonphysical, mental subjective experiences such as a belief or even the subjective experience of color (see above). So, the materialist position leads to the astonishing claim that consciously experienced phenomena (e.g., thoughts) have no effect on a person's behavior; psychological content is irrelevant to what a person does. Reason and argument, therefore, are also irrelevant to our behavior. All action is due to the physical contents of the brain. This problem of the

88. Collins, "Scientific Case."
89. Hasker, "Souls."

irrelevance of psychological states to behavior presents a conundrum for the materialist because if psychological states have no effect on behavior, how can they be affected by evolution? According to evolutionary psychology, any particular cognitive state evolved because it offered some selective advantage to the organism. However, according to the materialist account, psychological or cognitive states have no bearing on behavior at all. If this is the case, how can evolutionary processes shape these psychological and cognitive states? While physical brain states affect behavior and are subject to natural selection, mental states do not. If the mental state has no bearing on behavior, then it would be "invisible" to natural selection and not subject to evolution.[90]

One way for a materialist to understand the problems of consciousness described above is to adopt the approach taken by Christof Koch, who sees consciousness, and the phenomena associated with consciousness (such as reason), as a fundamental or elementary property of living matter, not derived from anything else. "Consciousness comes with organized chunks of matter," and cannot be reduced to anything more basic and does not emerge out of simpler elements. We live, according to Koch, in a universe in which all systems consisting of organized matter have some level of consciousness. "The larger and more highly networked the system (like a human brain), the greater the degree of consciousness."[91] Like the Catholic priest and paleontologist Pierre Teilhard de Chardin, who in the first half of the twentieth century postulated a rudimentary form of consciousness in all matter, Koch believes that we are surrounded by consciousness: "it is in the air we breathe, the soil we tread on, the bacteria that colonize our intestines, and the brain that enables us to think."[92] Whether or not the approach taken by Koch actually solves the problems a materialist has with consciousness, it is certainly a perspective that recognizes the reality of consciousness and does not merely dismiss mental life as irrelevant to understanding human behavior and experience.

Christian Materialism

Just as there are different forms of dualisms (see above) there are variations on materialism, and some of these kinds of materialism are comfortably

90. Ibid., 202–21.

91. Koch, *Consciousness*, 120.

92. Teilhard de Chardin, *Phenomenon*, 53–90; Koch, *Conscious*, 132.

held by theists, including Christian theists. As theists, these materialists will likely want to say that they do believe in dualism in that they believe that God is not a material thing and that there is a dualism of Creator and creation. What they would reject, however, is the dualism that postulates human nature as consisting of a material body and an immaterial mind or soul.[93] For example, the constitution view of human persons suggests that, while a person is not an immaterial soul, neither is a person identical with its physical body. Instead, a human person is constituted by a physical body in a similar way that a dollar bill or a diploma is *constituted* by pieces of paper without being *identical* with the pieces of paper.[94] The distinction between constituted by and being identical with is crucial in this perspective in that there are certain conditions that make a person (e.g., first-person perspective; and intentional states such as believing, desiring, intending, and the like) that do not make a physical body. Because of these differing conditions, proponents of this perspective would say that while human persons are constituted by our physical bodies, we are not identical with our physical bodies. In addition, while the physical material of an object (for example, a statue) might be copper, it would not be correct to say that the copper is identical with the statue. This is because we can imagine doing something to the copper statue (say, melting it down) that would change the statue itself (we would no longer have the statue) but would not change the physical material of the copper. We would still have the copper, but not the statue. In a similar way, the physical material out of which our bodies are made changes all the time. The physical molecules in my body today are not the same physical molecules that made up my body five years ago. Yet, I as a person (and the same person at that) am still here. So, this argument goes, while I am constituted by my physical body, I cannot be identical with my physical body. Clearly this approach takes the physical nature of the human person seriously (we do not have anything immaterial like a soul) while trying to avoid some of the problems associated with a purely materialist account of human personhood.

Nonreductive Physicalism

A further variation of the materialist perspective is nonreductive physicalism, which attempts to avoid some of the problems found in more reductive

93. Corcoran, "Constitution View."
94. Ibid., 156–61.

forms of materialism. Another term for this approach is emergent monism, *monism* being a general term for the view that there exists one kind of thing (generally a material thing) and contrasts with dualism. One of the reasons for postulating the existence of an immaterial soul is to explain higher mental capacities such as reason and morality. A reductive materialist such as Crick, who rejects belief in anything immaterial, would insist that there is only the physical brain. If only the brain exists, however, then how can we account for these higher mental capacities? The reductive materialist might answer by denying the existence of higher mental capacities. This perspective is also known as eliminativist materialism. Mental capacities (i.e., the mind) are simply eliminated from the discussion. If the mind cannot be explained using known physical laws and properties, then it cannot exist.

The nonreductive physicalist would say that if there is no immaterial soul, then these mental capacities (which the dualists would remind us we all believe we have) must be accounted for, at least in part, by the physical brain. But the physical brain and its function is not the entire story for the nonreductive physicalist. One cannot reduce mental capacities or the mind (or soul) to nothing but the physical workings of the brain (e.g., to neurons and neural chemicals). Much like the emergent dualism of Hasker (above), when the neurons of the brain are in a complex arrangement, new kinds of *properties*, which we call mind, emerge out of the brain. (The term "properties" is important in that it serves to differentiate nonreductive physicalism from various emergent dualisms. For emergent dualists, what emerges is a new entity such as a person or self or subject. For nonreductive physicalists, what emerges are new properties—mental capacities.) In addition, we must take into account that we are social creatures and we live in social environments. These social environments, particularly our social relationships with others, are important in producing mental capacities, as are cultural factors and our interactions with God.[95]

Fundamental to this nonreductive approach is the proposition that reality is multileveled, and each of these levels can, and indeed must, be studied using tools and methods appropriate for that level. In other words, we can think of nature as consisting of different levels of complexity, and as we move up this hierarchy of complexity, new entities and properties emerge that cannot be fully understood and explained by reference to the workings of the lower levels. For example, as we move up this hierarchy, we encounter atoms, molecules, cells, organisms, and consciousness, and

95. Murphy, "Nonreductive Physicalism."

at each of these levels we must use appropriate methods and tools. More than that, however, is the proposal that at each of these levels the entity or property that emerges is genuinely new. That is to say, cells cannot be completely explained and known by using the methods appropriate for studying molecules. Likewise, consciousness (while emerging out of the organism) cannot be fully explained by using the tools appropriate for the level of the organism. Consciousness is a new property that cannot be reduced to the lower level, thus the term "nonreductive physicalism."

Emergence, then, refers to the appearance of a new process. A controversy exists within this literature as to whether this new emergent has any causal influence over the lower physical entities. Weak emergence argues that while new processes or patterns emerge, causality remains at the lower physical level. Strong emergence, on the other hand, maintains that genuinely new causal processes come into existence that affect the lower levels and can be used to reject a reductionistic physicalist account of reality.[96] In this perspective, consciousness (or mind) is a higher-level emergent process (emerging out of the physical brain) and has a downward causal influence on the brain.[97] The mind, therefore, can and does affect the physical events of the brain. This perspective affirms our commonsense belief that mind can control the body or brain, but it does so as a new process or property that is completely dependent on the underlying brain for its existence. The mind is not an immaterial substance or entity; it is a new kind of process that emerges out of the brain. Without the physical brain there can be no mind.

Emergence and downward causation are considered by some to be relatively common in nature. Indeed, life itself is thought to be an example of an emergent process. Rothschild provides the following examples of causality that work in both a bottom-up and top-down direction.

> Sexual recombination determines the raw material for evolution, but evolution shapes sexual recombination. The nature of sexual encounters, the genetics of recombination, the biochemistry of the recombination process—all are subject to broader evolutionary processes that are not fully conditioned by lower causal processes. Sexual behavior, which may be induced by such emergent

96. Clayton, "Conceptual Foundations."
97. Chalmers, "Strong and Weak."

(or social) concepts as beauty and love, ultimately influences gene sequences of offspring, which in turn influence sexual behavior.[98]

Emergence and top-down causality are vital to the nonreductive physicalist perspective.

THE IMPORTANCE OF THE BODY/SOUL PROBLEM

Based on the number of approaches developed to the body/soul problem over the centuries, one would think that this is an issue of high importance. Based on the fact that the Bible, as mentioned earlier in this chapter, does not seem to present an explicit anthropology, one can be excused for thinking that perhaps the number of pages devoted to this topic by scholars goes well beyond any reasonable level of importance, at least to Christians. There are voices within philosophy, as well as in science, that agree with this latter assessment. There are also, however, scholars in these disciplines who argue that this is a very important issue and one that should be considered even more seriously.

Some theistic philosophers suggest that the very concept of the soul is rejected within science because the soul does not fit into the materialistic worldview many, if not most, scientist have. These scientists reply by saying that since the scientific revolution, materialism has been a highly successful approach in understanding and explaining the physical world. Beginning in the fifteenth century, this more mechanistic, naturalistic, and materialistic approach to the physical universe has revealed many of the universe's mysteries that were hidden before this scientific worldview was adopted. While consciousness, thinking, reason, and the other higher mental processes are still not completely understood, given enough time this materialistic approach will uncover the physical mechanisms for mind as it has for the body. Another reason why science tends to reject the concept of a soul is that a belief in an immaterial soul is linked to theism and religion, and for scientists who see a basic conflict between religion and science, any hint of theism must be avoided at all costs. So, even if there are legitimate reasons for considering the hypothesis of a soul (and many dualists say that there are), science, as science, simply must not.

One could argue, however, that if truth is being sought, one should honestly confront one's biases and try to limit them as much as possible.

98. Rothschild, "Role of Emergence," 156.

From this perspective, the choice between dualism and materialism should be made independently of any connections to one's opinions regarding theism or atheism. One can reasonably be a dualist and a theist or a dualist and an atheist just as one can be a materialist and a theist or a materialist and an atheist. The support for belief in soul and the support for a belief in God, while connected, are not logically the same.[99]

Many philosophers as well as scientists argue that the very question of personhood or soul, as it is being discussed here, is beyond the reach of a scientific investigation.[100] Science is very successful in what it does but is limited to investigation of the physical world and the discovery of natural mechanisms. While there may or may not be nonnatural phenomena and mechanisms, if they do exist they cannot be known via science and its methods. The experiencing self seems to be such a topic. As we have seen, one materialistic answer to this is to simply eliminate the possibility of a self or person (or soul) that is beyond science's purview. This approach is known as philosophical or ontological materialism, which holds that the very nature of reality itself consists entirely of material things. If this is the case, and it is, say many materialists, then science is the only way of knowing any truth. Another kind of materialism, however, is known as methodological materialism (or methodological naturalism), which simply argues that as a practicing scientist doing science, one must behave *as if* there were only natural mechanisms, because those are the only kind of mechanisms that science can discover. There may very well be nonnatural causes or substances, but if there are, science must of necessity be silent about them. They are beyond the ability of science to know. This perspective is taken by many philosophers as well as scientists.[101]

As discussed above, we might consider the soul a hypothetical construct, an entity like motivation that cannot be directly measured but is used to explain phenomena. Hypothetical constructs are commonplace in psychology as explanatory variables. Other examples would include intelligence and personality. While intelligence cannot be observed directly, psychologists have no problem using the term to explain what can be observed directly. Or, perhaps the soul can be likened to an intervening variable, another often used concept in psychology. Intervening variables cannot be observed directly either but are used to explain relationships between

99. Baker and Goetz, "Afterword."

100. Robinson, "Minds."

101. Goetz, "Making Things"; Klein, "Self and Science."

independent variables (manipulated in a study, the effects of which the experimenter is interested in) and dependent variables (measured by the experimenter). Thirst, for example, is an intervening variable that is used to explain relationships between various manipulations (such as water deprivation and eating salty foods) and different ways of measuring drinking behavior (for example amount of water consumed). In this respect, novelist and essayist Marilynne Robinson said, "If 'mind' and 'soul' are not entities in their own right, they are at least terms that have been found useful for describing aspects of the expression and self-experience of our very complex nervous systems."[102] It seems like the concept of soul can fit naturally into psychological terminology and psychological research if it is approached in this way.

WHAT IF WE DON'T HAVE AN IMMATERIAL SOUL?

If dualism is wrong (i.e., if we are really only one kind of thing and that is a physical thing), what are the implications? We must keep in mind that many theologians and biblical scholars maintain that dualism (at least the dualisms of Plato and Descartes) is not demanded by Scripture. There is certainly disagreement on this point, but the position that the Bible does not advocate a particular anthropology, or that dualism is not explicitly taught in Scripture, or that humans are essentially embodied creatures is not a radical or "liberal" theological position. Those who hold this view are found in mainstream seminaries, such as Asbury in Kentucky and Fuller in California and are, as in the case of biblical scholar and bishop N. T. Wright, often cited by "moderate" pastors and church leaders.[103] So, the idea of embodiment and of the physicality of the human person, and even the rejection of the idea of a disembodied soul, need not be dismissed out of hand because it is unbiblical or contrary to contemporary or even traditional Christian theological thought. There are theologically sound reasons for considering the position that the essential nature of human personhood is physical and that there is no immaterial soul that is added to our material body. The theological support provided by these biblical scholars can ease some concerns Christians might have as they read research findings such as those reviewed in this chapter. Author Marilynne Robinson, quoted above,

102. Robinson, *Absence of Mind*, xi.

103. Green, *Body*; Green, "Humanity"; Stone, "Soul"; Wright, "Mind"; and Wright, *Surprised*.

puts it this way, "If the mind is the activity of the brain, this means only that the brain is capable of such lofty and astonishing things that their expression has been given the names mind, and soul, and spirit."[104]

If this view is held, however, what are the implications for Christian belief and practice? This question is an important one and has been extensively considered by a variety of theologians, philosophers, and even theologically minded scientists. Brown and Strawn propose a number of ways a physicalist understanding of human nature might influence Christian belief and practice by contrasting this perspective with Cartesian dualism, the view that humans consist of two separate and distinct kinds of substances.[105] At one level, this contrast with Cartesian dualism is unfair in that philosophers tell us that few if any of their colleagues believe in the kind of dualism proposed by Descartes over 350 years ago. Dualism comes in many varieties (as indicated in the discussion above), and the approach of Descartes is just one of them. While it is no doubt true that professional philosophers have refined and modified dualism since the time of Descartes (and even more so Plato), the kind of dualism that most people seem to intuitive hold is very much like that of Descartes. The person on the street or in the pew on Saturday night or Sunday morning does not think of human personhood like an emergent dualist would. They tend to see personhood as Descartes did. There is a material body and a distinct and separable immaterial soul. When the body dies, the soul continues to exist in a disembodied condition. This soul (either immediately or perhaps after a period of time) will go to heaven (which is somewhere up in the sky, certainly not a part of this physical existence) and live with God for eternity. The soul might get another body (the resurrected body), but that seems to be almost a secondary feature of life after death in this account. It is the immaterial soul that is saved and is cared for and is the subject of continual development. So, while Brown and Strawn might be ignoring the many important nuances found in contemporary dualisms, they are addressing their comments to people who have a more intuitive understanding of body/soul, and they see ways in which Christian practices and beliefs that emerge from that intuitive understanding might be changed with acceptance of a physicalist account of the human person.

One change the authors suggest concerns the nature of worship. If we understand ourselves to be embodied persons embedded within a

104. Robinson, *Absence of Mind*, 112.

105. Brown and Strawn, *Physical Nature*, 140–52.

community of other embodied persons, then perhaps worship will be less about the "individual experience" and more corporate in nature, less about what is said and more about what is done within the community. Disembodied worship (seeing the person as an immaterial, disembodied soul) leads the worshiper to focus on what is happening within him or herself. A more physicalist perspective on personhood, the authors believe, will tend to direct the worshiper's focus outward, toward others. An inward focus also leads to conceptualizing God as being "inside" the individual, rather than in the worship space and outside of any particular individual. Brown and Strawn write, "The goal of worship is not to cultivate something inside, but, in unison with those gathered, to worship God who is outside of us as individuals, yet present between us—in our midst. We do not gather in order for each individual to have some kind of inner experience or feeling, but for each person and the gathered church to be formed through the context of worship."[106]

A physicalist perspective on personhood would also affect liturgy. For example, embodied worship might change how we participate during worship. What do we do with our bodies during prayer? During singing? During communion? Do we physically walk forward to take the Eucharist, or do we wait passively for the elements to be brought to us? Do we take the Lord's Supper together as a church body or as individuals? There is an interaction among our cognitions (including thoughts, feelings, and beliefs) and our actions. What we think (or feel or believe) affects our behavior, and our behavior affects these cognitions. "To participate in the Eucharist during worship . . . is for this bodily activity to have a deep influence on our thoughts, feelings, beliefs, and future behavior."[107]

Perhaps the most important implication deals with the resurrection and eternal life. With the existence of an immaterial soul that can exist outside of the physical body, life after death, while still a mystery, seems more coherent. There are still issues surrounding the resurrected body, but the essential personality of the individual is to be found in the soul, so if it can survive after death then I have hope for my own personal survival. If, as the physicalist account suggests, my essential identity (my memories, wishes, desires, beliefs) is closely tied to and requires a physical brain for its existence, then how can I be confident that I will survive when it is clear that my physical brain (along with the rest of my body) will return to the

106. Ibid., 148.
107. Ibid., 152.

dust of the earth? (There have been volumes written on this topic by theologians, philosophers, scientists, and others trying to develop a reasonable and coherent account of how this might happen, or why a physicalist account is or is not compatible with resurrection.)[108]

The body dies, and Christians believe "in the resurrection of the body and the life everlasting." When thinking about life after death, it seems unnecessary to try to develop a coherent and reasonable account of how that might work. Whether substance dualism, emergent dualism, Christian materialism, or some other perspective makes for a better and more coherent account of the resurrection of the body and continuing identity throughout eternity seems unimportant. When talking about life after death, it seems that all bets are off. Anything is possible. It is believing in eternal life that is necessary, not an account of how it is possible. In this regard, I think philosopher Trenton Merricks has it right when he says,

> It seems possible that, when God set about to create me, God was able to do just that: create me, not just somebody or other. To do this, God didn't need to make use of matter that had previously been mine, for none had . . . and if God could see to it that I—not just somebody or other—came into existence the first time around, what's to preclude God from doing it again, years after my cremation? . . . But for the physicalist, all hope of an afterlife resides only in the promises of God. For the physicalist believes that the death of her body is the death of her. And subsequent resurrection is surely not justified by any empirical evidence currently available. Moreover, while it might be 'natural' for a simple soul to leave its body behind at death, it surely isn't 'natural' for a decayed human person to rise again in glorious resurrection. Although resurrection may not be impossible, it will certainly take a miracle.[109]

While life after death might be more coherent philosophically from a dualist account of human personhood, resurrection nevertheless seems impossible from any perspective. Eternal life is a gift, not part of our intrinsic human nature because we have a soul that is immaterial. It takes God. It takes a miracle. If human nature is fundamentally physical instead of dualistic, if we do not have an immaterial soul, it does not change the need for God to accomplish this miracle.

---

108. Cooper, "Biblical"; Corcoron, *Rethinking*, 153–76; Green, *Body*; Green, "Resurrection"; Gutenson, "Time"; Hasker, *Emergent Self*; and Merricks, "How to Live."

109. Merricks, "How to Live," 197–200.

What about salvation? If there is no soul to save, what do we mean by salvation? Many understand salvation in terms of going to heaven when they die, and the principal work of the church is to save souls so that they can go to heaven. N. T. Wright in his book *Surprised by Hope* writes about the meaning of salvation and how that meaning might change if we place a stronger emphasis on our physicality. Wright reminds us that, according to Scripture, our ultimate salvation is in the resurrection into a new heaven and a new earth. God's future is not for us to escape this earth and go to heaven, but that God's rule would come to earth as it is in heaven. He also says that when Paul speaks about future immortality (for example in 1 Corinthians 15) he is talking about the whole mortal being, not the soul by itself. The soul was not understood by the earliest Christians as the part of us that survives death and that carries our "real" selves or identity.[110] The resurrection is always about a body (meaning the whole person), and the resurrection will give new life to the body. If this is so, then what we do with the body (the whole person) in the present life matters. The whole person is good in God's creation, and it is the whole person, not just the soul, that is to be saved. The work of the church is the salvation of the whole person, not so souls can go to heaven when the body dies, but so God's kingdom can come in the form of a new heaven and a new earth. This more embodied approach places, according to Wright, more emphasis on life in the here and now.[111] If our immaterial souls are saved for a future in a heaven that is "up in the sky," then there can be, and has been in the past, a deemphasis on the present and on the physical. If our own personal souls are saved for our own personal benefit (i.e., personal continuation in heaven), this can lead to, as it has in the past, an individualistic understanding of what my purpose as a Christian is—to make sure my own soul is saved and to make sure the souls of others are saved as well. A more physicalist perspective might serve to remind us of what we read in Romans 8—that it is the whole of the physical creation that is under bondage and awaiting redemption. As Wright puts it, the whole creation "is waiting with eager longing not just for its own redemption, its liberation from corruption and decay, but *for God's children to be revealed*: in other words, for the unveiling of those redeemed humans through whose stewardship creation will at last be brought back into that wise order for which it was made."[112] Certainly this understanding

110. Wright, "Mind."
111. Wright, *Surprised*, 194–201.
112. Ibid., 200.

of the future is possible from a substance dualism perspective, but an emphasis on the physicality of the human person makes this truth of salvation and redemption more familiar and easier to appreciate. Wright suggests this helps explain why the New Testament often refers to salvation in terms of bodily events, such as when Jairus begs Jesus to come and save his daughter, or when the woman with the issue of blood thinks that if she can only touch Jesus's clothes she will be saved.[113] What we do with the physical creation, including the physical body, is important to salvation.

A deemphasis of the personal and individual soul of dualism (at least of substance dualism) and an acknowledgement of the importance of our physicality, including our brains, also facilitates the recognition of the importance of relationships within the Christian community. Brains need other brains to develop fully and humanly. So, too, we need others to develop fully as Christians. Salvation or conversion is not solely an act of individual belief; it needs to be understood in the context of and requires interaction with the Christian community.[114] When Paul speaks of renewing your minds in Romans 12, he is not speaking to isolated individuals; he is using plural and communal language. This renewal of minds then leads to changes in behavior. The change in mind is for something; it is for community. God is love, and love requires others for its fullest expression. Psychiatrist and author Curt Thompson writes, "His [God's] love is most powerfully demonstrated in the context of this interdependent individual-community dynamic. And this dynamic is a most powerful means by which God builds his Kingdom."[115] Again, a substance-dualism view of self, personhood, or soul can see the importance of community as well, but the physicalist approach makes the role of the physical person interacting with other physical persons, as well as the rest of physical creation, more obvious.

CONTEMPORARY NEED FOR A SOUL?

When psychology emerged out of philosophy in the late nineteenth century and became a discipline in its own right, it patterned itself after the successful natural sciences of the day such as physics and physiology. In doing so, it sought to formally study human nature in a way that was distinctive from

113. Ibid., 198.

114. Markham, *Rewired*, 197.

115. Thompson, *Anatomy*, 254.

much of the philosophies of the past (especially Christian philosophies) that made reference to a human soul to account for human reason and immortality. The new psychology in Germany and the United States replaced discussion of the soul with that of the "mind" or "self," with these new terms taking over the functions of the soul such as thinking, feeling sensing, and moving.[116] There were a number of methodological reasons for this secularization of the soul, and a leading American figure in this transformation was William James, whose psychology was driven by naturalism and functionalism. As a functional psychology (asking what mind was for), James's naturalism was teleological; mind was active: it pursued goals. But James the psychologist was not interested in philosophical questions about mind. As a naturalistic science, James' psychology rejected metaphysical questions as much as physiology did. As Coon puts it, James argued that "it was unreasonable that the psychologist be asked to explain how he is able to analyze and report on his own or others thoughts. It was unreasonable to demand that the psychologist explain how she could be objective while viewing the world through her own subjective lens."[117] The psychologist should be objective, to the extent that any scientist can be objective, and avoid metaphysical questions, leaving them to philosophers. Included in the questions that, for James, should be left to philosophers was the issue of the soul's existence and, if it does exist, its nature. Those questions, James believed, were not answerable by psychology.

As a philosopher, James knew that the soul had served important functions, but in the new naturalistic science of psychology, many of these soul functions were replaced by the self, and the functions of unity of consciousness and personal identity were taken care of by James's notion of the stream of consciousness. Nevertheless, James had a difficult time rejecting any use of the concept of soul in his psychology, because he found it too useful to completely discard, particularly as a concept in ethics and morality. The concept served as a comforting presence for James as well as for his audience, serving metaphysical functions but also, perhaps, meeting psychological needs as well. As Coon, in her discussion of James and the self, put it, despite the secularization of the soul, "we still lack in our scientific vocabulary a compelling replacement for the soul, something to

116. Coon, "Salvaging."
117. Ibid., 89.

hold our multiple selves together and to help us judge their relative worth, something to serve as a common cultural referent to anchor us."[118]

The difficulty James had with the concept of the soul, wanting to reject it in his naturalistic psychology but recognizing the usefulness of the concept to help understand some functions of the mind and in encouraging morality, is perhaps reflected in today's psychology as well. In this regard, psychology both reflects and helps to shape the secularization of the soul. As noted in this chapter, a variety of terms have been proposed to name this thing that we all believe we have, an identity that is unified and mostly continuous across time. Some call it a soul, some a self, some personhood, some consciousness, some emergent properties. (Of course, some simply eliminate it and think they have dealt with the "problem" that way.) But whether we call it an immaterial substance, a self, an emergent property of the brain, or simply the brain itself, there seem to be some aspects of this "thing" that is beyond the purview of science. Psychology, cognitive science, and neuroscience can tell us a lot about what this self/property/soul/brain is like, but these disciplines cannot answer all of our questions. Perhaps in this respect James as psychologist was right when he said psychology (science) should not be expected to explain how it is that humans enjoy unified consciousness and subjectivity. Psychologists need not deal with metaphysics. These might be important questions, but they just might also be unanswerable using scientific methodologies. On the topic of the soul, James went on to say that those who wished to believe in the soul should feel free to do so because scientific findings "have not established the non-existence of the Soul"; the findings have only made belief in the soul unnecessary for scientific purposes.[119]

118. Ibid., 98–99.
119. Ibid., 93.

6

Moral Psychology
What is the Source of Morality?

But the main article of faith of the humanist, namely, the goodness of mankind and man's consequent capacity to be moral, is refuted by any careful study of human nature.[1]

Morality antedates religion and much can be learned about its origin by considering our fellow primates. Contrary to the customary blood-soaked view of nature, animals are not devoid of tendencies that we morally approve of, which to me suggests that morality is not as much of a human innovation as we like to think.[2]

In his fascinating memoir *Shantung Compound*, theologian Langdon Gilkey vividly describes the two and a half years he spent in an internment camp during World War II. Gilkey was a teacher at a Chinese university when the conquering Japanese military made the decision to send all foreigners to civilian internment camps. Gilkey was sent to a camp near Weihsien in the Shantung Province. Men, women, and children from a variety of walks of life (business, medicine, and education as well as junkies

1. Gilkey, *Shantung Compound*, 230.
2. De Waal, *Bonobo and the Atheist*, 3–4.

and prostitutes) were residents of the camp. Most were American or British in nationality. His time in this camp changed Gilkey's perspective from a humanist view that saw humans as basically good and society as making steady moral progress to one that understood that humans are selfish and love themselves more than anyone or anything else. At a fundamental level, Gilkey writes, "lie deep forces beyond our easy control which often push us seemingly in spite of ourselves into selfish acts."[3]

In this miniature community with a cross-section of human beings, Gilkey describes, not only the physical living conditions, but the social and moral living conditions as well. In one extended passage of the book (pp. 96–116), Gilkey writes about what happened when some food and clothing parcels arrived from the American Red Cross. The packages were divided equally among the 1,500 or so people in the camp so that each person got about one and one-half parcels of supplies. Divided among the approximately two hundred Americans in the camp, however, there were enough parcels from the American Red Cross to provide seven to eight parcels for each American. Initially, the decision was made (by the Japanese who ran the camp) to divide the parcels equally among all camp prisoners. The goodwill directed toward the Americans as a result of this decision was quickly replaced by anger when a handful of Americans in the camp protested to the Japanese that because the parcels were from the American Red Cross, they should all go to Americans. In describing the change in relationships among the prisoners, Gilkey writes, "A community where everyone had long forgotten whether a man was American or British, white, Negro, Jew, Parsee, or Indian, had suddenly disintegrated into a brawling, bitterly divided collection of hostile national groups . . . Had this food supply simply been used for the good of the whole community, it would have been an unmitigated blessing in the life of every one of us. But the moment it threatened to become the hoarded property of a select few, it became at once destructive rather than creative, dividing us from one another and destroying every vestige of communal unity and morale."[4] Gilkey's account illustrates how people can quickly fall back on tribal thinking and identity in times of stress and challenge. It is easy enough to think of other people, even people who are not a part of our group, when times are good, but under pressure we tend to revert back to our innate, animal instinctive patterns.

3. Gilkey, *Shantung Compound*, 230.
4. Ibid., 104–5.

But is that really true? While the events Gilkey experiences in the internment camp certainly illustrate how humans can act, is it a description of who we are as human beings at the deepest level? Is it really the case that we are fundamentally selfish and loveless towards others? Do we really not care that much about others, about what happens to them, or about how they feel? Are we really just looking out for ourselves?

A central issue that occupies religion is that of morality. What makes us moral? Many Christians believe that because of original sin we are at our core bad and prone to evil, and that our sinful character necessitates the offer of forgiveness provided by the sacrifice of Christ on the cross. Are humans basically immoral, selfish, evil creatures whose morality is only skin-deep? Is the capacity to act morally important in distinguishing humans from other animals? Are there any indications of moral behavior in other animals? Are the roots of morality found in our biology? Scientists from a variety of disciplines have recently begun an empirical investigation into human morality.

Psychologists study the cognitive, emotional, developmental, and social mechanism involved in behaviors thought to define morality. In addition, primatologists investigate the great apes, humans' closest relatives, to detect similarities and differences between human moral behavior and the behaviors of these primates that most would consider relevant to an understanding of morality. One of the goals of this kind of comparative research is to try to answer the question of the phylogenetic origin of morality.[5] Are there premoral behaviors in the great apes that might have evolved into the kinds of behaviors in humans that we recognize as moral acts? What impact does this research have for our understanding of moral codes as originating from religion (e.g., the Ten Commandments)? What role does God play? These are some of the questions addressed in this chapter, questions important for us as individuals, but also for us as we live in community with others.

NEED TO LIVE IN SOCIAL GROUPS

Human beings are a social species. Humans as a species are not fast enough or strong enough to find, track, and kill large prey. Neither are we capable of successfully defending ourselves as individuals against larger and stronger predators. In order to increase success in these endeavors, humans

5. Tomasello and Vaish, "Origins of Human."

throughout human history have affiliated with others, probably originally those related genetically, for protection and hunting/gathering, as well as for shared childcare. Working together, individual humans affiliated in groups can provide mutual protection. Acting as a group, humans can hunt even large game, which, or course, is then shared among the participants in the hunt. Within a group, individual members can divide the responsibilities so that some can gather food while others watch those too young to search for food back at the "camp."

Over many centuries these originally small groups of hunters and gatherers expanded to include individuals who were not genetically related, and as the groups got larger in size, new demands were placed on those who composed the group. Social interactions became more complicated because relating to "nonkin" was now part of the group dynamic. As long as group ties were primarily based on kinship, relationships among group members were relatively straightforward and required rather simple cognitive processes. Because participation in the group was based on family relatedness, trust, cooperation, and assistance among group members could be seen as a kind of helping oneself to the extent that all members of the group shared similar genes. As nonkin were included, however, simple cognitive processes no longer were sufficient. More sophisticated processes (sometimes called social cognition) were needed to keep track of the more complex relationships in the larger social groups. These larger social groups required trust and cooperation among the members and occasionally involved assisting other group members, often at a cost to the actor. From an evolutionary perspective, why would anyone act in such a way that another person is benefited at the expense of the actor? Why do something that will help another's success at surviving but reduce one's own chances? These kinds of altruistic acts to nonkin required more complex social cognition and memory in order to keep track of who was indebted to whom.

Humans are not the only animal species that socialize into groups. Many others live in social groups as well, including insects such as bees and ants, and the great apes, such as gorillas, bonobos, chimpanzees, and orangutans (and humans). For nonhuman great apes this social life typically involves competition (within and between social groups), but also a fair amount of cooperation as well, and this cooperation with allies is necessary for successful access to resources. The social interaction is complex in that the individual must take note of multiple relationships, both within the preferred group and without, which requires a great deal of social cognition.

(Social cognition includes those cognitive or mental processes necessary to develop and maintain social relationships.) Observations of the nonhuman great apes (including controlled experimental observations) reveal behaviors of helping and sharing and collaborating with others for mutual benefit.[6] Chimpanzees, for example, will help other chimpanzees (and in some cases humans) by opening gates, delivering food, sharing tools for the gathering of food, and handing out-of-reach objects to others. The helping and sharing among chimpanzees most often involves reciprocity, but not always. Many times the behavior seems indicative of altruism, in which the helping individual has positive affect toward the other. On the negative side, a chimpanzee will often retaliate against another when wronged, even if no material reward (like food) is obtained, which appears to have the effect of punishing the individual so that the transgression is less likely to occur in the future. Collaboration is also common in the great apes (chimpanzees have been studied the most), including forming alliances (even among nonkin) for group defense and for obtaining food.[7]

To note that cooperative social relationships exist in nonhuman primate species is not to say that those species behave in human-like moral ways. It is simply to acknowledge that human morality might have a biological basis to it. The idea that humans, because of their partial animal natures, are fundamentally bad, and that moral behavior is only superficially human is sometimes called the veneer theory. From this perspective, moral behavior is only a thin layer on top of many layers of selfish or evil behavior that composes the basic nature of human beings. If the veneer theory is incorrect—if, in fact, humans have a deep layer of selflessness, empathy, and altruism—we would expect to see these kinds of moral behaviors in other closely related species. This is the approach to the study of morality taken by psychologists and primatologists who use comparative studies of animals to look for signs of empathy and altruism.

EMOTIONS AND REASONING

One of the features that is thought by many to define human uniqueness is the ability to reason. Once considered a characteristic of the soul (see chapter 5), the capacity to reason is also considered to be a way of

6. Ibid.
7. Ibid.

understanding what it means to be made in the image of God.[8] Following Descartes, psychology for many decades viewed reasoning as a mental process independent of the more bodily and physical capacities such as emotion. In the middle to late part of the twentieth century, it would not be unusual for college psychology curricula to have separate courses in emotion and cognition. Cognition as a mental process, so it was believed, was a different kind of process than the more physical emotions, which were thought to be more closely tied to what was happening in the body. Today in psychology, the concept of embodied cognition is gaining support, and it is increasingly being recognized that mental processes such as reasoning are intimately tied to what is happening physically in the body.[9] As a result, in psychology today cognition and emotion are no longer separated but are recognized as interacting in crucial ways.

Over the past twenty years, dual-process theories have been proposed to more formally recognize that mental processing seems to occur in two basic forms.[10] These dual-process theories postulate that humans engage in two kinds of cognition: a fast, immediate, and automatic form of cognition, and a slower, more deliberative kind. These two forms of cognition are given different labels by different theorists, but the essential characteristics of the two forms of cognition are similar from theory to theory. The first type of cognition (variously labeled Type 1, System 1, Intuitive, or Natural) is fast, does not require conscious effort (is nonconscious), is present very early in life, and is similar to animal cognition. This type of cognition enables a person to detect emotions in a person's face or voice; understand that if an object is released, it will fall to the ground; know that tigers do not give birth to lions, etc. The second kind of cognition (called Type 2, System 2, Rational, or Unnatural) is slower and more deliberate, requires conscious effort, evolved late, and is thought to be distinctively human. It enables a person to prepare for an anticipated noise, know that 156 divided by twelve is thirteen, and understand that a solid object like a table is actually composed mostly of space.[11] (Dual-process theories are discussed more fully in chapter 3.)

Reasoning is considered to be a prime product of Type 2 cognition. Type 1 cognition, on the other hand, includes a principal role for emotion.

8. Jeeves, "Neuroscience," 178.
9. Glenberg et al., "From Revolution to Embodiment."
10. Evans and Stanovich, "Dual-Process Theories."
11. Ibid.; Kahneman, *Thinking*; McCauley, *Why Religion*.

These two kinds of cognition are clearly displayed in the psychology of decision-making. When we make decisions, we tend to believe that we make those decisions based on reflection and reasoning—Type 2 cognition. Research in cognitive psychology, however, increasingly suggests that many if not most of our decisions are made using Type 1 cognition. We make countless decisions throughout the day. These decisions about what we do, think, and believe are usually made intuitively and automatically. We generally do not use reflection or reason to make these decisions. We just make them without expending any effort. Even when the decision is about an important issue, research suggests that these choices too are made using Type 1 or intuitive thought; rational thought only comes into play after the choice has been made in order to try to justify the decision. We may, in fact, come up with good "reasons" for doing what we did or believing in a particular way. But the decision about what to believe or how to act was ultimately made quickly and automatically by Type 1 cognitive processes heavily influenced by our intuitions or emotions.[12] The important point is that reasoning and emotion are not two separate processes. Much of our reasoning about an issue is influenced by how we feel about the issue emotionally, and part of that emotional picture is provided by what the body is doing physically. Antonio Damasio writes about the use of somatic markers in rational decision-making, and these markers come from the response the body has to a particular situation.[13] Does the situation feel right or bad? Should I approach or pursue a particular act or thought, or should I avoid it? These intuitions emerge from what our body is telling us about a given situation, and we use these fast and automatic intuitions to make the decision. Sometimes these decisions we make are about moral or ethical issues. How do we know if a particular action is morally acceptable? Where do these ideas of what is right and wrong originate?

EMPATHY, ALTRUISM, AND MORALITY

Empathy can be defined as the ability to feel what others are feeling and is a basic component of our social and emotional lives.[14] This fundamental phenomenon is important to a number of situations including parental care, forming groups, and theory of mind (ToM), and can be applied

12. Haidt, "Emotional Dog."
13. Damasio, *Descartes' Error*, 165–201.
14. Bernhardt and Singer, "Neural Basis."

to interactions with kin, nonkin, or even to member of other species.[15] Finding examples of empathy in animals and identifying neurobiological mechanisms involved in empathy supports an evolutionary perspective for the origins of empathy and, by extension, perhaps morality as well. The direction, therefore, is from emotion (empathy) to behavior (altruism) to morality.

What is the evidence of empathic emotions and altruistic behavior in nonhuman animals, and what does research suggest about the neural mechanisms involved in empathy and altruism? Empathic behaviors have been observed in rats that appear responsive to the distress of a conspecific (a member of the same species).[16] Behaviors indicative of empathy have also been noted in birds, monkeys, bonobos, and chimpanzees, among other species.[17] When animals are aware of the emotional response of a conspecific (e.g., distress from observing a predator), cooperation can occur for mutual self-defense or even targeted helping of another in the absence of any apparent personal benefit—what seems to be true altruism. For example, both chimpanzees and bonobos help conspecifics either achieve a goal of the conspecific or help conspecifics escape from a dangerous situation that was not a threat to the individual doing the helping.[18] Various species display empathic and altruistic responses in social settings where conspecifics are attempting some task or are in physical danger. There is also anecdotal evidence of nonhuman primates helping a human in need as in the case of Binti Jua, a gorilla at the Brookfield Zoo near Chicago, who, in 1996, carried an unconscious boy who fell into the gorilla area to the safety of the zookeepers.

There is evidence of empathic and altruistic behavior in human (adults, children, and infants) as well as in nonhuman animals from rats to the great apes. What about evidence that the brain is involved in empathic behavior? That too would support the idea of a biological basis to the empathy, altruism, and morality connection. In a review of the literature on the neural basis of empathy, Bernhardt and Singer report that the anterior portion of the insula, sections of the cingulate cortex, and a variety of other brain areas play important roles in responses that can be considered illustrative

---

15. Decety, "Neuroevolution."
16. Bartal et al., "Empathy."
17. De Waal, "Putting."
18. Ibid.

of empathy.[19] Singer and colleagues investigated brain responses in females during painful shocks to their own hands via electrodes as well as similarly administered electric shocks to the hands of their romantic partners (the female subjects could see the hands of their partners being shocked). fMRI imaging indicated that cingulate cortex, insula, brain stem, and cerebellar regions were activated by both the first-person shock experience as well as by witnessing the shock delivered to the partner, suggesting a vicariously felt pain.[20] Similar overlap in brain activity has been found in studies investigating disgust, anxiety, anger, sadness, social exclusion, and social emotions such as embarrassment and admiration.[21] In other words, there is at least partial overlap between those brain areas (i.e., insula and cingulate cortex) active when a person experiences these responses in themselves or sees another person expressing these emotions. Animal research, brain imaging, and lesion studies using neurological patients show that empathy is broadly represented in the brain and uses a number of cortical (insula, anterior cingulate, orbitofrontal) and subcortical regions and includes the autonomic nervous system, endocrine system, and the hypothalamic-pituitary-adrenal axis.[22]

We humans are a groupish species. Because we need to live in groups, cognitive mechanisms or ways of thinking have evolved that facilitate living among others. These ways of thinking make it easier for us to get along with those in our group. Joshua Greene argues that there are two moral problems that humans face.[23] The first is the Me vs. Us problem—how to balance selfishness with a concern for others. The cognitive mechanisms mentioned above evolved to solve this problem. We are not the completely selfish individuals that the veneer theory suggests. We can and do behave with concern for others, and the work of primatologists such as de Waal suggests we share this concern with other primates.[24] It is not just a surface characteristic of being human; it is at least in part a product of our deepest biological inheritance. We do cooperate with members of our ingroup, and empathy facilitates this cooperation and cohesion by providing the necessary moral intuitions that help us to identify with those like us. Morality

19. Bernhardt and Singer, "Neural Basis."
20. Singer et al., "Empathy for Pain."
21. Bernhardt and Singer, "Neural Basis."
22. Decety, "Neuroevolution."
23. Greene, *Moral Tribes*, 19–102.
24. De Waal, *Bonobo and the Atheist*, 25–54.

also facilitates groupishness by encouraging (or requiring) behaviors that promote cohesiveness and cooperation. How should we treat others in our group with whom we share resources? How should we act toward others with whom we cooperate for group success?

There is, however, a second, larger moral problem that humans face, created by the very mechanisms in our brain that evolved to solve the first problem. This is the Us vs. Them problem. Our intuitions lead us to form groups with those who are like us in important ways and to trust those members of our group. Those same mechanisms, however, often lead us to be suspicious or mistrustful, or even to hate those who are not part of our group or tribe. The second problem then is whether we can transcend these intuitions to mistrust outgroup members. Can we go beyond our tribal gut reactions?[25] Greene argues that our biology encourages cooperation, "*but only with some people. Our moral brains evolved for cooperation within groups*, and perhaps only within the context of personal relationships. Our moral brains did not evolve for cooperation *between groups* (at least not all groups)."[26] The same morality that facilitates cooperation for the Me vs. Us problem undermines cooperation between groups. Morality developed to encourage ingroup cooperation but leads to outgroup competition.

MORAL FOUNDATIONS

A leading figure in the study of morality from a psychological perspective is Jonathan Haidt, who has with a number of other researchers led a resurgence of interest in moral psychology.[27] For Haidt, a proponent of dual-process theory, moral intuitions come before moral reasoning. When presented with a moral question, we typically make our moral judgment based on a "gut feeling" about whether the situation is right or wrong. An example of a moral situation used by Haidt in his research is the story of Julie and Mark, who are brother and sister, traveling together through France on summer vacation. One night while staying alone in a cabin, they decide to make love. Julie is already taking birth control pills, but Mark uses a condom for extra protection against any pregnancy. They both enjoy the experience, but decide not to do it again and to keep what they did their

25. Greene, *Moral Tribes*, 16.

26. Ibid., 23.

27. Graham and Haidt, "Sacred Values"; Greene, *Moral Tribes*; Haidt, "New Synthesis"; Haidt, *Righteous Mind*; Haidt and Graham, "When Morality."

own "special secret," which makes them feel even closer to each other. The question Haidt asks his research subjects is whether or not what Julie and Mark did was wrong. Was it okay for them to make love?[28]

Most people who hear this story (or read the story in the above paragraph) say that what Julie and Mark did was wrong. But why was it wrong? Many people will provide reasons why Julie and Mark making love was wrong: There is the danger of inbreeding, what they did might ruin their relationship as siblings, they might be emotionally damaged, and so on. In the story, however, Julie and Mark use two different forms of birth control so the chance of pregnancy is extremely small. They report that they felt closer emotionally to each other following what they did. The reasons for why it was wrong are not supported by the events of the story. Nevertheless, almost everyone believes sex between siblings is morally wrong. Haidt argues that we decide what Julie and Mark did was wrong based on an intuition, a feeling, not because of any well-thought-out reasons. Moral intuitions are primary, reasons secondary. We decide on the basis of a feeling that a given situation is morally wrong or right and then, afterwards, come up with reasons to justify our intuitions. It seems like we make our moral judgment based on good reasons, but that is an illusion. The reasons come after the moral decision has already been made based on how we feel about the situation.

The foundation for these intuitions is what our body (our somatic markers) is telling us, and these intuitions are the result of thousands of years of human history as well as our own individual history. Using these kinds of stories as well as other questionnaire data, Haidt developed his moral foundation theory, which identifies six foundations upon which people tend to form their beliefs about what is good or bad, right or wrong.[29] Each foundation has a positive and negative side, and we are influenced by some of these foundations more than others. These six moral foundations are (1) care/harm, (2) fairness/cheating, (3) liberty/oppression, (4) loyalty/betrayal, (5) authority/subversion, and (6) sanctity/degradation. Because these foundations evolved through evolutionary inheritance, each foundation has an original trigger as well as current triggers. So, for example, the original trigger for the care/harm foundation was the suffering or distress of one's child, while current triggers include seeing pictures of starving children in Africa or even cute puppies in a commercial for an animal shelter.

28. Haidt, "Emotional Dog," 814.
29. Haidt, *Righteous Mind*, 123–27, 170–76.

The original trigger for the loyalty/betrayal foundation was a threat to the ingroup, but current triggers would include a favorite sports team or a national flag eliciting pride (on the positive side) or anger at those who pose a threat to the group.

We are not all oriented to these six foundations in the same manner. Some of us are more affected by care/harm or fairness/cheating while others are more oriented toward loyalty/betrayal or authority/subversion. In fact, research in moral psychology suggests that individuals from different political parties also differ on which of these moral foundations are most important to them. Those who are politically liberal are more influenced in their beliefs by the foundations of care/harm and fairness/cheating than by the other foundations. People who identify with the conservative political position are motivated more equally by all six of the moral foundations.[30] When trying to understand why a person takes a particular position on some moral issue (abortion, immigration, climate change, gun control), it is necessary to know what moral foundations are motivating that person's decisions. It is also important to remember that these moral intuitions come first, so these foundations are usually going to be influencing the person at an automatic or nonconscious level. The same is true for the moral positions we hold. We might be able to justify with good reasons why we have a particular position on some moral issue, but it is likely that we hold the position we do because of our intuitions about whether something is right or wrong. Moral intuitions come first, reasons second.

MIRROR NEURONS AND VON ECONOMO NEURONS

The discovery of mirror neurons reveals a possible mechanism whereby the responses of others (physical, emotional, or social) can be translated into similar behaviors in the observer. Mirror neurons are brain cells that respond (fire) when the individual performs a particular response or sees that same response enacted by another. Discovered in monkey premotor cortex, mirror neurons are present in a variety of species, including humans, and in a variety of brain areas.[31] These neurons are thought to be involved in a number of social cognitive responses, including imitation, empathy and theory of mind, and have even been implicated (controversially) in autism

30. Haidt and Graham, "When Morality."

31. Pellegrino et al., "Understanding Motor Events"; Molenberghs et al., "Brain Regions"; Mukamel et al., "Single-Neuron."

spectrum disorders, conditions where in part the affected individual seems to have difficulty recognizing and responding appropriately to social cues in others.[32]

When we see another person experiencing an emotion (e.g., happiness or sadness), we are able to feel that emotion as well. Think about the times you have been at a movie or perhaps a stage play and seen the actor on the screen or on the stage express the emotion of sadness. We might find ourselves starting to tear up during the movie or play. We can empathize with the actor because, at least in part, of the action of these mirror neurons. The same neurons that mediate our sadness are activated when we see sadness portrayed by another. We can in a very real sense feel what the other person is feeling.

Von Economo neurons (VENs) are relative large neurons characterized by a spindle-shaped cell body and a single dendrite facing in the opposite direction from the single axon. Named after the neurologist Constantin von Economo (1876–1931), these cells are found in the anterior cingulate cortex (ACC), dorsolateral prefrontal cortex (DLPFC), and the fronto-insular cortex (FI) in humans and the great apes. VEN-like cells are also present in some species of whales, dolphins, and elephants. VENs are found in what are considered to be highly social animals and are thought to be vital in connecting brain regions that mediate social behaviors, including the perception of bodily states or gut feelings that are utilized in determining social interactions, even moral ones.[33]

SOCIAL COGNITION

Social cognition refers to the mental processes used in developing and maintaining our relationships with other people. As social species we need to form these relationships, and the brain/mind has certain cognitive mechanisms that mediate these interactions. To form and maintain relationships with other people certain cognitive capacities are critical. Examples of these abilities include the capacity to communicate with another; a conscious memory of past events, persons, and places; an ability to anticipate the future, to try out various possible scenarios, and see their implications; and a theory of mind, a capacity to understand what another person is thinking

32. Fan et al.," Unbroken"; Press et al., "Intact Imitation"; Schulte-Rüther et al., "Dysfunctions."

33. Butti et al., "Von Economo Neurons."

and feeling, and what that person might do next.[34] These capacities help to facilitate relationships with others. Theory of mind (ToM) is especially important. Without understanding that other people might (and do) think and feel differently from us, we would find it extremely difficult to develop relationships with those individuals. ToM emerges during early childhood, around four to five years of age. One way to assess for a ToM in a child is to perform what is called the false belief test. If a three-year-old child is shown a crayon box that actually contains pieces of chalk, the child will believe that everyone will know that the box contains chalk. The child knows there is chalk in the crayon box and cannot understand that another person could possibly believe anything else. If a five-year-old child is shown the crayon box that contains chalk, however, that child will understand that someone else shown the box will believe that the box contains crayons. The older child has developed a ToM, which enables the child to understand that other people can believe different things. In this case, the other people will have a false belief that there are crayons in the box.

Perhaps not surprisingly, mirror neurons and VENs are believed to be implicated in generating this ToM, and there is some evidence (challenged vigorously by many researchers) that individuals who have difficulty relating to others (e.g., individuals with autism spectrum disorders) have a deficiency in ToM.[35] Whether mirror neurons and VENs are involved in conditions such as autism is disputed, but the role of these neurons in ToM and social cognition in general is strongly suggested by the research.

ROLE OF EVOLUTION IN COOPERATION

The mental mechanisms of social cognition also include the ability to get along and cooperate with others. If there is a connection between the emotional response of empathy, the behavioral response of altruism, and the moral sense (a biological basis for morality), why might this development have occurred? From an evolutionary standpoint, there is a selective advantage to individuals of a species that show emotional responses of empathy and behavioral responses of altruism if and when those responses result in more offspring for those individuals. One way that individuals with those behavioral traits might have a selective advantage is through cooperation.

34. Brown, "Cognitive."

35. Butti et al., "Von Economo Neurons"; Fan et al., "Unbroken"; Glenberg, "Positions."

In other words, if the emotional and behavioral responses of empathy and altruism lead to greater cooperation among individuals with those responses (compared to individuals without those behavioral characteristics), and if those individuals live longer to produce more offspring (passing on the genes affecting the behaviors characteristic of empathy and altruism), then those behaviors are more likely to occur in the future and to become "typical" of members of that species. There is evidence from comparative animal studies, as well as studies using mathematical modeling, that altruism and cooperation (prosocial behavior) among conspecifics can and does lead to increased success of the group compared to other interactive strategies.[36] From an evolutionary perspective, pleasurable psychological states (e.g., awe, forgiveness, gratitude, and others) become associated with "successful" prosocial behaviors while unpleasant psychological states (e.g., shame and guilt) become associated with "unsuccessful" nonsocial behaviors. These "successful" and "unsuccessful" behaviors can become codified into the fabric of the community, leading to generally agreed-upon rules of behavior or morals. Those behaviors that promote group success (perhaps via the success of the individual members of that group) become moral and good behaviors (helping others, being reliable, being honest) whereas those behaviors that do not promote group success (lying, betrayal, theft, and others) become immoral or bad.

Physiology of Cooperation

If we are indeed social creatures in need of social affiliations, we should expect to find physiological mechanisms that facilitate these social connections. Is there any evidence of a physiological basis for positive relationships with others? If cooperation is so important for group cohesiveness and success, should there not be an underlying biological mechanism that promotes cooperation? A physiological mechanism, oxytocin, has been identified, one that is thought to be part of a broader biological foundation for social relationships. Oxytocin is a chemical that is implicated in a variety of physiological responses in the body, including lactation, facilitation of birth, and genetic regulation of brain growth. It is also implicated in social bonding and other social cognitions and behaviors, including romantic, parental, and filial attachments.[37] Oxytocin has been shown to

36. Krebs, "Morality."
37. Carter, "Oxytocin Pathways"; Feldman, "Oxytocin and Social."

increase ingroup conformity, trust, generosity, and empathic accuracy in humans—each of which is important in developing and maintaining social affiliations.[38] Oxytocin has even been correlated with elevated scores on spirituality in a group of Christians.[39] While some of these findings have been criticized for not being robust or strong (especially the research on the relationship between oxytocin and trust), a variety of researchers, from several different labs, utilizing different research methodologies find an intriguing connection between this physiological mechanism and cognitions and behaviors involved in sociality.[40]

SOCIAL CAPITAL[41]

I have mentioned a number of times already that humans are social creatures. We need social relationships and are driven by our biology and our cognitive mechanisms to make these connections with others. Is there any evidence that we need social contacts with others and that without these connections we will suffer? There is a great deal of evidence to support the idea that relationships with others is important, and the evidence comes in the study of social capital and social networks

In September 2003, the Commission on Children at Risk, a group of doctors, research scientists, and mental health specialists, issued their report titled "Hardwired to Connect." The Commission was called together to address a specific problem: Why are children today at such heightened risk for behavioral and mental disorders? The conclusion of the Commission was that children are "hardwired" for enduring connections to others and for moral and spiritual meaning. Children in the latter part of the twentieth century and the first part of the twenty-first century are not making these connections, and when these connections are not made, serious problems can result, problems such as depression, anxiety, conduct disorders, and suicidal thoughts.[42] What is true of America's children is also likely true of America's adults. Over the last third of the twentieth century through

38. Bartz et al., "Oxytocin Selectively"; Kosfeld et al., "Oxytocin Increases Trust"; Stallen et al., "Herding Hormone; Zak et al., "Oxytocin Increases Generosity."

39. Holbrook et al., "Self-Reported Spirituality."

40. Nave et al., "Does Oxytocin Increase."

41. Much of the material from this section on social capital comes from Seybold, "Social Ties and Health."

42. Commission on Children at Risk, *Hardwired*.

today, Americans have become increasingly disconnected from one another. Social structures such as churches, community service organizations (e.g., Kiwanis, Lions, or Elks), card clubs, and bowling leagues, have suffered from decreased participation as Americans join less, give less, trust less and socialize with others less. The political scientist Robert Putnam documents this decline in social connections in his book *Bowling Alone*. Putnam refers to the connections among individuals as social capital—the "social networks and norms of reciprocity and trustworthiness" that arise from these connections.[43] Just as a society must have physical capital (such as buildings or machinery) or cultural capital (such as knowledge, skills, and education), so too must a society have interconnections among the members of that society. Like physical and cultural capital, social capital has real value for the people in a society. There are objective benefits to a society that is rich in social capital.

Social capital exists in different forms, including structural (what people do) and cognitive (what people feel with regard to social relations). Additionally, bonding social capital consists of resources that help strengthen ties among members of a particular network (e.g., friends bringing meals to you when a loved one has died) while bridging social capital is characterized by links among individuals from separate networks, such as might be developed during an interfaith, international conference on human trafficking.[44]

Social networks consist of the relationships that exist in a person's life and can include family, friends, colleagues at work or school, and co-members of clubs, churches, or societies. Qualities that make up a specific social network include the number of members in the network, the interconnections among the members (for example, how many of one's friends are also members of the same church?), and the age of the relationships—how long have the friends or co-members been a part of one's social network. Generally speaking, the older the relationships and the richer the interconnections among the network's members, the more social capital is provided by the network and the greater the benefit to the individual.

Support coming from social networks is a well-documented factor influencing physical and mental health. The origin of this connection between social support and health is thought to come from early familial transactions such as caring, affection, and positive involvement.

43. Putnam, *Bowling Alone*, 19.
44. Putnam and Feldstein, *Better Together*, 1–10.

Expectations about social relationships in adulthood are largely affected by infant-caretaker attachment processes. Infant-caretaker interactions are thought to form a basis for developing trusting and dependable relationships in adulthood. Early family environment can also influence an array of psychosocial processes relevant to physical and mental health such as coping strategies, self-regulation and control, and emotional reactivity, and the early environment within the family (e.g., the mother's response to infant cues) can also impact the development of basic social competencies and peer acceptance. Perceived support from the family is also related to lower stress exposure and improved health behaviors, such as diet, exercise, smoking cessation, and medical regimens.[45] Not all social network effects produce positive health outcomes. Caregiving directed toward members of one's own social network can produce high stress, reduced immunity, and an increased risk of infection, doctor visits, serious illness, and even death.[46] Poor mental health in a spouse can also alter the physical health of the caregiving partner, and negative marital functioning is correlated with dysfunction in the immune system which can lead to chronic physical ailments.

Despite these documented negative effects, the overall impact of social support is positive. Support from social networks (family, friends, colleagues) is associated with lower levels of cardiovascular disease, cancer, myocardial infarction, atherosclerosis, and overall mortality. Social support is also linked to lower blood pressure, improved immune function, and higher levels of psychological well-being.[47] As in any correlational research, the problem of directionality is an issue: do poor social relationships lead to impaired physical/mental health or does impaired health lead to poor social relationships? The use of longitudinal studies, testing a given cohort of subjects repeatedly over a number of years, can provide some information regarding the direction of the effect, and these studies give the stronger influence to the social relationships affecting health.[48]

Social networks can affect health (both physical and mental) through a variety of possible processes. Many of the health issues experienced today

45. Uchino, "Understanding."

46. Robles et al., "Marital Quality"; Smith and Christakis, "Social Networks."

47. Robles et al., "Marital Quality"; Smith and Christakis, "Social Networks"; Uchino, "Understanding"; Umberson and Montez, "Social Relationships and Health"; Umberson et al., "Social Relationships and Health Behavior."

48. Ibid.

are due to behavior (rather than infections, for example). Influences from social networks (e.g., friends or family members) can improve health by encouraging healthy behaviors and discouraging unhealthy behaviors. For example, a friend who runs with you in the morning, a spouse who encourages you to stop smoking or eat a healthier diet, church requirements (for members) that insist on abstinence from drug use or moderating alcohol consumption can each direct behavior and result in improved overall health.

In addition to social networks, social ties can affect the health of an individual through various psychosocial processes. Social networks can provide a sense of meaning, control, fulfillment, and purpose to an individual that can serve as a buffer to stress and improve the individual's health. Social networks can also provide an environment through which positive and negative life events can be interpreted. For example, being connected to a community of like-minded individuals (e.g., a church) can motivate a person experiencing difficulty to reframe the problem, changing it into a positive life event (or at least one that is neutral), which can serve to reduce the detrimental effects that event might have on overall health.

Being a member of a group can provide a source of identity for a person. Much of our sense of personhood is derived from group membership, and this membership can provide an organizing strategy to help the person comprehend and put perspective on events that occur. There are downsides to this effect of the group on individual understanding, of course. How an individual thinks about a particular issue can be heavily shaped by the group to which one belongs. We often assume the beliefs or perspectives of the group in order to maintain our identity with that group, sometimes fearing that expressing views contrary to those of the group might lead to our rejection from the group and the loss of those group connections (see chapter 7).

The ability of social networks to reduce stress illustrates a third mechanism whereby social ties can affect health and that is via certain physiological processes, such as the hypothalamic-pituitary-adrenal (HPA) axis, the immune system, and the autonomic nervous system.[49] The HPA axis consists of a neural and hormonal communication system whereby the brain ultimately controls the body's response to environmental stressors. When physical, social, or psychological stressors are experienced, the hypothalamus (a brain region involved in a number of important biologi-

49. Seybold, "Physiological."

cal behaviors such as eating, drinking, temperature regulation, and sexual behavior) causes either through direct neural connections or indirectly through the release of chemical modulators the pituitary gland to release adrenocorticotropic hormone (ACTH), which eventually results in the release of the stress hormone cortisol from the adrenal cortex. Cortisol helps the body to respond to the stressor and, under normal, healthy conditions, also causes the pituitary gland (via the hypothalamus) to inhibit the release of ACTH, which results in lowered levels of cortisol in the body. This negative feedback system is vital in the healthy regulation of the body's stress response. Under abnormal conditions, this negative feedback system does not respond properly, and the levels of cortisol in the body remain elevated, contributing to various stress-related disorders such as high blood pressure and cardiovascular disease to name but two.

The autonomic nervous system (ANS) is also involved in the stress response of the body. While the HPA axis is responding to a stressor, the ANS is as well. The ANS consists of two systems that serve to keep each other balanced. The first is the sympathetic nervous system (SNS), which functions to arouse the body physiologically when confronted with a stressor. For example, the SNS increases blood pressure, heart rate, and respiration, and causes pupil dilation (among other effects) each of which serves to prepare the body to respond actively to the environmental event. These effects are sometimes referred to as the "fight or flight" response. The second system, the parasympathetic nervous system (PNS), has the opposite effect on the body. It decreases blood pressure, heart rate, and respiration, and causes pupil constriction (among other effects), which serve to put the body at rest. When functioning in a healthy manner, these two systems are complementary and keep the body in the proper balance between arousal and relaxation.

The immune system is also involved in the body's response to stressors. This system consists of numerous biological processes and structures that detect a variety of pathogens, distinguish these from the body's own tissue, and respond to the pathogens to try to neutralize them. Together with the HPA axis and ANS, the immune system, when functioning as it should, helps to maintain health and fight against the deleterious effects of stressors in the environment. Rich social networks help to maintain health in an individual through facilitating the positive effects of each of these systems. When social networks are impoverished, the individual is more susceptible to stress and the diseases that can result from extended exposure to stressors because the HPA axis, ANS, and immune systems are compromised and not functioning normally. It is important to keep in mind that these mechanisms are not mutually exclusive. Certainly physiological mechanisms will be implicated in any pathway involving behavior (e.g., increasing exercise is a behavioral mechanism but clearly has implications for one's physiological responses as well), and psychosocial mechanisms (e.g., control and meaning) will affect the individual's overall physiological responses (e.g., the HPA axis).

TRUST GAMES AND GAME THEORY

There is ample evidence in the psychological and medical literature that social living benefits the individuals in those groups. In relationship, humans tend to live longer and be in better health. We could say that group living is adaptive. As we have discussed in this chapter, in order to have social groups and positive relationships with other members of our group, cooperation is important. Whenever there are organized forms of life, cooperation is involved. We see cooperation in genes, cells, multicellular organisms, insect societies, and human ingroup relationships.[50] Cooperation is a vital component of ingroup relationships and success and is considered to be adaptive. But how might cooperation be adaptive and improve the likelihood of success in either an individual or group? The principal (and for many evolutionists the only) type of selection is at the level of the individual. From this perspective, adaptation is only considered at the level of the individual organism. Any modification in anatomy, physiology, behavior, or cognition that does not favor the survival success of the individual cannot possibly be considered adaptive. In the case of cooperation, how could this type of behavior have been selected for given that cooperative behavior does not always help the individual who is cooperating? Recently, however, multilevel selection has become a viable alternative to selection only at the individual level. Selection does occur at the level of the individual, but also at other levels as well.[51]

One possible alternative level is that natural selection favored cooperation among individuals who are genetically related, a process known as kin selection. This type of selection, also known as inclusive fitness, is seen in a number of insect species. A bee, for example, might cooperate

50. Coakley and Nowak, "Introduction," 9.

51. Wilson, *Does Altruism*, 31–45.

with others in the hive, not only for its own benefit, but also because the members of the hive share genes. Cooperation can facilitate the survival of the genetic "pool" within the hive even at the expense of the individual bee.

But what about situations in which there is cooperation among individuals who are not related genetically? What would motivate their cooperation? Direct reciprocity refers to cooperation among two members of a group, even if those two members are not genetically related. The idea behind reciprocity is that one individual will help or cooperate with another because helping the other will (it is expected) be repaid at a later date. Direct reciprocity could help explain cooperation among individuals who are in frequent contact with each other. Indirect reciprocity, on the other hand, refers to situations where cooperation occurs between individuals who are unlikely to encounter each other again, making direct reciprocity impossible. In this kind of reciprocity, cooperation can occur because reputation is important. People who have a reputation of being cooperative and helpful are likely to be the recipient of help and the cooperation of others when needed. Indirect reciprocity is thought to be prominent in groups of unrelated individuals and requires cognitive processes such as episodic memory and the monitoring of the social network (social cognition).It also is thought to form the basis of the evolution of morality and of social norms.[52]

Group selection, selection between groups, is another option according to the multilevel approach. While group selection has been controversial in evolutionary thinking, this controversy is "receding into the past."[53] The existence of different groups and variation between groups provides the fitness difference necessary for natural selection to favor some groups over others. There is competition between groups. Some groups will be successful; others will not. Those groups that cooperate (i.e., are composed of individuals who have the cognitive mechanisms that mediate cooperation) will be more successful than those who do not. As a result of this greater success, the individuals in those groups will pass their genes to the next generation, including those genes responsible for the mechanisms of social cognition involved in cooperative behaviors.

Psychologists, economist, game theorists, evolutionary biologists, and researchers in other disciplines often utilize trust games in studying interactions among (generally two) individuals. Trust games (also called

52. Nowak, "Five Rules."
53. Wilson, *Does Altruism*, 34.

economic games) consist of three elements: the players, the actions the players choose, and the payoff functions for each player's action generally measured in terms of money earned during the game.[54] Players typically can choose between a response that is considered "selfish" (it benefits the person making the response, often at the expense of the other player) and a response that is considered "cooperative" (a response that helps the other player, perhaps at the expense of the player making the response). When these types of games are studied, they show that individuals not only seek to maximize their own payoffs, but often show cooperative responses as well.

Trust games, which can be played as one-shot (one trial) games or as multiple trials between two participants, come in a variety of forms. One type of game is called the dictator game and involves two participants who do not know each other and who will not meet during or after the game. One player (player 1) is randomly assigned the role of dictator and is given the responsibility of dividing a sum of money between the two players. The money can be divided in any way the dictator chooses. Player 1 can keep all the money and give none to the other player (player 2), or player 1 can divide the money between the two participants, keeping some and giving some to player 2. Player 2 has no choice but to accept the "gift" from player 1, whatever that gift might be, including a "gift" of no money at all. When these games are played, the mean gift is around 20 percent, but gifts of up to 50 percent are frequently seen. The fact that any money at all is given by the dictator to the other player can be considered cooperation or even altruism because the gift is costing the dictator something and benefiting the other participant.

Another version of trust games is called the ultimatum game. Again, there are two players, and one player (player 1) is randomly assigned the role of distributing the money in any way this player chooses. In this version of the game, however, player 2 can either accept the division proposed by player 1 or reject it. If player 2 accepts, the money is distributed as proposed. If player 2 rejects the proposed distribution, neither player gets any money. From a purely rational perspective, player 2 should accept any distribution posed by player 1 (except a distribution where player 2 gets no money at all) because any money given to player 2 by player 1 is better than getting none. If I am player 2 and player 1 proposes to keep nine dollars and give me one dollar, reason would lead me to accept the proposal.

54. Almenberg and Dreber, "Economics and Evolution."

After all, one dollar is better than nothing. If I accept, I have more money than if I reject the offer. But as player 2, I will reject what I consider to be unfair offers, and player 1 knows this. (After all, player 1 knows she would reject unfair offers as well.) As a result, player 1 will make offers that she believes I will accept. This is to her advantage because if I do not accept her offer, she also gets no money. In the ultimatum game, mean offers of 40–50 percent are typical, and the likelihood of rejecting the offer is 50 percent if the offer is less than 20 percent of the money available. These trust games suggest that there is a social preference for fairness, and there is evidence of reciprocity in these games as well—a be-nice-to-me-and-I-will-be-nice-to-you relationship.[55]

As mentioned above, these games can be played as one-shot games or with multiple trials between the same two participants. The multiple-trial versions more closely match the social situations in which human beings find themselves. We evolved in social settings where there were typically repeated interactions among members of the group. So why would player 1 give any money to player 2 in the dictator game? If player 1 has any concern about her reputation, she will give money to player 2 (even though the rules of the game do not require she do so) to help protect that reputation. Other evidence suggesting the importance of reputation comes from research in which the dictator game is played in a setting where there are eyes watching the game being played. For example, playing the game in a room with posters of people's faces results in more generous offers from player 1 than if the game is played in rooms without these reminders that someone might be watching your behavior. Also, priming God concepts, for example nonconsciously exposing participants to reminders of God or the Divine, increases money allocated in the dictator game and also increases other prosocial behaviors.[56]

These games lend support to the notion than cooperation is a universal human characteristic, but the work of Frans de Waal suggests that cooperation is seen in nonhuman primates who also show signs of concerns for fairness.[57] Nevertheless, two characteristics are thought to make human cooperation unique: theory of mind, and language. Both increase the probability and severity of negative consequences for selfish behavior. Belief in supernatural punishment is also thought by some researchers to

---

55. Ibid., 137.

56. Shariff and Norenzayan, "God Is Watching."

57. Almenberg and Dreber, "Economics and Evolution," 144.

be adaptive because it helps to avoid the real-world costs of selfish actions such as retaliation and rejection.[58]

In group living, there are not only the advantages of group life (in the case of human societies those advantages include better defense, more effective hunting, and expansion of territory) there are also costs (such as participating in the dangers of the hunt or of defense). A central problem of group life, therefore, is defection, when an individual takes advantage of being a part of the group but is unwilling to pay any of the costs. The free rider or defector wants to share in the safety of the group but does not put himself in harm's way to provide that defense. Too many free riders or too much defection can threaten the entire group as unpunished defection can spread to other members of the group. This is the central problem of organized group life, whether it is organized human society or the organization found in multicellular organisms.[59]

A system of punishment for free riders is important if a group is going to be successful, but effective punishment is not easy to create because there are costs involved for the individuals who dole out the punishment. As a result, some have argued that certain religious beliefs, particularly beliefs in gods or in God, can been seen as an effective way of discouraging defective behavior in group members. If divine beings are given responsibility in a religious system for rewarding good or moral behavior and punishing bad or immoral behavior, then ultimate responsibility for punishing free riders belongs to the gods. An important part of any organized society's structure consists of rules that specify what kinds of behaviors are acceptable (or moral) and what behaviors are unacceptable (or immoral). Many of these rules for proper behavior deal with interactions among individuals of the group and function to help ensure positive relationships among group members. For example, regulations dealing with another's property ("You shall not steal."), relationships with another's spouse ("You shall not commit adultery."), trusting others ("You shall not bear false witness against your neighbor."), and life itself ("You shall not kill.") are all important in preserving cooperation among members of the group. It is easy enough, perhaps, to get away with some of these ethical and moral commands if the only ones who can catch you and punish you for violating them are your fellow group members. If, however, belief in an all-powerful, supernatural, divine being is also part of the group's system of control, then it

58. Johnson, "Uniqueness," 170.
59. Schloss and Murray, "Evolutionary Accounts."

becomes more difficult to "get away" with violating the group's standards. These supernatural beings can "take the burden of punishing off of group members by imposing sanctions and rewards via their presumed control of natural or supernatural processes."[60] Believing in such a divine being (or God) can decrease defection and increase cooperation within the group, making that group more likely to be successful against groups that lack such cooperation. As described above, being exposed, even nonconsciously, to suggestions that you are being watched or to God concepts tends to increase prosocial or cooperative behavior, and communities that do believe in moralizing and punishing gods have higher levels of cooperation.[61] In addition, individuals who view God as a more punishing figure tend to cheat less than individuals who see God through a more loving lens.[62] While these data support the idea that beliefs in supernatural beings are adaptive because they promote cooperation among groups (and, therefore, increase the success of those groups), it is important to note that these same studies also found increased prosocial behavior when research participants were exposed to more secular moralizing concepts such as police or juries. So, rather than religious beliefs being adaptive per se, it might be the case that what is adaptive is a general cognitive bias toward cooperation that many religious beliefs utilize.[63]

TOP-DOWN AND BOTTOM-UP MORALITY

Does morality and knowledge of what is right and wrong come from above, from a God who decrees what is good and bad from on high, or does knowledge of how we are to treat others emerge from below, from our basic biological natures? The story of the Israelites and their covenant with God as read in the book of Exodus tells of Moses bringing The Ten Commandments to the Israelites. Did our understanding of morality come to us in this top-down way? The work of primatologists such as Frans de Waal and evolutionary biologists like David Sloan Wilson suggests that we can see at least the precursors of morality, if not moral behavior itself, in animals, primarily primates but in other animals as well. Did our knowledge of how to treat other people emerge out of our biology in a more bottom-up fashion?

60. Ibid., 48.
61. Ibid., 51.
62. Shariff and Norenzayan, "Mean Gods."
63. Schloss and Murray, "Evolutionary Accounts," 59.

Is our morality embodied in us without being instructed from the outside? Are these mutually exclusive options or might both be true?

Many different mammals are sensitive to the emotions of conspecifics and can "come to their aid" on occasion. Empathic behavior (helping a conspecific in need) is seen in dogs and even in rats. Birds show comforting behaviors as do chimpanzees and other primates. Frans de Waal argues strongly and with a lot of empirical evidence that the great apes (chimpanzees, orangutans, gorillas, and bonobos) exhibit true altruism. Nonhuman primates show many of the same basic wants and needs that humans have, desires centering on power, sex, security, affection, aggression, trust, and cooperation.[64] Some primates also recognize inequity and evidence an aversion for it. While being rewarded for a task with a cucumber slice is perfectly satisfying for a capuchin monkey, if the capuchin sees a conspecific being rewarded with a more highly preferred grape for the same task, it will start to refuse the cucumber. Dogs also will perform tricks for no reward until they see other dogs receiving a treat for the same behavior.

There is certainly something special about human morality that makes it the result of a more deliberative, Type 2 cognitive process. Nevertheless, some moral actions in humans seem to come about as the result of natural or intuitive Type 1 cognition. These moral behaviors emerge out of our social instincts. Humans, like many other mammals, have an altruistic impulse; we respond to signs of distress in others and are motivated to take the feelings of others seriously and to try to improve their situation. We also have impulses toward trusting others, particularly those in our ingroup. Humans desire positive relationships with others; we are driven to try to get along with others when we can. These bottom-up responses emerge from our biological makeup, and the most fundamental factor driving these prosocial responses is the human need to live in groups. Our moral emotions of fairness and empathy, but also of shame, embarrassment, love, gratitude, honor, loyalty, and guilt, as well as our social cognitions and behaviors (such as altruism) facilitate group living, and out of these emerges morality. These emotions are all useful in maintaining group norms. These moral impulses or intuitions also present a challenge to the veneer theory, which suggests that human goodness is only superficial, that deep down we are selfish and aggressive. This alternative view argues that morality evolved

64. De Waal, *Bonobo and the Atheist*, 16.

for within-group reasons. We share with other primates, which are also groupish, a similar biological background.[65]

Religion, another contributing source of morality, appeals to this background. Without our being social creatures, religion's appeal to morality would not make any sense to us. It does make sense because we value relationships, and religion might serve the function of encouraging group cohesiveness. We are, many religious believers say, made in God's image, and one way of conceptualizing the *Imago Dei* is to think of it from a Trinitarian perspective. God (Father, Son, and Holy Spirit) is relationship, and as creatures made by God, we are made for relationship—with others and with something beyond ourselves, the transcendent. As creatures in need of social relationship, however, we have a preference for our own group. These moral emotions listed above can promote a sense of "us" but can also lead to negative attitudes and behaviors directed toward "them" or the "other." This is clearly seen in Langdon Gilkey's experiences during World War II as told in *Shantung Compound*. In that account, we see the good and the bad of human social interactions. The drive to unify and organize the camp in order to accomplish the day-to-day tasks that any social community needs to fulfill, but also the selfishness expressed when the members of one particular group (defined by nationality) received needed supplies that the members of other nationalities did not get.

Human morality is complex, and there is no necessary contradiction to try to understand this complexity from multiple perspectives. In what ways is human morality influenced by bottom-up biological tendencies that we share with other primates? In what ways can human morality be understood from an evolutionary perspective? To what extent has the fact that we are social creatures shaped the way that our brains mediate our relationships to others through various cognitive mechanisms? But what about religion's role in human morality? Is there a top-down perspective to understanding moral action? To what extent does religion appeal to our biological background when it comes to morality? Many if not most religions do promote altruism. In Christianity, for example, Jesus instructs his disciples to "offer the other also" to him who strikes you on your cheek; to "not withhold even your shirt" to him who takes your coat; and to "love your enemies, do good to those who hate you." (Luke 6:27–29). Indeed, much of Jesus's teaching seems to be centered on acting in an altruistic way toward others, even to those who are not a part of our ingroup. Matthew

---

65. Ibid., 223–40; Greene, *Moral Tribes*, 61–62.

25:31–46 contains the well-known passage where Jesus encourages his followers to feed the hungry, clothe the naked, and welcome the stranger. Luke 10:25–37 has the equally well-known parable of the Good Samaritan, where Jesus broadens our understanding of who is a part of our group, tribe, or nation.

We have dual-processing brains. We have both Type 1 automatic cognition, which is heavily influenced by our emotions, and we have Type 2 cognition, which is more deliberate and characterized by the use of reason. We need both the fast and automatic mode of thinking and the slower more deliberative mode because we face problems that require an efficient kind of thinking as well as problems that utilize more rational thought. Joshua Greene argues that the automatic Type 1 mode evolved to help us cooperate with those of our ingroup, but to get along with those outside of our group we need to use more deliberative Type 2 cognition.[66]

We are in a period of American cultural life where there is much fear of the "Other," where the outgroup is identified by religion or nationality. Many Americans express fear of increasing numbers of immigrants coming into the country, particularly if those immigrants follow Islam instead of Christianity. It seems like there is an increasing emphasis on the ingroup (Christian, American, perhaps even white) in contrast to the outgroup (Muslim, non-American, minority). (These divisions into "Us" and "Them" can have profound effects on public policy and politics, issues discussed in the next chapter of this book.) To what extent does Jesus in his teachings appeal to the more deliberative Type 2 cognitive style? Do Matthew 25 and the parable of the Good Samaritan cause us to think more slowly and rationally about who is part of our ingroup? Do these teachings cause us to think more judiciously about outgroups and how we treat them? Or, somewhat differently, is Jesus encouraging us via his teachings to broaden our understanding of the ingroup so we have automatic, intuitive reactions to people who would normally be classified as "Them" or "Other"?

Perhaps one way to think about bringing a bottom-up and top-down perspectives together is to consider how religion might act upon our biological background to encourage us to see more and more people as part of our group, to redefine what it means to be a social creature in relationship with others. Religion can certainly contribute to greater loyalty to the ingroup at the expense of the outgroup as events in the first couple decades of the twenty-first century have demonstrated. But religion cannot be blamed

66. Greene, *Moral Tribes*, 171–204.

for all intergroup conflict, and at its best, perhaps as it is intended to be practiced, religion can help to blur group boundaries and encourage a new answer to the question, who is my neighbor? Or, who is in my group?

7

Cultural Cognition

Why Do Conservatives and Liberals
Think Differently?
(Or, Can't We All Just Get Along?)

Listening to people's political views can sound like listening to a reflex ... it just sounds like something in the wiring. —Colin Firth

As frustration grows, there will be voices urging us to fall back into tribes, to scapegoat fellow citizens who don't look like us, or pray like us, or vote like we do, or share the same background. We can't afford to go down that path.[1]

Over the past twenty years, polarization along political lines has increased in America.[2] The percentage of Americans who have consistently conservative or consistently liberal views has doubled over this period. At the same time, ideological overlap has diminished. Approximately 92 percent of Republicans are to the right of the average (median) Democrat, while about 94 percent of Democrats are to the left of the average Republican. A

1. Obama, "State of the Union."
2. Abramowitz and Webster, "All Politics"; Iyengar and Westwood, "Fear and Loathing."

substantial proportion of Americans today live their lives in what has been called "ideological silos" where down the line consistency is followed on all political, social, and cultural issues. As a result, more and more Americans are likely to select their friends, where they will live, and even who they would want in their families on the basis of political ideology.[3] This is not the sentiment of the majority of Americans, but it is the view of a growing number of Americans who see a consistent conservative or liberal position on all the major issues of our day as crucial in determining with whom they will associate, and it is these Americans who are most likely to participate in the political process. In other words, the more ideologically pure you are, the more politically active you are.[4]

Not only are we becoming more ideologically polarized in America; we are also developing a more negative view of people who think differently than us. The percentage of Americans who have very negative views of the opposing politically party has doubled over the past two decades. The negativity even reaches the point of seeing those who disagree with us politically as threats to the well-being of the country. Twenty-seven percent of Democrats and 36 percent of Republicans view the opposing party as not only wrong, but as actual threats to the nation.[5] These negative and even hostile feelings directed toward those who do not have the same ideological positions as we do are often implicit, and the discrimination that results is as strong as any based on race.[6] Again, these extremely negative views of the opposing political party are not held by the majority of Americans, but tend to be held by those who are the most active politically and who identify most strongly as either Democrats or Republicans.[7]

ORIGINS OF DIFFERENCES

What are the origins of these differences? Do people acquire these political views through experience only, or might there be a biological basis to some of the differences seen among individuals? Perhaps surprisingly there is an increasing amount of evidence to suggest that political differences are influenced by the same kind of factors that produce other differences

3. Pew Research Center, "Political Polarization," overview.
4. Ibid.
5. Ibid.
6. Iyengar and Westwood, "Fear and Loathing," 690.
7. Westfall et al., "Perceiving Political."

in the way people respond to the world. Political liberals and conservatives differ not just in politics but also in the food, art, and humor they enjoy. Liberals and conservatives differ in the kind of pastimes they pursue, the way they gather information and think, in personality, and in the way they perceive other people and events. They also tend to differ in the way they respond to arousing stimuli, in what they attend to, in their preference for simplicity and realism as opposed to complexity and abstraction, in their neural architecture, and, perhaps, genetically as well.[8] Parenting attitudes, child temperament, gray matter volume, disgust sensitivity, and need for closure have all been found to distinguish political liberals from political conservatives.[9] One way of organizing these many differences is to see them as indicative of variations in negativity bias, how liberals and conservatives respond to negative features in the environment. Using this approach, Hibbing, Smith, and Alford found that conservatives, compared to liberals, tend to show greater physiological responsivity to negative or aversive stimuli (such as angry faces) in the environment and to use more psychological resources in reaction to these stimuli. Conservatives are also less open to novel experiences; prefer predictable, orderly, and expected situations; and are less likely to take chances. It is not surprising, therefore, that conservatives tend to prefer public policies that minimize threat, emphasize traditional solutions to problems, and appeal to authority.[10]

CULTURAL COGNITION

Whatever the origins of these differences might be, it is interesting to note how positions on seemingly unrelated issues tend to cluster together. For example, a political conservative will tend to be pro-life, pro–death penalty, anti–gun control, against same-sex marriage, against vaccination for human papillomavirus (HPV), and skeptical about climate change and evolutionary theory—to name just a few issues of importance in today's society. On the other hand, political liberals will tend to be pro-choice, anti–death penalty, pro–gun control, for same-sex marriage, in favor of HPV vaccinations, and accepting of the scientific consensus regarding climate change and evolutionary theory. Why these positions on seemingly unrelated

8. Hibbing et al., *Predisposed*, 6; Hibbing et al., "Differences," 300–301.

9. Hibbing, "Differences"; Fraley et al., "Developmental"; Jost, "Elective Affinities."

10. Hibbing et al., "Differences," 297–304.

issues? What is the connection, if any, between gun control and same-sex marriage? Between the death penalty and HPV vaccinations?

One answer to the question of what shapes these distributions of beliefs is cultural cognition, which refers to a set of processes whereby what a person believes about an issue (e.g., gun control, abortion, climate change) derives from their cultural commitments or values. Even on a factual issue such as climate change that seems to be answerable by empirical data, culture comes before fact, so one's adoption of a particular cultural perspective shapes what one believes about that issue.[11] One implication of the role cultural cognition plays in shaping opinion is that more evidence or information (i.e., more facts) on a particular topic, such as climate change, is unlikely to change minds. Cultural commitments act as a kind of heuristic for assessing evidence on public policy issues. Regular citizens are not in a position to know for themselves whether the climate is really changing, or if gun control really does reduce violent crime, or if evolutionary theory really is the best explanation for speciation. Regular citizens have to depend on information they get from others, and the psychological processes of cultural cognition lead us to listen to and depend upon information we get from those we trust, and we trust those who share our beliefs and values. We are going to find information we get from a person who shares our cultural commitments more credible and believable than evidence provided from a person who does not have the same values and commitments we have.[12]

A study by Kahan et al. found that how an individual evaluates information received from an expert in a field (i.e., a person with elite academic credentials) depends on if the expert has the same cultural commitments as the person receiving the information. If the expert is perceived as having the same commitments, then the evidence is accepted as credible and accurate. If the expert is perceived as having different cultural commitments than the person receiving the information, then that same factual information is evaluated as not credible or accurate.[13] So, if David Barton shares the same cultural commitments as I do, then I am likely to accept what he says about American history as truth and fact even though he is not a historian. If Ken Ham shares the same commitments as I do, then I am likely to accept

11. Kahan and Braman, "Cultural Cognition and Public Policy," 148.

12. Lewandowsky et al., "Misinformation."

13. Kahan et al., "Cultural Cognition of Scientific Consensus."

as credible and true his version of creation and speciation over the theory of evolution, which is the consensus view held by scientists.

A heuristic is a thinking strategy that typically allows us to be more efficient in making decisions or judgments and is contrasted with an algorithm, which, while leading to fewer errors, is slower. So, using heuristics is faster but more error prone while using algorithms is slower but will generally lead to fewer mistakes in our reasoning. Cognitive and social psychologists have identified several heuristics that we use as we think, reason, and make decisions. One is the availability heuristic whereby what we think about a subject (e.g., is it safer to fly than drive) is influenced by how easily flying and driving accidents come to mind. Even though statistically it is much safer to fly than to drive, most of us can readily remember tragic airplane crashes where hundreds of people were killed in an instant. On the other hand, thinking of a car crash or even multiple car crashes that resulted in the same loss of life is difficult or impossible. If we decide that flying is more dangerous than driving on the basis of how easily we can bring plane crashes to mind, then the availability heuristic is at work in the way we reason about the relative safety of flying and driving. In a similar way, when thinking about whether climate change is a legitimate threat to the environment, some pieces of evidence are going to be more easily retrieved than others. Cultural cognition predicts that the evidence that is more easily retrieved is likely to come from a person who holds similar cultural commitments as I do. Not only will the information from that person be more easily remembered (availability heuristic), but I am going to consider that information more credible because of the greater trust I have in that person because of our shared cultural commitments.[14]

Another factor in shaping the distribution of beliefs is biased assimilation, which refers to the tendency of a person to accept the reliability of new information if it conforms to what they already think is true and to reject information that is inconsistent with what they already believe. So, if I believe that the death penalty reduces violent crime rate, information to the contrary will be rejected by me no matter how empirically based that evidence might be. Evidence consistent with my prior belief on the death penalty will be evaluated as true and accurate by me even if it comes from a single source and is not empirically strong. Additionally, the psychological mechanisms of naïve realism and reactive devaluation support the tendency

14. Kahan and Braman, "Cultural Cognition and Public Policy"; Kahan et al., "Cultural Cognition of Scientific Consensus."

to see new information as unreliable if it goes against my cultural beliefs. Naïve realism refers to the phenomenon whereby individuals see beliefs held by their cultural group as the result of objective assessment of the evidence and to view the beliefs of individuals in other cultural groups as biased. Reactive devaluation occurs when individuals in one group dismiss the persuasiveness of evidence presented by people belonging to a different cultural group. So, information presented by a Christian might be seen as more persuasive than evidence provided by a Muslim simply because of group membership.[15]

Preference falsification also helps shape the distribution of beliefs. In group discussions, if there is even a slight preference for one position over another (for example, a slight preference among the group that climate change is not a concern), then those who agree with that position are likely to participate more in the discussion than those who might disagree with that position. As a result, over the course of the discussion, the position that climate change is not a concern will seem to have stronger and stronger support within the group. Those who might think climate change is a real threat to the environment are likely to remain silent to avoid censure from the group. If the group to which I belong (because of similar cultural commitments) develops a particular view on climate change (e.g., not really a danger), then to remain in good standing with that group, I will either adopt a similar view of climate change or at least remain silent about my true thoughts.

As indicated above, the commitments we have to a particular culture (e.g., a liberal political/theological position or a conservative political/theological position) influences the way we process information, which tends to affect the way beliefs are distributed among liberal or conservative groups. One might think that increased education and knowledge about science would decrease the polarization of positions on issues such as climate change, HPV vaccinations, and evolutionary theory, but greater scientific literacy is associated with higher levels of polarization on these issues.[16] The tendency of individuals to conform their evaluation of information to be consistent with a goal or purpose besides accuracy is known as motivated cognition. For example, if a person's identity is tied to membership in a group or community that shares important values and that group adopts a particular position on some public policy issue (e.g., gun control), then

15. Kahan and Braman, "Cultural Cognition and Public Policy."
16. Kahan, "Ideology."

that person is likely to adopt that position on gun control as well. Taking a different position on that public policy issue might threaten membership in the group and, therefore, that person's identity. That kind of threat can be a powerful motivator to assess and process information on gun control in a way that is biased in favor of the group's position, even if that position is contrary to the objective, empirical data.[17]

INGROUPS AND OUTGROUPS

Identity, on the other hand, appeals to a constellation of the worst human impulses. It is worse than ordinary tribalism because it assumes a more than virtuous *us* on one side, and on the other a *them* who are very doubtful indeed, who are, in fact, a threat to all we hold dear.[18]

Group identity is an important factor that affects thinking, perception, judgments, and behavior toward other people, both those in the group and those out of the group. Changing group status, for example, can affect political ideology and attitudes and can also lead to increases in group polarization and decreases in toleration of others. A majority of Americans believe that American culture has changed for the worse since the 1950s, and 58 percent of Americans who believe this also believe that white men are losing influence and status.[19] Almost half of Americans (48 percent) report that they are bothered when they hear immigrants speak a language other than English (up from 40 percent just three years ago), and over half report they feel like strangers in their own country and no longer identify with what America has become.[20] It is predicted that by 2042 at the latest, the United States will be a "majority-minority" nation, meaning that no single racial/ethnic group will make up a majority of the population. White Americans will be the largest racial/ethnic group, but will no longer represent a majority. How might this changing demographic influence how white Americans view members of other racial/ethnic groups? Craig and Richeson found that the change from a majority status to a

17. Ibid.

18. Robinson, *Givenness*, 104.

19. Public Religion Research Institute, "Anxiety," 25.

20. Ibid., 26; Young and Jackson, "Rise of Neo-Nativism."

majority-minority status is perceived by many white Americans as a threat to their social and political status. This perceived threat was associated with expressions of racial bias: white Americans showed stronger preferences for interactions with their own ethnic group over interactions with other ethnic groups. The perceived change in status was also associated with an increase in negative attitudes toward other racial/ethnic groups and increased preference for political conservatism, suggesting the increased diversity in the United States over the next twenty years will lead to further polarization and a widening of the partisan divide.[21]

Ingroup and outgroup membership represents an important factor in how we relate to others. As discussed in chapter 6, group membership is even implicated in the development of morality and religion. Social relationships are vital for human survival, and humans have evolved various cognitive processes that help to identify efficiently and effectively who is a part of "my group" and who is not. These same processes can lead us to relate differently to those who are part of our group compared to those who are members of the outgroup.

Psychologists use the term "social categorization" to refer to the process whereby we organize our knowledge of groups and people. This categorization occurs swiftly and automatically, involving Type 1 thinking (see chapter 3), and affects how we behave toward members of assorted groups. We tend to use various categories, such as race, gender, age, and sexual orientation as we organize and place people into groups. The field of social cognitive neuroscience is interested in understanding how the social, cognitive, and neural processes involved in categorization into groups affects our behavior toward members of the group and how the concepts of "us" and "them" are represented in the brain.[22] Social identification occurs when people categorize themselves into a particular group and obtain part of their self-concept from membership in the group. The self is seen from a more collective perspective; a change from "me" to "us," and the act of self-categorization also influences how we respond to others within our group as well as to those outside of our group. We tend to be biased in favor of the ingroup and against the outgroup.[23]

21. Craig and Richeson, "More Diverse"; Craig and Richeson, "On the Precipice"; Danbold and Huo, "No Longer."

22. Molenberghs and Morrison, "Role of the Prefrontal."

23. Cikara and Van Bavel, "Neuroscience," 245–48.

Research suggests that it does not particularly matter how the groups are formed for these biases to exist. The minimal group paradigm is a research technique used to create groups for laboratory investigation of intergroup relations. The method involves assigning the research participants into groups based on arbitrary, random differences. Even if created according to this technique, bias for the ingroup and against the outgroup is found. An example of this kind of study is the well-known Robbers Cave Experiment conducted by Sherif and colleagues in the early 1960s at Robbers Cave State Park in Oklahoma.[24] Two groups of fifth-grade boys were created with neither group knowing the existence of the other. Eventually the groups named themselves the Rattlers and the Eagles. After this initial phase of the experiment was concluded, the two groups were brought into contact in various competitive situations, for example baseball games and tug-of-war, where prizes were awarded to the winning group. These games were intended to create intergroup conflict, which occurred with name-calling and references to the members of the other group using derogatory terms. These relatively harmless forms of conflict escalated into low-level physical violence between the groups. In the final stage of the experiment, the researchers tried to reduce the intergroup conflict by bringing the groups together for a cooperative task, such as fixing the water supply to the camp. This effort at cooperation did, in fact, have the desired effect of diminishing the conflict between the two groups and reducing the bias against members of the outgroup.[25] The Robbers Cave experiment is used to illustrate how studies of group dynamics can occur outside of the laboratory in a "real-life" setting, but also to show how easily group identity can lead to prejudice, bias, and even aggression against outgroup members, even if the groups are created arbitrarily by randomly assigning individuals to specific groups. Groups created on the basis of ethnic, racial, or religious characteristics are also subject to the same kind of ingroup/outgroup biases.

Ingroup and Outgroup Biases and Prejudice

There are many examples of how these biases affect the way people in one group respond to or perceive members of the outgroup. For example, we tend to see selfish motives in outgroup members, but selfless motives for our own group. We also tend to underestimate the generosity of members

24. Sherif et al., *Intergroup Conflict.*
25. Ibid.

of the outgroup and to see members of the ingroup as being more honest, prosocial, considerate, and trustworthy.[26] Our brains also respond differently to ingroup compared to outgroup members. Researchers randomly divided participants into two teams, a "red" team and a "blue" team, and asked the team members to judge the speed of hand movements performed by both groups. Perhaps not surprisingly, the "red" team members judge their teammates movements as faster than those of the opposing team. The "blue" team had the same biased perceptions, and these biases were correlated with activity in the left inferior parietal lobe, a region implicated in changing visual representations of actions into motor representations of actions.[27] We perceive the actions of ingroup members more positively than those of outgroup members, and this difference in perception is correlated with increased activity in the inferior parietal lobe. We literally perceive ingroup members differently than people belonging to the outgroup.[28]

We also respond with greater empathy to members of our ingroup. When we see a member of our ingroup in pain, the neural circuits mediating pain perception in our own brains (i.e., the anterior cingulate cortex and the anterior insula) are activated as they would be if we were experiencing the pain ourselves. No such activation occurs if we see a member of the outgroup in pain. In addition, we find it easier to take the cognitive perspective of a member of our ingroup (or read their minds) in part because brain regions involved in this kind of perspective taking are activated when we are exposed to people in our own group, but not when we are around members of the outgroup.[29] Face recognition for ingroup members is also faster and more accurate compared to faces of people belonging to the outgroup. The fusiform face area (FFA) mediates facial recognition, and this area shows greater activity when responding to an ingroup face. There also tends to be greater activity in the amygdala, a brain area involved in emotional processing and fear conditioning, when viewing outgroup faces. Both blacks and whites show increased amygdala activity when viewing faces of the other group, and this activity is correlated with implicit measures of racial bias such as the Implicit Association Test (IAT) and the startle response. Other studies show increased amygdala activity to novel faces, even if ingroup membership is determined on a trivial basis by the

26. Van Lange, "Generalized Trust."
27. Cikara and van Bavel, "Neuroscience," 251.
28. Molenberghs, "Neuroscience," 1532.
29. Ibid., 1533.

minimal group paradigm, suggesting that group membership can guide neural responses to social stimuli.[30]

We obtain much of our personal identity through membership in particular groups, ethnic, religious, racial, and so forth. Part of that identity results from the status of the group to which we belong. As the social status of that group changes (for example the predicted change from a white majority status to a white majority-minority status described above), doubts about our own identity can develop. These doubts can motivate a person to align themselves with clearly defined beliefs and behavioral prescriptions to reduce the identity uncertainty. These kinds of beliefs and behavioral prescriptions are often found in more extreme groups that provide strong and certain leadership, an often exclusionary approach to outgroup members, and an ideological belief system that discourages or forbids dissent and insists upon particular group-normative behavior.[31]

If one identifies with evangelical Christians, the identity afforded by that membership might seem threatened by recent changes in the American political/judicial landscape. We sometimes hear about Christians in the United States (often, but not necessarily evangelical) feeling as if they are being discriminated against because of their faith. (Indeed, Americans who belong to a particular religious group are more likely than those who do not to report that their group faces discrimination. For example, 51 percent of white evangelical Protestants believe that evangelical Christians experience a lot of discrimination, while less than 40 percent of black Protestants and about 25 percent of mainline Protestants believe evangelicals face a lot of discrimination. Half of white Americans believe that discrimination against whites is as big a problem today as discrimination against minorities, but less than 30 percent of Hispanics and black Americans hold that belief.)[32] This perceived discrimination often emerges in the context of same-sex marriage. Many Christians (again, often but not always evangelical) believe that same-sex marriage is wrong, despite what the courts have decided. These same Christians might not want any involvement in a marriage they believe is immoral. Some have refused to bake cakes, provide flowers, or even issue marriage licenses for gay or lesbian couples. When public opinion and the courts rule against these Christians, the individuals might think they are no longer free to practice their religion as they once were allowed

---

30. Ibid., 1534; Cikara and Van Bavel, "Neuroscience," 248–52.

31. Hogg, "From Uncertainty."

32. Public Religion Research Institute, "Anxiety," 36–38.

to do, the practice of which is a vital part of their personal identity. It is this kind of societal change that can, according to the uncertainty-identity theory, lead a person to align with more self-inclusive groups in an attempt to reduce the identity uncertainty. Some evidence does indicate that such group identification reduces uncertainty and also decreases neural activity in brain areas involved in anxiety.[33] Sometimes identity uncertainty can lead an individual to groups that are extreme in their belief systems and behavioral prescriptions. In a series of laboratory studies Hogg and colleagues have found that identity uncertainty can lead to identification with radical groups, increased intentions to engage in specific extreme group behaviors, increased support for violent group action, and increased support for authoritarian leadership.[34] While these studies were conducted in a laboratory, the implications of the findings for group identification and behavior in real-life settings are important and unsettling.

Racial and religious groups are two of the most obvious in American public life today, and both race and religious categories affect how we perceive, understand, and act toward members of the outgroup. We tend to evaluate our own racial or religious group more positively than others, and some studies have found greater humanitarian concern directed toward ingroup members.[35] Group labels can have material consequences for group members. Hall and colleagues found that whites perceive those labeled blacks (as opposed to those labeled African Americans) as lower in status, competence, and warmth, and that whites see a criminal suspect labeled black more negatively than a criminal suspect labeled African American.[36] At the same time, white Americans tend to implicitly and explicitly convey what might be called superhuman traits on black Americans, which can lead to a perception that members of the racial outgroup do not have the same kind of experiences that members of the racial ingroup have.[37]

Social context, however, is important in evaluating others. If race is the most salient group distinctive, then racial attitudes, stereotypes, and values will probably be more relevant in evaluating members. If race is not a distinctive feature of the group (i.e., if the group consists of people from a

33. Hogg, "From Uncertainty," 340.

34. Hogg et al., "Religion"; Hogg et al., "Solace"; Hogg and Adelman, "Uncertainty-Identity Theory"; Hogg et al., "Uncertainty and the Roots."

35. Axt et al., "Rules"; Hall et al., "Why Don't."

36. Hall et al., "Rose."

37. Waytz et al., "Superhumanization."

variety of races), then race becomes less salient and will be less likely used for evaluations of the group members. Indeed, studies show that assigning people to mixed-race groups can override any racial bias seen on implicit measures (e.g., IAT); this suggests that forming mixed-gender, mixed-age, or mixed–sexual orientation groups might also reduce outgroup prejudice.[38]

What are the relationships among political and racial or religious groups? In other words, are there differences between how political liberals and political conservatives respond to ingroups and outgroups? By and large, the answer seems to be no. While political conservatives show higher scores on measures of dogmatism, both conservatives and liberals show similar levels of intolerance toward groups that are seen as either threatening or ideologically different. Both also show similar levels of superiority in viewing their beliefs as better than the political outgroup's.[39]

HOW WE THINK AND BELIEVE DIFFERENTLY

An important dimension along which current American culture is polarized is political, and there is a substantial literature in psychology attempting to identify what these differences are. But why do we hold the beliefs we have? How do these beliefs affect our interactions with others? How do these beliefs influence our thinking about new information? And to what extent do we have conscious control over our beliefs and their influence on our behavior? These questions are important and suggest that there might be important differences in people who are political conservatives and political liberals, not only in the beliefs they hold, but also in how they relate to others and even in how they think.

One difference between political conservatives and political liberals is in the predisposition to feel disgust. A number of investigations show that conservatives are more easily disgusted by issues related to the moral foundation of purity or sanctity, the foundation that make it easier for us to consider some things untouchable or forbidden. Disgust, an emotion easily elicited by a smell, sound, or sight, evolved to help us avoid pathogens and other threats spread by physical contact or proximity. This research shows, for example, that compared to political liberals, conservatives show increased disgust toward issues of abortion and gay marriage.[40] This in-

38. Cikara and Van Bavel, "Neuroscience," 248–52.
39. Brandt et al., "Ideological-Conflict Hypothesis"; Toner et al., "Feeling Superior."
40. Inbar et al., "Conservatives"; Inbar et al., "Disgust Sensitivity."

creased disgust reaction occurs automatically, without conscious reflection. Other studies find that reminders of physical purity and cleanliness (such as hand washing) results in greater disapproval of moral behaviors such as watching pornography, using drugs, or even littering. These reminders of purity also result in those randomly exposed to the reminders reporting more political conservativism than those not so reminded.[41]

Conservatives and liberals also differ in their sensitivity to and perception of threat. Threat can come in a variety of forms from fear of death to unstable economic or social conditions, and many studies show a correlation between measures of threat perception and indicators of political conservativism, such as authoritarianism. People with left-wing ideological beliefs are less likely to perceive threat than individuals with right-wing beliefs. Right-wing attitudes consist of high regard for authority and an adherence to mainstream norms and traditions. In particular, people holding right-wing political beliefs are more likely to perceive as threatening changes in external social/cultural factors.[42]

Differences are also seen between liberals and conservatives in cognitive style, cognitive abilities, and in motivated cognition. Jost and colleagues argue that all ideological belief systems are held because they satisfy certain psychological needs or desires. This statement does not mean that the beliefs are wrong or unreasonable, but psychologists are interested in the origins of the beliefs and what purpose the beliefs have. People adopt those beliefs, in part, that are most likely to meet their psychological needs centering not only on threat, but structure, certainty, order, authority, tradition, and closure. Several studies suggest that political conservatives, for example, have a higher need for stability, structure, and predictability and are most sensitive to perception of threat. Conservatives seem to be less tolerant of ambiguity, to favor traditional norms, and to value authority compared to political liberals. Consequently, a conservative is likely to adopt a belief system that emphasizes certainty, structure, stability, gradual change (instead of rapid), tradition, and authority. These beliefs will be held, in part, because they reduce anxiety experienced through ambiguity, threat, and change.[43]

A number of interesting associations are found involving prejudice. For example, prejudice is correlated with cognitive style and with cognitive

41. Helzer and Pizarro, "Dirty Liberals."

42. Onraet et al., "Relationships."

43. Jost et al., "Political."

abilities. A model that attempts to bring meaning and understanding to these correlations is provided by Dhont and Hodson, who propose that various psychological processing mechanisms mediate the relationship between cognitive abilities/style and prejudice.[44] Some people seem to have a greater need to find an answer, any answer, on a given issue or question. They feel a desire for quick and definitive answers and prefer secure and stable knowledge that can be applied across all situations. The term psychologists give for these preferences is "need for cognitive closure" (NFC), which is also characterized by a preference for order and structure, discomfort with ambiguity, and an unwillingness to have obtained knowledge challenged. This NFC serves as a kind of framework for knowledge acquisition and maintenance.[45] NFC is positively correlated with both gender and racial prejudice; in other words, people who have a high need for cognitive closure tend to score high on measures of prejudice based on gender and race. It has been suggested that individuals with a high NFC tend to satisfy this need for quick, stable, and decisive knowledge by turning to essentialist categories and authoritarian ideologies, which are what lead to the increased prejudicial attitudes. Essentialist categories result from thinking in terms of meaningful, defining attributes that each member of a particular category possesses. While this kind of thinking has the advantage of enabling easy (and sometimes accurate) inferences about group membership, it can also lead to overgeneralizations and stereotyping. Authoritarian ideologies are defined by the preference for authorities that impose discipline, define clear hierarchical structures, and discourage ambiguity.[46]

Several research studies find correlations between cognitive abilities and prejudice. In this case, the correlations are negative, meaning that people who score low on measures of various cognitive abilities (such as abstract-reasoning skills and verbal and nonverbal intelligence) score high on prejudice. Why would lower cognitive ability negatively correlate with prejudice? Is there a meaningful connection between the two? Dhont and Hodson propose that right-wing social/cultural ideology (RWSC) is the mediator between cognitive ability and prejudice.[47] According to this model, RWSC provides an ordered and structured view of society that seeks to preserve traditional social conventions, a view that would also tend to

44. Dhont and Hodson, "Does Lower."
45. Roets and van Hiel, "Allport's Prejudiced."
46. Ibid.
47. Dhont and Hodson, "Does Lower."

appeal to people with a high need for cognitive closure. Dhont and Hodson provide evidence of a negative correlation between cognitive abilities and RWSC, and a positive correlation between RWSC and prejudice. In other words, individuals who score low on measures of cognitive abilities show high scores on RWSC, and people with high scores on RWSC have high scores on prejudice. As a result, the relationship between cognitive abilities and prejudice is mediated by RWSC. The authors also provide evidence that low childhood cognitive-abilities scores predict higher levels of prejudice in adulthood through the endorsement of right-wing social/cultural ideology.[48]

While there are many causes of prejudice, these studies suggest a role for cognitive factors as well. How might one bring together the roles cognitive abilities, cognitive styles (e.g., NFC), and threat play in producing prejudice? Lower cognitive abilities and NFC might influence psychological mechanisms involved in how we perceive, process, and assess information, including information regarding the social and cultural environment. So, shifts in demographics such as the change of white Americans from a majority to majority-minority status in the next couple of decades (see above) might be assessed as more threatening, motivating the person to try to prevent the change through emphasizing the known and familiar, and through decreasing uncertainty and anxiety. These are not necessarily unreasonable reactions to perceived threat, but over time the focus on prevention can lead to stronger reactions, including the adoption of right-wing social/cultural ideologies producing a prejudicial perspective on members of the outgroup. Indeed, studies do show that adherents of right-wing ideologies feel threatened by social problems, and also show correlations between RWSC and stereotyping, discrimination, segregation, as well as prejudice.[49]

MORAL FOUNDATIONS

In eighteenth- and nineteenth-century America, the psychology that was taught in colleges such as Harvard, Yale, and Princeton was typically found in courses on moral philosophy.[50] While the psychology taught in today's colleges and universities is much more naturalistic, there is still a part of

48. Hodson and Busseri, "Bright Minds," 187–95.

49. Dhont and Hodson, "Does Lower"; Malka and Soto, "Rigidity"; Onraet and van Hiel, "Are Right-Wing Adherents."

50. Coon, "Salvaging."

psychological science that is interested in moral behavior. Moral psychology is the name given to the contemporary psychological study of moral, ethical, and virtuous behavior. Some researchers in this field of psychology are interested in the foundations of morality and how these foundations might differ from one person or group to another. To what extent are differences between conservatives and liberals, Republicans and Democrats based on different fundamental moral positions? Given the lack of civility we see in much of our political discussions and the polarization we see in politics and religion today, how can an understanding of moral foundations help to increase dialogue between individuals whose political or religious ideas are so different?

One approach to these questions comes from the work of Jonathan Haidt, who argues that many of the differences that divide people politically or religiously stem from the fact that we are making our political or religious judgments based on a different collection of moral foundations.[51] Haidt bases his approach on what he calls the social intuitionist model of moral judgment whereby decisions about the morality of a particular act are determined less through slow, conscious, and deliberate rational analysis and decision-making processes than by quick, nonconscious, automatic, and relatively effortless intuition. According to the social intuitionist model, moral judgments are typically made on the basis of an emotional, bodily response in the person, who then, after the moral decision has been made, will use reason to justify that decision.[52]

Haidt's social intuitionist model comes out of the developing literature on dual-processing theories discussed in chapter 3. These theories postulate the existence of two separate types of cognition or thinking.[53] The first is automatic, fast, and effortless and is often classified as Type 1 thinking. In Haidt's model, this kind of thinking is termed "intuitionist" because it does not seem to require conscious effort and is based upon an emotional or intuitive response to the particular situation. The second kind of cognition is typically classified as Type 2 and requires conscious effort and takes time. This style of thinking Haidt terms "rational cognition." For Haidt, many if not most, of our decisions and judgments, even in the moral realm, are the product of intuitive thought. We make a quick and automatic decision

51. Graham and Haidt, "Sacred Values"; Haidt, "Emotional Dog"; Haidt, "New Synthesis"; Haidt, *Righteous Mind*, 128–86; Haidt and Graham, "When Morality."

52. Haidt, "Emotional Dog."

53. Evans and Stanovich, "Dual-Process Theories."

about a situation (e.g., is it right or wrong?) and then, after the fact, might use rational thought to try to find reasons to justify the decision we made at an intuitive level. Haidt illustrates this by providing examples where a particular moral decision is made (e.g., some behavior is wrong), even though we might not have a good rational reason for believing that the behavior is immoral, a phenomenon called moral confounding.

Using the social intuitionist model as a starting point, Haidt and his colleagues developed the Moral Foundations Questionnaire to assess subjects' views about a number of ethical and moral situations. Using the results of that questionnaire, six psychological systems were identified that provide the foundations for many of the world's moralities.[54] These six foundations, each shaped through evolution, prepare the person to detect and respond emotionally to issues of (1) care/harm, (2) fairness/cheating, (3) liberty/ oppression, (4) loyalty/betrayal, (5) authority/subversion, and (6) sanctity/ degradation.[55] The first foundation, care, prepares us to be sensitive to signs of suffering, first in one's own offspring and then more generally to others, and elicits the emotion of compassion. The second foundation, fairness, motivates reciprocal altruism and produces the social emotions of anger, guilt, gratitude, and the like. Loyalty is the fourth foundation and involves cooperation with one's kin group and the emotion of trust. This preference for kin groups generalizes to other "ingroups" that are composed of nonkin. Feelings of loyalty, patriotism, and heroism are associated with this foundation as are distrust and even aggression or hate directed against those in the "outgroup." The fifth foundation is authority (and respect for authority), which developed evolutionarily through living in hierarchically structured ingroups where dominant males (and females) receive privileges unavailable to others. Feelings of awe and respect are associated with this foundation. (The third foundation of liberty/oppression also involves social interactions with members of one's group and feelings that develop in response to perceptions of restraints on one's liberty, be they perceived threats from government, business, employers, and so forth). Sanctity (purity) is the sixth foundation and motivates approach and avoidance toward certain situations and elicits feelings of disgust (avoidance) or pleasure (approach). These approach/avoidance responses are initially directed toward physical situations (e.g., corpses, rotting food) but generalize to social situations as well (e.g., deformity, obesity).

54. Haidt and Graham, "When Morality."
55. Ibid.; Graham and Haidt, "Sacred Values."

Based on the social intuitionist model, Haidt and colleagues investigated the extent to which people from various political and religious groups differed in how they are motivated by these six moral foundations. The authors found that self-identified political liberals were motivated, primarily, by the first two foundations (care and fairness) and less by the remaining four foundations, while self-identified conservatives were motivated by all six foundations equally. More specifically, political liberals were more motivated by care and fairness than were conservatives. Conservatives were more motivated by loyalty, authority, and sanctity than were liberals.[56] In general, while there are those who disagree with Haidt's basic premise of differences between conservatives and liberals, political conservatives seem to have a more balanced set of moral foundations, although conservatives value loyalty and respect more than liberals, and liberals value fairness and care more than conservatives.[57] While both liberals and conservatives might use different moral foundations, liberals tend to be less accurate about the moral foundations of conservatives than conservatives are about political liberals, and these moral foundations affect how ingroup members perceive outgroup members.

When trying to talk to or reason with a person from the other end of the political spectrum, it will be helpful, Haidt's research implies, to understand that the other person might be operating from a different set of moral foundations than you. While there is overlap in the foundations between liberals and conservatives, there is a difference in emphasis that might drive the thinking of the two camps. The same can be said of religiously "liberal" or "conservative" individuals.[58] We might find it difficult to understand how people can have particular opinions or think in particular ways because their moral foundations motivate a different set of emotions and virtues than we experience. Added to this, in today's society an individual's identity can be closely tied to his or her political positions. In describing this trend of linking identity to political causes and positions, James Davison Hunter writes, "Next to their occupation or profession, their commitments as Democrats, or Republicans, pro-lifers or pro-choicers, conservative, liberal, gay, and so on, compete to form the largest part of a person's identity in public . . . Taken to an extreme, identity becomes so

56. Ibid.; Graham et al., "Liberals and Conservatives"; Graham et al., "Mapping"; Haidt et al., "Above and Below"; Haidt and Graham, "When Morality."

57. Frimer et al., "Liberals and Conservatives."

58. Haidt, *Righteous Mind*, 274–313.

tightly linked with ideology, that partisan commitment becomes a measure of their moral significance; of whether a person is judged good or bad."[59]

This connection between identity and ideology is one factor that contributes to our increasingly polarized society where people with particular political beliefs tend to live in particular parts of the country. In the 2008 presidential election, 89 percent of the counties with a Whole Foods store were carried by Barack Obama; 62 percent of the counties with a Cracker Barrel restaurant were carried by John McCain. In the 2012 election, 77 percent of counties with a Whole Foods went for Barack Obama.[60] This "self-sorting" can contribute to the kind of polarization we find in the United States today. The same "self-sorting" is seen in our churches. People attend and perhaps belong to a church based in large part on what the beliefs of the church are. In several Protestant denominations (e.g., in the Episcopal Church and in the Presbyterian Church [USA]) individual church congregations are voting to leave their denomination (and separate from churches that compose that denomination) because the local church members do not agree with some of the beliefs that the people who make up the larger denomination hold (e.g., the ordination of gays and lesbians). One of the results of this is decreased diversity in opinions about issues within local churches, and increased polarization within the broader body of Christ.

Haidt's research suggests that to enter into a dialogue, especially one where you might be trying to change another person's (political or religious) opinion, it will be necessary to understand the moral foundations from which the other person is operating. For example, on the issue of ordination of gay clergy or on gay marriage, a "liberal" on this position will probably emphasize the foundations of fairness and care and use language that emphasizes "equality" and "justice." Former president Bill Clinton's words in a *Washington Post* opinion piece are a good example of this emphasis on the foundations of care and fairness when he said, in reference to the Supreme Court considering the constitutionality of the Defense of Marriage Act, "the justices must decide whether it is consistent with the principles of a nation that honors freedom, equality and justice above all, and is therefore constitutional."[61] A person on the "conservative" side will probably be motivated by, in addition to fairness and care, loyalty, authority, and sanctity and will talk about "respect for the institution of marriage"

59. Hunter, *To Change the World*, 105.

60. Delmore, "Whole Foods? Cracker Barrel?"

61. Clinton, "It's Time."

and "sanctity of the family." Donald Wildmon, founder and president of the American Family Association wrote the following on the Association's webpage, "The homosexual movement's promotion of same-sex marriage undermines the God-ordained institution of marriage and family which is the foundation of all societies."[62] Individuals from the "right" and "left" on this issue might share the six moral foundations, but each will be primarily motivated in their opinions by a different set. Knowing what set of foundations is motivating the other person might help in reaching common ground.

REDUCING BIAS AND POLARIZATION

As I write this chapter, several events from the last couple years are front and center in American public consciousness. In Ferguson, Missouri, an eighteen-year-old black man named Michael Brown was shot and killed by a white policeman, resulting in numerous protests (in the streets of Ferguson as well as in other cities) and eliciting an investigation by the United States Department of Justice into that city's police department. Although the police officer who shot Michael Brown was cleared of any wrongdoing, the Justice Department report determined that there had been a general pattern of police misconduct against the citizens of Ferguson, including long-term discrimination and use of racial stereotypes against African Americans.

Other incidents also led to protests of perceived police mistreatment of minorities. Freddie Gray, a twenty-five-year-old African American, was arrested and put into a police vehicle in Baltimore, Maryland, and died of injuries to his neck and spine, which occurred while he was being transported to the police station. Twelve-year-old Tamir Rice, an African American boy in Cleveland, Ohio, was shot by a white policeman while the boy held a pellet gun. Witnesses to the shooting said that the police officer shot Tamir within seconds of arriving on the scene. An unarmed black man was shot in the back by police in North Charleston, South Carolina. Eric Garner, also unarmed and African American, died while being arrested by New York City police for allegedly selling illegal cigarettes. Each of these incidents, as well as many others (e.g., the death of Trayvon Martin at the hands of George Zimmerman in Florida in 2012) was part of the motivation

62. Wildmon "Principles."

that resulted in the emergence of the Black Lives Matter movement in the United States.

On June 17, 2015, a white man twenty-one years of age entered the historic Emanuel African Methodist Episcopal Church (known as Mother Emanuel) and killed nine members of the congregation, including the senior pastor of the church, who were participating in a Bible study. The shooter, survivors said, sat next to the pastor, Rev. Clementa Pinckney, and for over an hour took part in the Bible study before pulling a gun from a fanny pack and shooting the victims. He purportedly shouted racial epithets during the shooting. After his arrest, the shooter allegedly told police he murdered the nine people because he wanted to start a race war. A couple months later near Houston, Texas, a black man walked up to a white sheriff's deputy who was putting gas in his patrol car and executed him by shooting him multiple times from behind. When the officer fell to the ground, the killer continued to shoot him.

Not all the incidents that are in the news as I write involve such tragedy. Another presidential election is in full swing, and proposals aimed at barring Muslims from immigrating to the United States, statements about immigrants being rapists and criminals, and personal attacks on the appearance of political rivals have been common during the primary campaign. More evidence of polarization within the political process can be found in Congress, which recent polls suggest is at an all-time low in public approval. The poll numbers vary somewhat, but approximately 10 percent of the American people think Congress is doing a good job, and a major reason for the low approval rating seems to be the public's belief that members of Congress cannot get along with each other or compromise on the important issues of the day or manage the government as they are supposed to do. It is easy to offer an overly simplistic account of Americans' disapproval of their congressional leaders, but clearly lack of civility is a big part of the problem.

Members of the different political parties no longer seem to find agreement on any issue. In many cases, they cannot even agree on what counts as a fact. As an example, Congress in the fall of 2015 debated and voted on a deal with Iran that was supposed to prevent Iran from obtaining nuclear weapons, at least into the foreseeable future. But members of Congress could not even agree on the elements of the deal itself. Did the deal allow inspectors to monitor Iran's nuclear facilities to make sure Iran abides by the pact? Some said yes, it clearly did. Some said, equally confidently, no, it did not. Should it not be obvious whether monitoring can or cannot occur? Other parts of the deal were equally controversial. The point is not that members of Congress must agree on what is good or bad for the United States. The point is that the polarization is so wide among congressional members that they seemingly cannot even agree on what words on a page mean. Not only can they not agree, but they do not seem to recognize that there are legitimate views that can be held by people on the other side of an issue.

Forget a complicated issue like a treaty between two countries; there is even vehement disagreement on the citizenship of the forty-fourth president of the United States, Barack Obama. Surely an issue as simple as where a person was born is easy enough to determine, but the disagreement runs squarely along party lines, with recent polls reporting that up to 29 percent of Republicans believe that Barack Obama was not born in the United States and 54 percent believe that President Obama is a Muslim. Other seemingly empirical questions are also the subject of strong disagreement between groups. Do gun control laws actually decrease gun violence? Can nuclear waste material be safely stored underground? Has the average temperature in a given region of the world increased over the past fifty years? Do immigrants contribute to or harm economic prosperity in the United States? These are all questions that one would think could be answered by collecting empirical data, but they are also questions that divide Americans, typically along political lines.[63] Again, the interesting question for a psychologist is, why do people disagree so strongly over what one would think are easily determined facts?

What the literature reviewed in this chapter suggests is that group membership has profound effects on how we process information. We endorse whichever view supports our connection to others with whom we have vital commitments. The values and beliefs of our ingroup affect how we perceive and process information we obtain from our environment. That is part of the reason why groups who share similar views on the moral issues of abortion and same-sex marriage also hold similar views on issues such as climate change and the safety of genetically modified food.[64] We are all biased by our biology to prefer members of our own group. As discussed in chapter 6, groups are necessary for human survival, and there are various cognitive- and social-psychological processes to ensure that we become

63. Public Religion Research Institute, "How Immigration."
64. Kahan, "Fixing."

members of a group. These psychological processes lead us to prefer members of our ingroup over people in outgroups. These groups come in many forms, including racial, ethnic, political, and religious. We prefer people who look like us, who think like us, who behave like us, and who believe like us. We get part of our personal identity from the groups to which we belong, and we will adopt behaviors and beliefs similar to those of other ingroup members because not to do so might result in our exclusion from the group.

While there is a strong preference for ingroup over outgroup members, these preferences, even though they are partially the result of evolutionary processes, are not deterministic. The literature reviewed above also indicates that there are steps we can take to decrease these biases for ingroup and against outgroup members. One of the ways that bias against outgroups can be reduced is through intergroup contact. There is an abundance of evidence in the literature that increased contact among groups improves intergroup relations and attitudes. While the importance of intergroup contact for improving intergroup relations was initially observed in people who were not particularly prejudiced toward or intolerant of the outgroup in the first place, later evidence shows that intergroup contact helps to reduce intolerance even in those individuals who are highly ideological. This finding appears in studies of groups from a variety of cultures, countries, and communities (e.g., prisons, universities). Contact with other racial groups or other groups that differ in sexual orientation improves relationships between groups by increasing empathy toward and trust of outgroup members. Contact also decreases threat and anxiety these outgroups generate.[65] Empathy, trust, and decreased threat and anxiety are all factors that characterize relationships toward members of the ingroup. It appears that contact with outgroups has the effect of changing our perceptions of the outgroup members; we begin to see them as more like us and other members of our own group. Intergroup contact also reduces prejudice toward outgroups, and one mediator of this effect is need for cognitive closure (NFC) with people having the higher NFC showing the greatest decrease in prejudice.[66]

Another way relationships between ingroups and outgroups can be improved is through increasing a person's awareness of their moral identity. Moral identity refers to the extent to which a person is clearly aware of how

65. Hodson, "Do Ideologically."
66. Dhont et al., "Opening."

his or her actions, feelings, and thoughts are motivated by moral traits and values such as fairness, generosity, helpfulness, friendliness, honesty, and kindness. The moral foundations discussed above can be divided into the binding foundations (loyalty, authority, and sanctity) and the individual-izing foundations (care and fairness). The binding foundations encourage a group/collective orientation while the individualizing foundations focus on the protection of individual rights. While the binding foundations in-crease ingroup trust and cooperation, they can also lead to negative views of outsiders. Increasing awareness of moral identity tempers the negative effects of the binding foundations, suggesting that making moral identity more accessible and salient might improve intergroup relationships.[67]

A study by Westfall and colleagues suggests that while both actual and perceived political polarization has almost doubled over the last five decades, Americans still overestimate the amount of polarization that ex-ists in the United States. The authors identify three psychological factors that contribute to the perception of polarization among Americans. First, merely dividing people into groups (e.g., Republicans and Democrats) makes the groups seem further apart. Even categorizing two purplish colors into red or blue makes these colors appear more different than if the colors are not categorized.[68] In addition to categorization, the strength with which a person identifies with a particular group (e.g., with a political party) affects the degree of polarization the person perceives. If a person strongly identifies as a Republican or as a Democrat, that person will per-ceive greater polarization among the parties than a person who does not strongly identify with a particular group. Third, the extremity of a person's attitude affects how polarized that person perceives the political process. People holding extreme political views, whether extreme toward the right or the left, see the outgroup as more ideological and extreme than their own group. Persons with extreme political attitudes who also identify strongly with a particular party will perceive the greatest polarization in the political process.[69] Attempts to reduce an emphasis on party identification might serve to decrease not only perceived polarization but actual polarization as well.

A further way to try to reduce polarization between groups is to appeal to the moral foundations of the outgroup. If you want to convince people

67. Smith et al., "Moral Ties."
68. Roberson et al., "Development of Color."
69. Westfall et al., "Perceiving Political Polarization."

of the "opposing" group that your position on a particular issue should be adopted by them, try to present information in a way that does not threaten the other side's values.[70] The work of Haidt discussed above suggests that political liberals and political conservatives see and understand the world according to different moral foundations. Liberals tend to rely on the moral foundations of care and fairness in interpreting evidence while conservatives rely on a broader spectrum of moral foundations including loyalty, authority, and sanctity in addition to care and fairness. So, if a liberal wants to convince a conservative that same-sex marriage is not only constitutionally protected but also consistent with a pro-family agenda, then appeal to the conservative's sense of loyalty and sanctity by pointing out that many gay couples, like many straight couples, show great respect for the institution of marriage, have loyal and long-lasting relationships with their partners, and desire the same kind of responsibilities for another person that marriage (and family) can provide. If a conservative wants to convince a liberal that legislation designed to limit carbon emissions should not be adopted, then appeal to what moves the liberal: care and fairness. Talk about how these environmental laws might harm small businesses who are trying to provide much-needed employment for the poor. Talk about how it is unfair for smaller businesses to be subject to the same kind of regulations as big businesses because of the discrepancy in their ability to pay for them.

Making these kinds of petitions to the moral foundations of another person (or group) is essentially appealing to Type 1 thinking. It is not so much making a strong, reasoned argument that counts (Type 2 thinking), as working on the other person's intuitions that will win the day. What works seems to be getting the other person to come to the conclusion that this new way of thinking, believing, or seeing the world is more intuitively correct that the old way.

IS RESEARCH IN PSYCHOLOGY SCIENTIFIC?

In many ways, psychology is not like the natural sciences of physics, chemistry, or biology. Psychology often deals with constructs (like intelligence, personality, attitudes, and learning) that cannot be directly measured or observed. They are not "public" in the language of objective science. Psychologists have to find some way to indirectly measure learning or attitude, and this typically involves selecting a behavior (or behaviors) that are

70. Kahan, "Fixing."

thought to represent the concept in which we are interested. Behavior is public; it can be observed. So, psychologists define learning, for example, as a more or less permanent change in behavior due to experience. You observe and measure behavior at time one, provide the subject with some kind of experience, and then observe and measure the behavior again at time 2. If you detect a change in the behavior, then you can reasonably attribute the behavioral change to learning. The problem is trying to find a behavior (broadly defined) that is valid, that is actually measuring what you claim to be interested in.

There are other ways that psychology as a scientific discipline is different from other sciences; for example, the degree to which the findings of psychology are replicable. Replication is essential to science. Water freezes at 0 degrees Celsius. Given similar conditions (e.g., altitude), water will freeze at 0 degrees Celsius every time. In psychology, replication of results from one study to the next is not always found. An attempt to replicate the findings of one hundred psychological experiments and correlational studies found that the original robust findings were generally weaker in the follow-up study. While 97 percent of the original studies reported statistically significant findings, only 36 percent of the replications did. While 47 percent of the original studies reported effect sizes at the 95 percent confidence level, only 39 percent of the replications had effect sizes at this high confidence level.[71] One might look at the results of this study as evidence that psychology is not a "real" science. One might also, however, recognize that all scientific results need to be held provisionally. All scientific evidence is subject to change pending later research findings.

Psychology is a discipline that tries to use scientific methods (methods appropriately adjusted for psychology) to study human behavior and mental processes. One could argue that the subject matter of psychology (human behavior, brain/mind) is the most complex subject matter there is. That is to say, we use our brains/minds to investigate everything else in the universe. But psychology is interested in how that brain/mind works to produce behavior, beliefs, feelings, and thoughts. Therefore, many different approaches (psychology, neuroscience, cognitive science, anthropology, sociology, theology, biology) will be required to obtain a complete understanding of human behavior and brain/mind (as complete as we can make it). If replications in this subject matter are not as robust as they are in chemistry, that probably reflects the nature of the subject matter rather

71. Open Science Collaboration, "Estimating."

than the competence of the researchers or the inappropriateness of scientific methods being applied to the study of psychology.

Another study reports on the lack of political diversity in some areas of psychological research, including some of the areas discussed in this chapter. By and large, psychologists tend to lean to the left politically. While political orientation is unlikely to affect research in many if not most areas of psychology (e.g., physiological, sensation, cognitive), it could in other areas where value statements and ideological claims are being investigated. For example, research on prejudice shows that both left-leaning and right-leaning people show evidence of prejudice directed toward ideologically dissimilar others.[72] If, however, the majority of psychologists who study prejudice are political liberals, they will naturally be interested in studying prejudice of the right rather than prejudice coming from the left. As a result, the bulk of the studies, some of which are described in this chapter, report on right-wing ideology and how it is connected to prejudice. We do not get as many studies in the literature where the prejudicial behavior was coming from the left.

Another example of the potential problems associated with psychological research that is generally conducted by left-leaning experimenters is that negative attitudes about conservatives the researchers hold can result in mischaracterizations of conservative positions. People from the political left and political right are similar in the extent to which their ideology affects their views of the outgroup, yet if the bulk of the research is reported by liberal researchers, then the "other side of the story" might not get as much attention.[73] The well-known confirmation bias suggests that we all search for evidence to confirm what we already believe, including what we already believe about people in the outgroup. While science, with its peer review process, tries to control for this bias, it cannot eliminate it.

I do not mean to suggest that all psychological research is suspect because of the concerns raised above. Even if the concerns are legitimate, and I believe they are, they do not necessitate a dismissal of all research in psychology, even research in social psychology where much of the "problem" seems to reside. The research reported in this chapter suggests that how we relate to other people within our group and outside our group is controlled to some extent by psychological mechanisms involved in how we process and assess information, and these mechanisms often run below the level of

72. Duarte et al., "Political Diversity," 1–58.
73. Ibid.

our conscious awareness. All the studies described in this chapter do not have to be 100 percent correct to give us pause as we think about where our ideas, beliefs, and attitudes about other people come from, and why we act toward other people the way we do. Christ calls us to a new standard of thinking and behaving. In Matthew 5–6 we read Christ's words detailing what this new way looks like. The meek inheriting the earth. The poor in spirit gaining the kingdom of heaven. Turning the other cheek in the face of aggression. Giving to others, loving enemies, praying for persecutors. Christ's ingroup is everyone: Jew, Gentile, male, female, free, and slave. Empathy, cooperation, trust, compassion is extended to all. Not just those who think, feel, believe, and look like me, but even those who do not. The "other" is to be taken in as a member of our ingroup. "They" are to become "us." This is radical. It goes against our natural inclinations, preferences, and biases. It requires a change in our natural selves. Psychology by itself cannot produce that change. Is it possible, however, for what we learn from psychological science, as it studies the general revelation, to go alongside what we learn from our study of the special revelation? Might what psychological science reveals, when examined with the lens of good scientific practice, give us additional insight into who we are as human beings made in the image of God? Can it not help us to achieve, with God's help, the kind of radical change in our nature Jesus is talking about? We are complex beings. It will take a variety of perspectives—biological, psychological, sociological, anthropological, and theological (among others)—to get a complete picture (to the extent we humans can get a complete picture) of who we are and what we might become. Psychological science, as flawed as it might be at times, helps to fill in the picture.

Postscript

Like the meridians as they approach the poles, science, philosophy and religion are bound to converge as they draw nearer to the whole. I say 'converge' advisedly, but without merging, and without ceasing, to the very end, to assail the real from different angles and on different planes.[1]

Christians should have no need to be afraid or shocked by the results of scientific research, whether in physics, biology or history (or psychology) . . . Science should not disturb our faith by its analyses. Rather it should help us to know God better.[2]

Pierre Teilhard de Chardin (1881–1955) was, like John Hapgood, both a scientist and a theologian. A French Jesuit, de Chardin was also a highly regarded paleontologist and was involved in the discovery of Peking Man, an important evolutionary link between apes and humans. Despite being censored by his church and superiors for his views on the compatibility of evolutionary theory and Christianity (and acceptance of the implications of evolutionary theory on theological issues such as Original Sin), Teilhard remained committed to both his faith and his science. Only after his death on Easter Sunday, 1955, did his writings become widely distributed and published, and it is in these writings where we see de Chardin's efforts in linking what he knew as a scientist with what he knew as a Christian believer.

1. Teilhard de Chardin, *Phenomenon*, 30.
2. Teilhard de Chardin, *Science*, 35–36.

For de Chardin, everything is pointed to Christ, including the unfolding of creation. Science, like religion, is one of the ways we come to better understand God. There can be no contradiction or incompatibility between science and religion because they are both, in different ways, pointing the way to God. Teilhard was certainly not the first nor the last person to see religion and science in this way. There is a long history of looking to nature as a way to know about God. (This history includes philosophers, theologians, and scientists. Individuals such as Augustine, Aquinas, Isaac Newton, Robert Boyle, Galileo Galilei, William Paley, B. B. Warfield, Asa Gray, and, from more recent times, John Polkinghorne, Alister McGrath, Francis Collins, Kenneth Miller, and Simon Conway Morris to name just a few.) For de Chardin, as illustrated in the quotes above, science and religion converge on a single reality. A reality that is viewed from different perspectives, but a whole, nevertheless.

This understanding of reality sees reality as stratified, as being composed of different levels. Each level or stratum is studied using particular procedures and methods. Reality in this perspective is also seen as a hierarchy, with some levels more "fundamental" or basic than others. For example: (these are just a few of the disciplines used to study reality)

Theology

Anthropology

Sociology

Psychology

Biology

Chemistry

Physics

The lower and more fundamental levels must be investigated using more fundamental procedures. Physics might be thought of as the discipline (or set of procedures and methods) for studying reality at this most basic level. Chemistry also investigates reality at a more basic or lower level and uses methods suitable for that stratum. Above physics and chemistry we might find levels of reality that can be investigated using biology, psychology, sociology, anthropology, and theology. The methods of biology are different from the methods of sociology, but both are needed to give us a more complete picture and understanding of reality.

A particular phenomenon, morality for example, can be studied from a variety of different levels. We can understand morality from a theological perspective, from what is often called a top-down view. We can also study morality cross-culturally using the methods appropriate for anthropology. It is reasonable to study morality from the perspective of sociology and to investigate the psychology and the biology of morality, as was done in chapter 6. We could also go "deeper" and begin to think and learn about the chemistry and even the physics involved in moral behavior. The point is that each of these levels of analysis is important. Each has something useful to tell us about the phenomenon of morality. It is important, however, to avoid the mistake of believing that once we know the physics, chemistry, and biology of morality there is nothing else to know. We still have the other disciplines, including theology, to tell us additional information about our subject. While each level might be exhaustively known using the methods appropriate for that level, other levels need to be examined using different methodologies to have a fuller picture of what we are studying.[3] The knowledge we obtain from each of the different disciplines converge "without merging, and without ceasing, to the very end, to assail the real from different angles and on different planes."[4]

Science and religion are both important in our culture and society. Most Americans believe in God and, despite some declines, still worship on a fairly regular basis. Religion is strong in many other parts of the world as well, especially in countries in the southern hemisphere. Science is also an important part of life in the twenty-first century, and, for the most part, people take the findings of science seriously and utilize the developments in science and technology to their advantage. Psychology, too, is important in our twenty-first-century culture. Some have called ours a "psychological society" because of the role psychology plays in not only understanding but also shaping human behavior and mental processing.[5] For Christianity to continue to keep its relevance in this age of science and psychology, it must be seen as compatible with what we are learning about our world through the work of scientists, including psychological scientists. Christianity must continue, as it has throughout most of its history, to see both the Book of Nature and the Book of Scripture as true and complementary. If our knowledge of God (and ourselves) is not based on our understanding of nature, as

3. Seybold, *Explorations*, 56–58.
4. Teilhard de Chardin, *Phenomenon*, 30.
5. Leahey, *History*, 484–91.

well as scripture, more and more people in our society will reject God, and we will continue to see further declines in religious participation and belief. As Ilia Delio, a Teilhard scholar put it recently, "Without engaging the book of nature in the task of theology, theology can become a mere abstraction of a nonexisting God."[6] People are going to follow the findings of science and psychology. We as a society are going to continue to see ourselves from the perspective of psychology and the other sciences. It is important, therefore, for Christians to understand what psychological science is telling us about who we are, particularly as we consider the important issues of religious experience, the nature of the soul, morality, ingroup and outgroup dynamics, and many other questions at the interface of psychology and religion.

6. Delio, "Evolution," 40.

Bibliography

Aarts, Henk, and Kees van den Bos. "On the Foundations of Beliefs in Free Will: Intentional Binding and Unconscious Priming in Self-Agency." *Psychological Science* 22 (2011) 532–37.

Abramowitz, Alan, and Steven Webster. "All Politics Is National: The Rise of Negative Partisanship and the Nationalization of U.S. House and Senate Elections in the 21st Century." Presentation at the Midwest Political Science Association, Chicago, April 16–19, 2015.

Agrillo, Christian. "Near-Death Experience: Out-of-Body and Out-of-Brain." *Review of General Psychology* 15 (2011) 1–10.

Alcorta, Candace S., and Richard Sosis. "Ritual, Emotion, and Sacred Symbols: The Evolution of Religion as an Adaptive Complex." *Human Nature* 16 (2005) 323–59.

Allman, John M., et al. "The Von Economo Neurons in Frontoinsular and Anterior Cingulate Cortex in Great Apes and Humans." *Brain Structure and Function* 214 (2010) 495–517.

Almenberg, Johan, and Anna Dreber. "Economics and Evolution: Complementary Perspectives on Cooperation." In *Evolution, Games, and God: The Principle of Cooperation*, edited by Martin A. Nowak and Sarah Coakley, 132–49. Cambridge: Harvard University Press, 2013.

Apicella, Coren L., et al. "Social Networks and Cooperation in Hunter-Gatherers." *Nature* 481 (2012) 497–501.

Areni, Charles S., and David Kim. "The Influence of Background Music on Shopping Behavior: Classical versus Top-Forty Music in a Wine Store." *Advances in Consumer Research* 20 (1993) 336–40.

Atkinson, Quentin D., and Pierrick Bourrat. "Beliefs about God, the Afterlife and Morality Support the Role of Supernatural Policing in Human Cooperation." *Evolution and Human Behavior* 32 (2011) 41–49.

Atran, Scott. *In Gods We Trust: The Evolutionary Landscape of Religion*. Evolution and Cognition. New York: Oxford University Press, 2002.

Atran, Scott, and Joseph Henrich. "The Evolution of Religion. How Cognitive By-Products, Adaptive Learning Heuristics, Ritual Displays, and Group Competition Generate Deep Commitments to Prosocial Religions." *Biological Theory* 5 (2010) 18–30.

Axt, Jordan R., et al. "The Rules of Implicit Evaluation by Race, Religion, and Age." *Psychological Science* 25 (2014) 1804–15.

Azari, Nina P., et al. "Neural Correlates of Religious Experience." *European Journal of Neuroscience* 13 (2001) 1649–52.

Baker, Mark, and Stewart Goetz. "Afterword." In *The Soul Hypothesis: Investigations into the Existence of the Soul*, edited by Mark C. Baker and Steward Goetz, 247–53. New York: Continuum, 2011.

Balaguer, Mark. *Free Will as an Open Scientific Problem*. Cambridge: MIT Press, 2010.

Bargh, John A., and Tanya L. Chartrand. "The Unbearable Automaticity of Being." *American Psychologist* 54 (1999) 462–79.

Bargh, John A., et al. "Automaticity of Social Behavior: Direct Effect of Trait Construct and Stereotype Activation on Action." *Journal of Personality and Social Psychology* 71 (1996) 230–44.

Bargh, John A., and Ezequiel Morsella. "The Unconscious Mind." *Perspectives on Psychological Science* 3 (2008) 73–79.

Barrett, Justin L. *Born Believers: The Science of Children's Religious Belief*. New York: Free Press, 2012.

———. "Cognitive Science of Religion: What Is It and Why Is It?" *Religion Compass* 1 (2007) 1–19.

———. "Cognitive Science, Religion, and Theology." In *The Believing Primate: Scientific, Philosophical, and Theological Reflections on the Origin of Religion*, edited by Jeffrey Schloss and Michael Murray, 76–99. New York: Oxford University Press, 2009.

———. "Exploring the Natural Foundations of Religion." *Trends in Cognitive Sciences* 4 (2000) 29–34.

———. "Is the Spell Really Broken? Bio-psychological Explanations of Religion and Theistic Belief." *Theology and Science* 5 (2007) 57–72.

———. "Theological Correctness: Cognitive Constraint and the Study of Religion." *Method & Theory in the Study of Religion* 11 (1999) 325–39.

———. *Why Would Anyone Believe in God?* Cognitive Science of Religion Series. Lanham, MD: AltaMira, 2004.

Barrett, Justin L., and Frank C. Keil. "Conceptualizing a Nonnatural Entity: Anthropomorphism in God Concepts." *Cognitive Psychology* 31 (1996) 219–47.

Barrett, Justin L., and Melanie A. Nyhof. "Spreading Non-Natural Concepts: The Role of Intuitive Conceptual Structures in Memory and Transmission of Cultural Materials." *Journal of Cognition and Culture* 1 (2001) 69–100.

Barrett, Justin L., and Rebekah A. Richert. "Anthropomorphism or Preparedness? Exploring Children's God Concepts." *Review of Religious Research* 44 (2003) 300–312.

Barrett, Justin L., et al. "God's Beliefs versus Mother's: The Development of Nonhuman Agent Concepts." *Child Development* 72 (2001) 50–65.

Bartal, Inbal Ben-Ami, et al. "Empathy and Pro-Social Behavior in Rats." *Science* 334 (2011) 1427–30.

Bartz, Jennifer A., et al. "Oxytocin Selectively Improves Empathic Accuracy." *Psychological Science* 21 (2010) 1426–28.

Bass, Diana Butler. *Christianity after Religion: The End of Church and the Birth of a New Spiritual Awakening*. New York: HarperOne, 2012.

Baumeister, Roy F. "Free Will in Scientific Psychology." *Perspectives on Psychological Science* 3 (2008) 14–19.

Baumeister, Roy F., et al. "Choice, Free Will, and Religion." *Psychology of Religion and Spirituality* 2 (2010) 67–82.

―――. "Ego Depletion: Is the Active Self a Limited Resource?" *Journal of Personality and Social Psychology* 74 (1998) 1252–65.

―――. "Free Will: Belief and Reality." In *Surrounding Free Will: Philosophy, Psychology, Neuroscience*, edited by Alfred R. Mele, 49–71. New York: Oxford University Press, 2015.

―――. "Prosocial Benefits of Feeling Free: Disbelief in Free Will Increases Aggression and Reduces Helpfulness." *Personality and Social Psychology Bulletin* 35 (2009) 260–68.

Beauregard, Mario, and Vincent Paquette. "Neural Correlates of a Mystical Experience in Carmelite Nuns." *Neuroscience Letters* 405 (2006) 186–90.

Bernhardt, Boris C., and Tania Singer. "The Neural Basis of Empathy." *Annual Review of Neuroscience* 35 (2012) 1–23.

Bloom, Paul. *Descartes' Baby: How the Science of Child Development Explains What Makes Us Human.* New York: Basic, 2004.

―――. "Is God an Accident?" *Atlantic Monthly* December (2005) 105–12.

―――. "Religion Is Natural." *Developmental Science* 10 (2007) 147–51.

Boyer, Pascal. *Religion Explained: The Evolutionary Origins of Religious Thought.* New York: Basic, 2001.

Bradford, David T. "Emotion in Mystical Experience." *Religion, Brain & Behavior* 3 (2013) 103–18.

Braithwaite, Jason J., et al. "Cognitive Correlates of the Spontaneous Out-of-Body Experience (OBE) in the Psychologically Normal Population: Evidence for an Increased Role of Temporal-Lobe Instability, Body-Distortion Processing, and Impairments in Own-Body Transformations." *Cortex* 47 (2011) 839–53.

Brandt, Mark J. et al. "The Ideological-Conflict Hypothesis: Intolerance among Both Liberals and Conservatives." *Current Directions in Psychological Science* 23 (2014) 27–34.

Brass, Marcel, and Patrick Haggard. "To Do or Not to Do: The Neural Signature of Self-Control." *Journal of Neuroscience* 27 (2007) 9141–45.

Brown, Warren S. "Cognitive Contributions to Soul." In *Whatever Happened to the Soul? Scientific and Theological Portraits of Human Nature*, edited by Warren S. Brown et al., 99–125. Theology and the Sciences. Minneapolis: Fortress, 1998.

Brown, Warren S., and Brad D. Strawn. *The Physical Nature of Christian Life: Neuroscience, Psychology, and the Church.* New York: Cambridge University Press, 2012.

Bulbulia, Joseph, and Richard Sosis. "Signaling Theory and the Evolution of Religious Cooperation." *Religion* 31 (2011) 363–88.

Butti, Camilla et al. "Von Economo Neurons: Clinical and Evolutionary Perspectives." *Cortex* 49 (2013) 312–26.

Caldwell-Harris, Catherine, et al. "Religious Belief Systems of Persons with High Functioning Autism." Presented at the Annual Meeting of the Cognitive Science Society, Boston, 2011.

Carter, C. Sue. "Oxytocin Pathways and the Evolution of Human Behavior." *Annual Review of Psychology* 65 (2014) 17–39.

Casasanto, Daniel. "Different Bodies, Different Minds: The Body Specificity of Language and Thought." *Current Directions in Psychological Science* 20 (2011) 378–83.

―――. "Embodiment of Abstract Concepts: Good and Bad in Right- and Left-Handers." *Journal of Experimental Psychology: General* 138 (2009) 351–67.

Chalmers, David J. "Strong and Weak Emergence." In *The Re-Emergence of Emergence: The Emergentist Hypothesis from Science to Religion*, edited by Philip Clayton and Paul Davies, 244–54. Oxford: Oxford University Press, 2006.

Chartrand, Tanya L., and John A. Bargh. "The Chameleon Effect: The Perception-Behavior Link and Social Interaction." *Journal of Personality and Social Psychology* 76 (1999) 893–910.

Chasteen, Alison L., et al. "Thinking about God Moves Attention." *Neuropsychologia* 48 (2010) 627–30.

Churchland, Patricia Smith. *Neurophilosophy: Toward a Unified Science of the Mind/Brain.* Computational Models of Cognition and Perception. Cambridge: MIT Press, 1986.

Cikara, Mina, and Jay J. van Bavel. "The Neuroscience of Intergroup Relations: An Integrative Review." *Perspectives on Psychological Science* 9 (2014) 245–74.

Clayton, Philip. "Conceptual Foundations of Emergence Theory." In *The Re-Emergence of Emergence*, edited by Philip Clayton and Paul Davies, 1–31. New York: Oxford University Press, 2006.

Clinton, Bill. "It's Time to Overturn DOMA." *Washington Post*, March 7, 2012, https://www.washingtonpost.com/opinions/bill-clinton-its-time-to-overturn-doma/2013/03/07/fc184408-8747-11e2-98a3-b3db6b9ac586_story.html?utm_term=.2ac1091eec50/.

Coakley, Sarah, and Martin A. Nowak. "Introduction: Why Cooperation Makes a Difference." In *Evolution, Games, and God: The Principle of Cooperation*, edited by Martin A. Nowak and Sarah Coakley, 1–34. Cambridge: Harvard University Press, 2013.

Cobb, Mark et al., eds. *Oxford Textbook of Spirituality in Healthcare.* Oxford Textbooks in Public Health. Oxford: Oxford University Press, 2012.

Cohen, Adam B. "Religion's Profound Influences on Psychology: Morality, Intergroup Relations, Self-Construal, and Enculturation." *Current Directions in Psychological Science* 24 (2015) 77–82.

Cohen, Emma, and Justin Barrett. "When Minds Migrate: Conceptualizing Spirit Possession." *Journal of Cognition and Culture* 8 (2008) 23–48.

Cohen, Emma, et al. "Religion, Synchrony, and Cooperation." *Religion, Brain & Behavior* 4 (2014) 20–30.

Collins, Robin. "A Scientific Case for the Soul." In *The Soul Hypothesis: Investigations into the Existence of the Soul*, edited by Mark C. Baker and Steward Goetz, 222–46. New York: Continuum, 2011.

The Commission on Children at Risk. *Hardwired to Connect: The New Scientific Case for Authoritative Communities.* New York: Institute for American Values, 2003.

Coon, Deborah J. "Salvaging the Self in a World without Soul: William James's *The Principles of Psychology*." *History of Psychology* 3 (2000) 83–103.

Cooper, John. "Biblical Anthropology and the Body-Soul Problem." In *Soul, Body, and Survival: Essays on the Metaphysics of Human Persons*, edited by Kevin Corcoran, 218–28. Ithaca: Cornell University Press, 2001.

Corcoran, Kevin. "The Constitution View of Persons." In *In Search of the Soul: Four Views of the Mind-Body Problem*, edited by Joel B. Green and Stuart L. Palmer, 153–76. Downers Grove, IL: InterVarsity, 2005.

———. *Rethinking Human Nature: A Christian Materialist Alternative to the Soul.* Grand Rapids: Baker Academic, 2006.

Craig, Maureen A., and Jennifer A. Richeson. "More Diverse yet Less Tolerant? How the Increasingly Diverse Racial Landscape Affects White Americans' Racial Attitudes." *Personality and Social Psychology Bulletin* 40 (2014) 750–61.

Craig, Maureen A., and Jennifer A. Richeson. "On the Precipice of a 'Majority-Minority' America: Perceived Status Threat from the Racial Demographic Shift Affects White Americans' Political Ideology." *Psychological Science* 25 (2014) 1189–97.

Craver, Carl F. *Explaining the Brain: Mechanisms and the Mosaic Unity of Neuroscience.* Oxford: Clarendon, 2007.

Crick, Francis. *The Astonishing Hypothesis: The Scientific Search for the Soul.* New York: Simon & Schuster, 1994.

Cushman, Fiery, and Joshua D. Greene. "Finding Faults: How Moral Dilemmas Illuminate Cognitive Structure." *Social Neuroscience* 7 (2012) 269–79.

Damasio, Antonio R. *Descartes' Error: Emotion, Reason, and the Human Brain.* New York: Avon, 1994.

Danbold, Felix, and Yuen J. Huo. "No Longer 'All-American'? Whites' Defensive Reactions to Their Numerical Decline." *Social Psychological and Personality Science* 6 (2015) 210–18.

David, Nicole. "New Frontiers in the Neuroscience of the Sense of Agency." *Frontiers in Human Neuroscience* 6 (2012) 1–5.

Dawkins, Richard. *River Out of Eden: A Darwinian View of Life.* New York: Basic, 1995.

Decety, Jean. "The Neuroevolution of Empathy." *Annals of the New York Academy of Sciences* 1231 (2011) 35–45.

Delio, Ilia. "Evolution and the Rise of the Secular God." In *From Teilhard to Omega: Co-Creating an Unfinished Universe*, edited by Ilia Delio, 37–52. Maryknoll, NY: Orbis, 2014.

Delmore, Erin. "Whole Foods? Cracker Barrel? What You Eat Tells How You Vote." The Cycle. MSNBC. November 14, 2012. (retrieved January 3, 2017). http://www.msnbc.com/the-cycle/whole-foods-cracker-barrel/.

Devinsky, Orrin. "Religious Experiences and Epilepsy." *Epilepsy & Behavior* 4 (2003) 76–77.

Devinsky, Orrin, and George Lai. "Spirituality and Religion in Epilepsy." *Epilepsy & Behavior* 12 (2008) 636–43.

Dhont, Kristof, and Gordon Hodson. "Does Lower Cognitive Ability Predict Greater Prejudice?" *Current Directions in Psychological Science* 23 (2014) 454–59.

Dhont, Kristof et al. "Opening Closed Minds: The Combined Effects of Intergroup Contact and Need for Closure on Prejudice." *Personality and Social Psychology Bulletin* 37 (2011) 514–28.

Dijksterhuis, Ap, et al. "The Unconscious Consumer: Effects of Environment on Consumer Behavior." *Journal of Consumer Psychology* 15 (2005) 193–202.

Donald, Merlin. "Consciousness and the Freedom to Act." In *Free Will and Consciousness*, edited by Roy F. Baumeister et al., 8–23. New York: Oxford University Press, 2010.

Duarte, José L. et al. "Political Diversity Will Improve Social Psychological Science." *Behavioral and Brain Sciences* 38 (2015) 1–58.

Dunbar, R. I. M. "The Social Brain: Mind, Language, and Society in Evolutionary Perspective." *Annual Review of Anthropology* 32 (2003) 163–81.

Evans, Jonathan St. B. T., and Keith E. Stanovich. "Dual-Process Theories of Higher Cognition: Advancing the Debate." *Perspectives on Psychological Science* 8 (2013) 223–41.

Evrard, Henry C., et al. "Von Economo Neurons in the Anterior Insula of the Macaque Monkey." *Neuron* 74 (2012) 482–89.

Fan, Yang-Teng, et al. "Unbroken Mirror Neurons in Autism Spectrum Disorders." *Journal of Child Psychology and Psychiatry* 51 (2010) 981–88.

Feldman, Ruth. "Oxytocin and Social Affiliation in Humans." *Hormones and Behavior* 61 (2012) 380–91.

Fingelkurts, Alexander A., and Andrew A. Fingelkurts. "Is Our Brain Hardwired to Produce God, or is Our Brain Hardwired to Perceive God? A Systematic Review on the Role of the Brain in Mediating Religious Experience." *Cognitive Processing* 10 (2009) 293–326.

Forbes, Chad E., and Jordan Grafman. "The Role of the Human Prefrontal Cortex in Social Cognition and Moral Judgment." *Annual Review of Neuroscience* 33 (2010) 299–324.

Fraley, R. Chris, et al. "Developmental Antecedents of Political Ideology: A Longitudinal Investigation From Birth to Age 18 Years." *Psychological Science* 23 (2012) 1425–31.

Freud, Sigmund. *The Future of an Illusion*. Edited by James Strachey. New York:. Norton, 1928/1961.

Frimer, Jeremy A., et al. "Liberals and Conservatives Rely on Common Moral Foundations When Making Moral Judgments about Influential People." *Journal of Personality and Social Psychology* 104 (2013) 1040–59.

Gailliot, Matthew T., et al. "Self-Control Relies on Glucose as a Limited Energy Source: Willpower is More Than a Metaphor." *Journal of Personality and Social Psychology* 92 Sosis (2007) 325–36.

Gazzaniga, Michael S. *Who's in Charge? Free Will and the Science of the Brain*. New York: HarperCollins, 2011.

Galen, Luke W. "Does Religious Belief Promote Prosociality? A Critical Examination." *Psychological Bulletin* 138 (2012) 876–906.

Gervais, Will M. "Perceiving Minds and Gods: How Mind Perception Enables, Constrains, and is Triggered by Belief in Gods." *Perspectives on Psychological Science* 8 (2013) 380–94.

Gervais, Will M., and Ara Norenzayan. "Like a Camera in the Sky? Thinking about God Increases Public Self-Awareness and Socially Desirable Responding." *Journal of Experimental Social Psychology* 48 (2012) 298–302.

———. "Reminders of Secular Authority Reduce Believers' Distrust of Atheists." *Psychological Science* 23 (2012) 483–91.

Gervais, Will M., et al. "Do You Believe in Atheists? Distrust is Central to Anti-Atheist Prejudice." *Journal of Personality and Social Psychology* 101 (2011) 1189–1206.

Gilkey, Langdon. *Shantung Compound: The Story of Men and Women under Pressure*. New York: HarperOne, 1966.

Glenberg, Arthur M. "Positions in the Mirror Are Closer Than They Appear." *Perspectives on Psychological Science* 6 (2011) 408–10.

Glenberg, Arthur M., et al. "From the Revolution to Embodiment: 25 Years of Cognitive Psychology." *Perspectives on Psychological Science* 8 (2013) 573–85.

Goetz, Stewart. "Making Things Happen: Souls in Action." In *The Soul Hypothesis: Investigations into the Existence of the Soul*, edited by Mark C. Baker and Stewart Goetz, 99–122. New York: Continuum, 2011.

———. "Substance Dualism." In *In Search of the Soul: Four Views of the Mind-Body Problem*, edited by Joel B. Green and Stuart L. Palmer, 33–60. Downers Grove, IL: InterVarsity, 2005.

Gould, Stephen Jay. *The Structure of Evolutionary Theory*. Cambridge: Belknap, 2002.

Graham, Jesse, and Jonathan Haidt. "Beyond Beliefs: Religions Bind Individuals into Moral Communities." *Personality and Social Psychology Review* 14 (2010) 140–50.

Graham, Jesse, and Jonathan Haidt. "Sacred Values and Evil Adversaries: A Moral Foundations Approach." In *The Social Psychology of Morality: Exploring the Causes of Good and Evil*, edited by Mario Mikulincer and Phillip R. Shaver, 11–31. Herzliya Series on Personality and Social Psychology. Washington, DC: American Psychological Association, 2012.

Graham, Jesse, et al. "Liberals and Conservatives Rely on Different Sets of Moral Foundations." *Journal of Personality and Social Psychology* 96 (2009) 1029–46.

Graham, Jesse, et al. "Mapping the Moral Domain." *Journal of Personality and Social Psychology* 101 (2011) 366–85.

Granqvist, Pehr, et al. "Sensed Presence and Mystical Experiences Are Predicted by Suggestibility, Not by the Application of Transcranial Weak Complex Magnetic Fields." *Neuroscience Letters* 379 (2005) 1–6.

Green, Joel B. *Body, Soul, and Human Life: The Nature of Humanity in the Bible*. Studies in Theological Interpretation. Grand Rapids: Baker Academic, 2008.

———. "Humanity—Created, Restored, Transformed, Embodied." In *Rethinking Human Nature: A Multidisciplinary Approach*, edited by Malcolm Jeeves, 271–94. Grand Rapids: Eerdmans, 2011.

———. "Resurrection of the Body: New Testament Voices Concerning Personal Continuity and the Afterlife." In *What about the Soul? Neuroscience and Christian Anthropology*, edited by Joel B. Green, 85–100. Nashville: Abingdon, 2004.

Greene, Joshua. "From Neural 'Is' to Moral 'Ought': What Are the Moral Implications of Neuroscientific Moral Psychology?" *Nature Reviews Neuroscience* 4 (2003) 847–50.

———. *Moral Tribes: Emotion, Reason, and the Gap between Us and Them*. New York: Penguin, 2013.

Greene, Joshua, and Jonathan Haidt. "How (and Where) Does Moral Judgment Work?" *Trends in Cognitive Sciences* 6 (2002) 517–23.

Greene, Joshua D., et al. "An fMRI Investigation of Emotional Engagement in Moral Judgment." *Science* 293 (2001) 2105–8.

Greenwald, Anthony G., and Mahzarin R. Banaji. "Implicit Social Cognition: Attitudes, Self-Esteem, and Stereotypes." *Psychological Review* 102 (1995) 4–27.

Greyson, Bruce. "Implications of Near-Death Experiences for a Postmaterialist Psychology." *Psychology of Religion and Spirituality* 2 (2010) 37–45.

Greyson, Bruce, et al. "Mystical Experiences Associated with Seizures." *Religion, Brain & Behavior* 5 (2015) 182–96.

Gutenson, Charles E. "Time, Eternity, and Personal Identity: The Implications of Trinitarian Theology." In *What about the Soul? Neuroscience and Christian Anthropology*, edited by Joel B. Green, 117–32. Nashville: Abingdon, 2004.

Gushee, David. "Donald Trump and the Travesty of Christian Tribalism." Religion News Service (blog), January 20, 2016. http://religionnews.com/2016/01/20/donald-trump-travesty-christian-tribalism/.

Habgood, John. *Confessions of a Conservative Liberal*. London: SPCK, 1988.

Haidt, Jonathan. "The Emotional Dog and its Rational Tail: A Social Intuitionist Approach to Moral Judgment." *Psychological Review* 108 (2001) 814–34.

———. "The New Synthesis in Moral Psychology." *Science* 316 (2008) 998–1002.

————. *The Righteous Mind: Why Good People Are Divided by Politics and Religion*. New York: Pantheon, 2012.

Haidt, Jonathan, and Jesse Graham. "When Morality Opposes Justice: Conservatives Have Moral Intuitions That Liberals May Not Recognize." *Social Justice Research* 20 (2007) 98–116.

Haidt, Jonathan, et al. "Above and Below Left-Right: Ideological Narratives and Moral Foundations." *Psychological Inquiry* 20 (2009) 110–19.

Hall, Deborah. L., et al. "Why Don't We Practice What We Preach? A Meta-Analytic Review of Religious Racism." *Personality and Social Psychology Review* 14 (2010) 126–39.

Hall, Erika V., et al. "A Rose by any Other Name? The Consequences of Subtyping 'African-Americans' from 'Blacks.'" *Journal of Experimental Social Psychology* 56 (2015) 183–90.

Hamlin, J. Kiley, et al. "Not Like Me = Bad: Infants Prefer Those Who Harm Dissimilar Others." *Psychological Science* 24 (2013) 589–94.

Han, Shihui, et al. "Neural Consequences of Religious Belief on Self-Referential Processing." *Social Neuroscience* 3 (2008) 1–15.

Harris, Sam. *Waking Up: A Guide to Spirituality Without Religion*. New York: Simon & Schuster, 2014.

Harris, Sam, et al. "Functional Neuroimaging of Belief, Disbelief, and Uncertainty." *Annals of Neurology* 63 (2007) 141–47.

————. "The Neural Correlates of Religious and Nonreligious Belief." *PLOS ONE* 4 (2009) e0007272. doi: 10.1371/journal.pone.0007272/.

Harris, Erica, and Patrick McNamara. "Is Religiousness a Biocultural Adaptation?" In *The Evolution of Religion: Studies, Theories & Critiques*, edited by Joseph Bulbulia et al., 79–85. Santa Margarita, CA: Collins Foundation, 2008.

Harrison, Peter. *The Territories of Science and Religion*. Chicago: University of Chicago Press, 2015.

Hasker, William. *The Emergent Self*. New York: Cornell University Press, 1999.

————. "Souls Beastly and Human." In *The Soul Hypothesis: Investigations into the Existence of the Soul*, edited by Mark C. Baker and Stewart Goetz, 202–21. New York: Continuum, 2011.

Hayward, R. David, et al. "Associations of Religious Behavior and Experiences with Extent of Regional Atrophy in the Orbitofrontal Cortex During Older Adulthood." *Religion, Brain & Behavior* 1 (2011) 103–18.

Helzer, Erik G., and David A. Pizarro. "Dirty Liberals! Reminders of Physical Cleanliness Influence Moral and Political Attitudes." *Psychological Science* 22 (2011) 517–22.

Hibbing, John R., et al. "Differences in Negativity Bias Underlie Variations in Political Ideology." *Behavioral and Brain Sciences* 37 (2014) 297–350.

Hibbing, John R., et al. *Predisposed: Liberals, Conservatives, and the Biology of Political Differences*. New York: Routledge, 2014.

Hill, Peter C., and Ralph W. Hood. *Measures of Religiosity*. Birmingham, AL: Religious Education, 1999.

Hill, Peter C., and Kenneth I. Pargament. "Advances in the Conceptualization and Measurement of Religion and Spirituality: Implications for Physical and Mental Health Research." *Psychology of Religion and Spirituality* S1 (2008) 3–17.

Hill, Peter, C., et al. "Conceptualizing Religion and Spirituality: Points of Commonality, Points of Departure." *Journal for the Theory of Social Behaviour* 30 (2000) 51–77.

Hirsch, Alan R. "Effects of Ambient Odors on Slot-Machine Usage in a Las Vegas Casino." *Psychology and Marketing* 12 (1995) 585–94.

Hirst, William, and Elizabeth A. Phelps. "Flashbulb Memories." *Current Directions in Psychological Science* 25 (2016) 36–41.

Hodson, Gordon. "Do Ideologically Intolerant People Benefit from Intergroup Contact?" *Current Directions in Psychological Science* 20 (2011) 154–59.

Hodson, Gordon, and Michael A. Busseri. "Bright Minds and Dark Attitudes: Lower Cognitive Ability Predicts Greater Prejudice through Right-Wing Ideology and Low Intergroup Contact." *Psychological Science* 23 (2012) 187–95.

Hofmann, Wilhelm, and Lotte van Dillen. "Desire: The New Hot Spot in Self-Control Research." *Current Directions in Psychological Science* 21 (2012) 317–22.

Hogg, Michael A. "From Uncertainty to Extremism: Social Categorization and Identity Processes." *Current Directions in Psychological Science* 23 (2014) 338–42.

Hogg, Michael A., and Janice Adelman. "Uncertainty-Identity Theory: Extreme Groups, Radical Behavior, and Authoritarian Leadership." *Journal of Social Issues* 69 (2013) 436–54.

Hogg, Michael A., et al. "Religion in the Face of Uncertainty: An Uncertainty-Identity Theory Account of Religiousness." *Personality and Social Psychology Review* 14 (2010) 72–83.

———. "The Solace of Radicalism: Self-Uncertainty and Group Identification in the Face of Threat." *Journal of Experimental Social Psychology* 46 (2010) 1061–66.

———. "Uncertainty and the Roots of Extremism." *Journal of Social Issues* 69 (2013) 407–18.

Holbrook, Colin, et al. "Self-Reported Spirituality Correlates with Endogenous Oxytocin." *Psychology of Religion and Spirituality* 7 (2015) 46–50.

Holland, Rob W., et al. "Smells Like Clean Spirit: Nonconscious Effects of Scent on Cognition and Behavior." *Psychological Science* 16 (2005) 689–93.

Hood, Ralph W., et al. *The Psychology of Religion: An Empirical Approach.* 4th ed. New York: Guilford, 2009.

Hunter, James Davison. *To Change the World: The Irony, Tragedy, and Possibility of Christianity in the Late Modern World.* New York: Oxford University Press, 2010.

Inbar, Yoel, et al. "Conservatives Are More Easily Disgusted Than Liberals." *Cognition and Emotion* 23 (2009) 714–25.

———. "Disgust Sensitivity Predicts Intuitive Disapproval of Gays." *Emotion* 9 (2009) 435–39.

Iyengar, Shanto, and Sean J. Westwood. "Fear and Loathing across Party Lines: New Evidence on Group Polarization." *American Journal of Political Science* 59 (2015) 690–707.

Inzlicht, Michael, and Brandon J. Schmeichel. "What Is Ego Depletion? Toward a Mechanistic Revision of the Resource Model of Self-Control." *Perspectives on Psychological Science* 7 (2012) 450–63.

Inzlicht, Michael, et al. "The Need to Believe: A Neuroscience Account of Religion as a Motivated Process." *Religion, Brain & Behavior* 1 (2011) 192–212.

———. "Neural Markers of Religious Conviction." *Psychological Science* 20 (2009) 385–92.

James, William. *The Varieties of Religious Experience.* New York: Modern Library, 1902/1999.

Jeeves, Malcolm. "Introduction: The Agenda." In *The Emergence of Personhood: A Quantum Leap?*, edited by Malcolm Jeeves, 1–9. Grand Rapids: Eerdmans, 2015.

———. "Neuroscience, Evolutionary Psychology, and the Image of God." *Perspectives on Science and Christian Faith* 57 (2005) 170–86.

Johnson, Dominic D. P. "The Uniqueness of Human Cooperation: Cognition, Cooperation, and Religion." In *Evolution, Games, and God: The Principle of Cooperation*, edited by Martin A. Nowak and Sarah Coakley, 168–85. Cambridge: Harvard University Press, 2013.

Johnson, Kathryn A., et al. "Fundamental Social Motives and the Varieties of Religious Experience." *Religion, Brain & Behavior* 5 (2015) 197–231.

Johnson, Kyle D., et al. "Pilot Study of the Effect of Religious Symbols on Brain Function: Association with Measures of Religiosity." *Spirituality in Clinical Practice* 1 (2014) 82–98.

Johnson, Megan K., et al. "Priming Christian Religious Concepts Increases Racial Prejudice." *Social Psychological and Personality Science* 1 (2010) 119–26.

———. "Religiosity and Prejudice Revisited: In-Group Favoritism, Out-Group Derogation, or Both?" *Psychology of Religion and Spirituality* 4 (2012) 154–68.

Johnstone, Brick, et al. "Right Parietal Lobe-Related 'Selflessness' as the Neuropsychological Basis of Spiritual Transcendence." *International Journal for the Psychology of Religion* 22 (2012) 267–84.

Jost, John T. "Elective Affinities: On the Psychological Bases of Left-Right Differences." *Psychological Inquiry* 20 (2009) 129–41.

Jost, John T., et al. "Political Conservatism as Motivated Social Cognition." *Psychological Bulletin* 129 (2003) 339–75.

Kahan, Dan. "Fixing the Communications Failure." *Nature* 463 (2010) 296–97.

———. "Ideology, Motivated Reasoning, and Cognitive Reflection." *Judgment and Decision Making* 8 (2013) 407–24.

Kahan, Dan M., and Donald Braman. "Cultural Cognition and Public Policy." *Yale Law & Policy Review* 24 (2006) 147–70.

Kahan, Dan M., et al. "Cultural Cognition of Scientific Consensus." *Journal of Risk Research* 14 (2011) 147–74.

Kahneman, Daniel. *Thinking, Fast and Slow*. New York: Farrar, Straus and Giroux, 2011.

Kapogiannis, Dimitrios, et al. "Cognitive and Neural Foundations of Religious Belief." *Proceedings of the National Academy of Science* 106 (2009) 4876–81.

Kapogiannis, Dimitrios, et al. "Neuroanatomical Variability of Religiosity." *PLOS ONE* 4 (2009) e7180. doi: 10.1371/journal.pone.0007180

Kelemen, Deborah. "Why Are Rocks Pointy? Children's Preference for Teleological Explanations of the Natural World." *Developmental Psychology* 35 (1999) 1440–52.

———. "Are Children 'Intuitive Theists'?" *Psychological Science* 15 (2004) 295–301.

Klein, Stanley B. "The Self and Science: Is it Time for a New Approach to the Study of Human Experience?" *Current Directions in Psychological Science* 21 (2012) 253–57.

Koch, Christof. *Consciousness: Confessions of a Romantic Reductionist*. Cambridge: MIT Press, 2012.

Koenig, Harold G., et al. *Handbook of Religion and Health*. Oxford: Oxford University Press, 2001.

Kosfeld, Michael, et al. "Oxytocin Increases Trust in Humans." *Nature* 435 (2005) 673–76.

Krebs, Dennis L. "Morality: An Evolutionary Account." *Perspectives on Psychological Science* 3 (2008) 149–68.

Kuhlmeier, Valerie, et al. "Attribution of Dispositional States by 12–month–olds." *Psychological Science* 14 (2003) 402–8.

LaRock, Eric. "Disambiguation, Binding, and the Unity of Visual Consciousness." *Theory & Psychology* 17 (2007) 747–77.

———. "From Biological Naturalism to Emergent Subject Dualism." *Philosophia Christi* 15 (2013) 97–118.

Laurin, Kristin, et al. "Outsourcing Punishment to God: Beliefs in Divine Control Reduce Earthly Punishment." *Proceedings of the Royal Society B* 279 (2012) 3272–81.

Leahey, Thomas Hardy. *A History of Psychology: From Antiquity to Modernity* (seventh edition). Boston: Pearson, 2013.

Leech, David, and Aku Visala. "The Cognitive Science of Religion: Implications for Theism." *Zygon* 46 (2011) 47–64.

Leotti, Lauren A., et al. "Born to Choose: The Origins and Value of the Need for Control." *Trends in Cognitive Sciences* 14 (2010) 457–63.

Lewandowsky, Stephan, et al. "Misinformation and Its Correction: Continued Influence and Successful Debiasing." *Psychological Science in the Public Interest* 13 (2012) 106–31.

Libet, Benjamin. "Do We Have Free Will?" *Journal of Consciousness Studies* 6 (1999) 47–57.

———. "Unconscious Cerebral Initiative and the Role of Conscious Will in Voluntary Action." *The Behavioral and Brain Sciences* 8 (1985) 529–66.

Lynn, Steven Jay, et al. "Near-Death Experiences: Out of Body and Out of Mind?" *Psychology of Religion and Spirituality* 2 (2010) 117–18.

MacIntyre, Alasdair. *Dependent Rational Animals: Why Human Beings Need the Virtues.* Chicago: Open Court, 1999.

Malhotra, Deepak. "(When) Are Religious People Nicer? Religious Salience and the 'Sunday Effect' on Pro-Social Behavior." *Judgment and Decision Making* 5 (2010) 138–43.

Malka, Ariel, and Christopher J. Soto. "Rigidity of the Economic Right? Menu-Independent and Menu-Dependent Influences of Psychological Dispositions on Political Attitudes." *Current Directions in Psychological Science* 24 (2015) 137–42.

Maoz, Uri, et al. "On Reporting the Onset of the Intention to Move." In *Surrounding Free Will: Philosophy, Psychology, Neuroscience*, edited by Alfred R. Mele, 184–202. New York: Oxford University Press, 2015.

Markham, Paul N. *Rewired: Exploring Religious Conversion.* Distinguished Dissertation Series in Theology 2. Eugene, OR: Pickwick Publications, 2007.

McCauley, Robert N. *Why Religion Is Natural and Science Is Not.* New York: Oxford University Press, 2011.

McCauley, Robert N., and E. Thomas Lawson. *Bringing Ritual to Mind: Psychological Foundations of Cultural Forms.* New York: Cambridge University Press, 2002.

McNamara, Patrick, and P. Monroe Butler. "The Neuropsychology of Religious Experience." In *Handbook of the Psychology of Religion and Spirituality*, edited by Raymond F. Paloutzian and Crystal L. Park, 215–33. 2nd ed. New York: Guilford, 2013.

McNamara, Patrick, et al., "The Chemistry of Religiosity: Evidence from Patients with Parkinson's Disease." In *Where God and Science Meet: How Brain and Evolutionary Studies Alter Our Understanding of Religion.* Vol. 2, *The Neurology of Religious Experience*, edited by Patrick McNamara, 1–14. Westport, CT: Praeger, 2006.

Merricks, Trenton. "How to Live Forever without Saving Your Soul: Physicalism and Immortality." In *Soul, Body, and Survival: Essays on the Metaphysics of Human Persons*, edited by Kevin Corcoran, 183–200. Ithaca: Cornell University Press, 2001.

Metzinger, Thomas. "Introduction: Consciousness Research at the End of the Twentieth Century." In *Neural Correlates of Consciousness: Empirical and Conceptual Questions*, edited by Thomas Metzinger, 1–12. Cambridge: MIT Press, 2000.

Molenberghs, Pascal. "The Neuroscience of In-Group Bias." *Neuroscience and Biobehavioral Reviews* 37 (2013) 1530–36.

Molenberghs, Pascal, and Samantha Morrison. "The Role of the Prefrontal Cortex in Social Categorization." *Social Cognitive and Affective Neuroscience* 9 (2014) 292–96.

Molenberghs, Pascal, et al. "Brain Regions with Mirror Properties: A Meta-Analysis of 125 Human fMRI Studies." *Neuroscience and Biobehavioral Reviews* 36 (2012) 341–49.

Muir, Edwin. "The Incarnate One." In *The Penguin Book of Religious Verse*, edited by R. S. Thomas, 55. Harmondsworth, UK: Penguin, 1963.

Mukamel, Roy, et al. "Single-Neuron Responses in Humans During Execution and Observation of Actions." *Current Biology* 20 (2010) 750–56.

Muraven, Mark, and Roy F. Baumeister. "Self-Regulation and Depletion of Limited Resources: Does Self-Control Resemble a Muscle?" *Psychological Bulletin* 126 (2000) 247–59.

Muraven, Mark, et al. "Longitudinal Improvement of Self-Regulation through Practice: Building Self-Control through Repeated Exercise." *Journal of Social Psychology* 139 (1999) 446–57.

Muraven Mark, et al. "Self-Control as a Limited Resource: Regulatory Depletion Patterns." *Journal of Personality and Social Psychology* 74 (1998) 774–89.

Murphy, Nancey. "Nonreductive Physicalism." In *In Search of the Soul: Four Views of the Mind-Body Problem*, edited by Joel B. Green and Stuart L. Palmer, 115–37. Downers Grove, IL: InterVarsity, 2005.

Murray, Michael J. "Scientific Explanations of Religion and the Justification of Religious Belief." In *The Believing Primate: Scientific, Philosophical, and Theological Reflections on the Origin of Religion*, edited by Jeffrey Schloss and Michael Murray, 168–78. New York: Oxford University Press, 2009.

Murray, Michael J., and Andrew Goldberg. "Evolutionary Accounts of Religion: Explaining and Explaining Away. In *The Believing Primate: Scientific, Philosophical, and Theological Reflections on the Origin of Religion*, edited by Jeffrey Schloss and Michael Murray, 179–99. New York: Oxford University Press, 2009.

Myers, David G. "Reflections on Religious Belief and Prosociality: Comment on Galen (2012)." *Psychological Bulletin* 138 (2012) 913–17.

Nave, Gideon, et al. "Does Oxytocin Increase Trust in Humans? A Critical Review of Research." *Perspectives on Psychological Science* 10 (2015) 772–89.

Neubauer, Raymond L. "Prayer as an Interpersonal Relationship: A Neuroimaging Study." *Religion, Brain & Behavior* 4 (2014) 92–103.

Newberg, Andrew, and Eugene D'Aquili. *Why God Won't Go Away: Brain Science and the Biology of Belief*. New York: Ballantine, 2001.

Newberg, Andrew, et al. "The Measurement of Regional Cerebral Blood Flow During the Complex Cognitive Task of Meditation: A Preliminary SPECT Study." *Psychiatry Research: Neuroimaging Section* 106 (2001) 113–22.

Nietzche, Friedrich. *The Gay Science*. Cambridge Texts in the History of Philosophy. New York: Cambridge University Press, 2001.

Norenzayan, Ara. *Big Gods: How Religion Transformed Cooperation and Conflict.* Princeton: Princeton University Press, 2013.

————. "Theodiversity." *Annual Review of Psychology* 67 (2016) 465–88.

Norenzayan, Ara, and Azim F. Shariff. "The Origin and Evolution of Religious Prosociality." *Science* 322 (2008) 58–62.

Nowak, Martin A. "Five Rules for the Evolution of Cooperation." In *Evolution, Games, and God: The Principle of Cooperation,* edited by Martin A. Nowak and Sarah Coakley, 99–114. Cambridge: Harvard University Press, 2013.

Obama, Barack. "The State of the Union." Speech, January 12, 2016. https://medium.com/@WhiteHouse/president-obama-s-2016-state-of-the-union-address-7c06300f9726#.rdw271lmm/.

O'Craven, Kathleen M., and Nancy Kanwisher. "Mental Imagery of Faces and Places Activates Corresponding Stimulus-Specific Brain Regions." *Journal of Cognitive Neuroscience* 12 (2000) 1013–23.

Onraet, Emma, and Alain Van Hiel. "Are Right-Wing Adherents Mentally Troubled? Recent Insights on the Relationship of Right-Wing Attitudes with Threat and Psychological Ill-Being." *Current Directions in Psychological Science* 23 (2014) 35–40.

Onraet, Emma, et al. "The Relationships between Internal and External Threats and Right-Wing Attitudes: A Three-Wave Longitudinal Study." *Personality and Social Psychology Bulletin* 40 (2014) 712–25.

Open Science Collaboration. "Estimating the Reproducibility of Psychological Science." *Science* 349 (2015) 943.

Owen, Amy D., et al. "Religious Factors and Hippocampal Atrophy in Late Life. *PLOS ONE* 6 (2011) e17006. doi: 10.1371/journal.pone.0017006/.

Paloutzian, Raymond F., and Crystal L. Park. "Recent Progress and Core Issues in the Science of the Psychology of Religion and Spirituality." In *Handbook of the Psychology of Religion and Spirituality,* edited by Raymond F. Paloutzian and Crystal L. Park, 3–22. 2nd ed. New York: Guilford, 2013.

Park, Crystal L. "Religion and Meaning." In *Handbook of the Psychology of Religion and Spirituality,* edited by Raymond F. Paloutzian and Crystal L. Park, 357–79. 2nd ed. New York: Guilford, 2013.

Pellegrino, Giuseppe di, et al. "Understanding Motor Events: A Neurophysiological Study." *Experimental Brain Research* 91 (1992) 176–80.

Persinger, Michael. "Religious and Mystical Experiences as Artifacts of Temporal Lobe Function: A General Hypothesis." *Perceptual and Motor Skills* 57 (1983) 1255–62.

Persinger, Michael A., and Faye Healey. "Experimental Facilitation of the Sensed Presence: Possible Intercalation between the Hemispheres Induced by Complex Magnetic Fields." *Journal of Nervous and Mental Disease* 190 (2002) 533–41.

Peterson, Gregory R. "Are Evolutionary/Cognitive Theories of Religion Relevant for Philosophy of Religion?" *Zygon* 45 (2010) 545–57.

Pew Research Center. "America's Changing Religious Landscape." May 12, 2015. http://www.pewforum.org/2015/05/12/americas-changing-religious-landscape/.

————. "Nones on the Rise." October 9, 2012. http://www.pewforum.org/2012/10/09/nones-on-the-rise/.

————. "Political Polarization in the American Public." June 12, 2014. http://www.people-press.org/2014/06/12/political-polarization-in-the-american-public/.

Pew Research Center. "U.S. Public Becoming Less Religious." November 3, 2015. http://www.pewforum.org/2015/11/03/u-s-public-becoming-less-religious/.

Pickren, Wade E. "A Whisper of Salvation: American Psychologists and Religion in the Popular Press." *American Psychologist* 55 (2000) 1022–24.

Press, Clare, et al. "Intact Imitation of Emotional Facial Actions in Autism Spectrum Conditions." *Neuropsychologia* 48 (2010) 3291–97.

Public Religion Research Institute. "Anxiety, Nostalgia, and Mistrust." November, 2015. http://publicreligion.org/site/wp-content/uploads/2015/11/PRRI-AVS-2015.pdf/.

———. "How Immigration and Concerns About Cultural Changes are Shaping the 2016 Election." June 23, 2016. http://www.prri.org/wp-content/uploads/2016/06/PRRI-Brookings-2016-Immigration-survey-report.pdf/.

Purzycki, Benjamin Grant, et al. "Moralistic Gods, Supernatural Punishment and the Expansion of Human Sociality." *Nature* 530 (2016) 327–30.

Putnam, Robert D. *Bowling Alone: The Collapse and Revival of American Community.* New York: Simon & Schuster, 2000.

Putnam, Robert D., and Lewis M. Feldstein. *Better Together: Restoring the American Community.* New York: Simon & Schuster, 2003.

Rand, David G., et al. "Religious Motivations for Cooperation: An Experimental Investigation Using Explicit Primes." *Religion, Brain & Behavior* 4 (2014) 31–48.

Reddish, Paul, et al. "Does Synchrony Promote Generalized Prosociality?" *Religion, Brain & Behavior* 4 (2014) 3–19.

Richert, Rebekah A., and Paul Harris. "Dualism Revisited: Body vs. Mind vs. Soul." *Journal of Cognition and Culture* 8 (2008) 99–115.

Rigoni, Davide, et al. "Inducing Disbelief in Free Will Alters Brain Correlates of Pre-conscious Motor Preparation: The Brain Minds Whether We Believe in Free Will or Not." *Psychological Science* 22 (2011) 613–18.

Robles, Theodore F., et al. "Marital Quality and Health: A Meta-Analytic Review." *Psychological Bulletin* 140 (2014) 140–87.

Roberson, Debi, et al. "The Development of Color Categories in Two Languages: A Longitudinal Study." *Journal of Experimental Psychology: General* 133 (2004) 554–71.

Robinson, Daniel N. "Minds, Brains, and Brains in Vats." In *The Soul Hypothesis: Investigations into the Existence of the Soul,* edited by Mark C. Baker and Stewart Goetz, 46–72. New York: Continuum, 2011.

Robinson, Marilynne. *Absence of Mind: The Dispelling of Inwardness from the Modern Myth of the Self.* The Terry Lectures. New Haven: Yale University Press, 2010.

———. *The Givenness of Things.* New York: Farrar, Straus and Giroux, 2015.

———. *Home.* New York: Farrar, Straus & Giroux, 2008.

Roets, Arne, and Alain van Hiel. "Allport's Prejudiced Personality Today: Need for Closure as the Motivated Cognitive Basis of Prejudice." *Current Directions in Psychological Science* 20 (2011) 349–54.

Roskies, Adina L. "Freedom, Neural Mechanism, and Consciousness." In *Free Will and Consciousness: How Might They Work?*, edited by Roy F. Baumeister et al., 153–71. New York: Oxford University Press, 2010.

Rothschild, Lynn J. "The Role of Emergence in Biology." In *The Re-Emergence of Emergence,* edited by Philip Clayton and Paul Davies, 151–65. New York: Oxford University Press, 2006.

Rowatt, Wade C., et al. "Associations among Religiousness, Social Attitudes, and Prejudice in a National Random Sample of American Adults." *Psychology of Religion and Spirituality* 1 (2009) 14–24.

Ruse, Michael. "Biologically Evolutionary Explanations of Religious Belief." In *Evolution, Religion and Cognitive Science*, edited by Fraser Watts and Léon Turner, 38–55. Oxford: Oxford University Press, 2014.

Sanders, Matthew A. et al. "The Gargle Effect: Rinsing the Mouth with Glucose Enhances Self-Control." *Psychological Science* 23 (2012) 1470–72.

Saramago, José. *Cain*. Boston: Houghton Mifflin Harcourt, 2011.

Saroglou, Vassilis. "Is Religion not Prosocial at All? Comment on Galen (2012)." *Psychological Bulletin* 138 (2012) 907–12.

Schjoedt, Uffe. "The Religious Brain: A General Introduction to the Experimental Neuroscience of Religion." *Method and Theory in the Study of Religion* 21 (2009) 310–39.

Schjoedt, Uffe, et al. "Highly Religious Participants Recruit Areas of Social Cognition in Personal Prayer." *Social Cognitive and Affective Neuroscience* 4 (2009) 199–207.

Schloss, Jeffrey P. and Michael J. Murray. "Evolutionary Accounts of Belief in Supernatural Punishment: A Critical Review." *Religion, Brain & Behavior* 1 (2011) 46–66.

Schmeichel, Brandon J., et al. "Intellectual Performance and Ego Depletion: The Role of the Self in Logical Reasoning and Other Information Processing." *Journal of Personality and Social Psychology* 85 (2003) 33–46.

Schooler, Jonathan W. "What Science Tells Us about Free Will." In *Free Will and Consciousness*, edited by Roy F. Baumeister et al., 191–218. New York: Oxford University Press, 2010.

Schooler, Jonathan, et al. "Measuring and Manipulating Beliefs and Behaviors Associated with Free Will." In *Surrounding Free Will: Philosophy, Psychology, Neuroscience*, edited by Alfred R. Mele, 72–94. New York: Oxford University Press, 2015.

Schulte-Rüther, Martin, et al. "Dysfunctions in Brain Networks Supporting Empathy: An fMRI Study in Adults with Autism Spectrum Disorders." *Social Neuroscience* 6 (2011) 1–21.

Scruton, Roger. *The Soul of the World*. Princeton: Princeton University Press, 2014.

Seligman, Martin E. P., and Mihaly Csikszentmihalyi. "Positive Psychology: An Introduction." *American Psychologist* 55 (2000) 5–14.

Seybold, Kevin S. "Biology of Spirituality." *Perspectives on Science and Christian Faith* 62 (2010) 89–98.

———. *Explorations in Neuroscience, Psychology and Religion*. Ashgate Science and Religion Series. Burlington, VT: Ashgate, 2007.

———. "God and the Brain: Neuroscience Looks at Religion." *Journal of Psychology and Christianity* 24 (2005) 122–29.

———. "Physiological Mechanisms Involved in Religiosity/Spirituality and Health." *Journal of Behavioral Medicine* 30 (2007) 303–9.

———. "Social Ties and Health: Mechanisms and Implications." Presentation at the Center for Vision and Values, Grove City, Pennsylvania, April 16, 2015.

———. "The Untidiness of Integration: John Stapylton Habgood." *Perspectives on Science and Christian Faith* 57 (2005) 114–19.

Shariff, Azim F., and Ara Norenzayan. "God Is Watching You: Priming God Concepts Increases Prosocial Behavior in an Anonymous Economic Game." *Psychological Science* 18 (2007) 803–9.

———. "Mean Gods Make Good People: Different Views of God Predict Cheating Behavior." *International Journal for the Psychology of Religion* 21 (2011) 85–96.

Shariff, Azim F., et al. "Religious Priming: A Meta-Analysis with a Focus on Prosociality." *Personality and Social Psychology Review* 20 (2016) 27–48.

Sharp, Patricia E. "Meditation-Induced Bliss Viewed as Release from Conditioned Neural (Thought) Patterns That Block Reward Signals in the Brain Pleasure Center." *Religion, Brain & Behavior* 4 (2014) 202–29.

Sheikh, Hammad, et al. "Religion, Group Threat and Sacred Values." *Judgment and Decision Making* 7 (2012) 110–18.

Sherif, Muzafer, et al. *Intergroup Conflict and Cooperation: The Robbers Cave Experiment.* Norman: University of Oklahoma Institute of Group Relations, 1961.

Singer, Tania, et al. "Empathy for Pain Involves the Affective but Not Sensory Components of Pain." *Science* 303 (2004) 1157–62.

Skinner, B. F. *Science and Human Behavior.* New York: Free Press, 1953.

Slingerland, Edward, and Mark Collard. "Introduction—Creating Consilience: Toward a Second Wave." In *Creating Consilience: Integrating the Sciences and the Humanities,* edited by Edward Slingerland and Mark Collard, 3–40. New Directions in Cognitive Science. New York: Oxford University Press, 2012.

Smith, Isaac H., et al. "The Moral Ties That Bind . . . Even to Out-Groups: The Interactive Effect of Moral Identity and the Binding Moral Foundations." *Psychological Science* 25 (2014) 1554–62.

Smith, Kirsten P., and Nicholas A. Christakis. "Social Networks and Health." *Annual Review of Sociology* 34 (2008) 405–29.

Soliman, Tamer M., et al. "It's Not 'All in Your Head': Understanding Religion From an Embodied Cognition Perspective." *Perspectives on Psychological Science* 10 (2015) 852–64.

Soon, Chun Siong, et al. "Unconscious Determinants of Free Decisions in the Human Brain." *Nature Neuroscience* 11 (2008) 543–45.

Sosis, Richard, and Candace Alcorta. "Signaling, Solidarity, and the Sacred: The Evolution of Religious Behavior." *Evolutionary Anthropology* 12 (2003) 264–74.

Southern Poverty Law Center. "The Year in Hate and Extremism." *Intelligence Report* I 160 (Spring 2016) 1–73.

Spezio, Michael L., et al. "Religion, SCAN, and Developing Standards of Inquiry." *Religion, Brain & Behavior* 5 (2015) 179–81.

Stallen, Mirre, et al. "The Herding Hormone: Oxytocin Stimulates In-Group Conformity." *Psychological Science* 23 (2012) 1288–92.

Stone, Lawson G. "The Soul: Possession, Part, or Person?" In *What about the Soul? Neuroscience and Christian Anthropology,* edited by Joel B. Green, 47–61. Nashville: Abingdon, 2004.

Tangney, June P., et al. "High Self-Control Predicts Good Adjustment, Less Pathology, Better Grades, and Interpersonal Success." *Journal of Personality* 72 (2004) 271–322.

Taves, Ann. "Building Blocks of Sacralities: A New Basis for Comparison across Cultures and Religions." In *Handbook of the Psychology of Religion and Spirituality,* edited by Raymond F. Paloutzian and Crystal L. Park, 138–61. 2nd ed. New York: Guilford, 2013.

———. *Religious Experience Reconsidered.* Princeton: Princeton University Press, 2009.

Teilhard de Chardin, Pierre. *The Phenomenon of Man.* Translated by Bernard Wall. New York: Harper, 1959.

———. *Science and Christ.* Translated by René Hague. London: Collins, 1968.

Thiselton, Anthony C. "The Image and the Likeness of God: A Theological Approach." In *The Emergence of Personhood: A Quantum Leap?*, edited by Malcolm Jeeves, 184–201. Grand Rapids: Eerdmans, 2015.

Thompson, Curt. *Anatomy of the Soul: Surprising Connections between Neuroscience and Spiritual Practices That Can Transform Your Life and Relationships*. Carol Stream, IL: Tyndale House, 2010.

Tomasello, Michael, and Amrisha Vaish. "Origins of Human Cooperation and Morality." *Annual Review of Psychology* 64 (2013) 231–55.

Toner, Kaitlin et al. "Feeling Superior Is a Bipartisan Issue: Extremity (Not Direction) of Political Views Predicts Perceived Belief Superiority." *Psychological Science* 24 (2013) 2454–62.

Tremlin, Todd. *Minds and Gods: The Cognitive Foundations of Religion*. New York: Oxford University Press, 2006.

Uchino, Bert N. "Understanding the Links between Social Support and Physical Health: A Life-Span Perspective with Emphasis on the Separability of Perceived and Received Support." *Perspectives on Psychological Science* 4 (2009) 236–55.

Umberson, Debra, and Jennifer Karas Montez. "Social Relationships and Health: A Flashpoint for Health Policy." *Journal of Health and Social Behavior* 51 (2010) S54–S66.

Umberson, Debra, et al. "Social Relationships and Health Behavior across the Life Course." *Annual Review of Sociology* 36 (2010) 139–57.

Urgesi, Cosimo, et al. "The Spiritual Brain: Selective Cortical Lesions Modulate Human Self-Transcendence." *Neuron* 65 (2010) 309–19.

Valdesolo, Piercarlo, et al. "The Rhythm of Joint Action: Synchrony Promotes Cooperative Ability." *Journal of Experimental Social Psychology* 46 (2010) 693–95.

Van Lange, Paul A. M. "Generalized Trust: Four Lessons from Genetics and Culture." *Current Directions in Psychological Science* 24 (2015) 71–76.

Voas, David, and Mark Chaves. "Is the United States a Counterexample to the Secularization Thesis?" *American Journal of Sociology* 121 (2016) 1517–56.

Vohs, Kathleen D., and Jonathan W. Schooler. "The Value of Believing in Free Will." *Psychological Science* 19 (2008) 49–54.

Vohs, Kathleen D., et al. "Making Choices Impairs Subsequent Self-Control: A Limited-Resource Account of Decision Making, Self-Regulation, and Active Initiative." *Journal of Personality and Social Psychology* 94 (2008) 883–98.

Waal, Frans W. B. de *The Bonobo and the Atheist: In Search of Humanism among the Primates*. New York: Norton, 2013.

———. "Putting the Altruism Back into Altruism: The Evolution of Empathy." *Annual Review of Psychology* 59 (2008) 279–300.

Walton, John H. "Human Origins and the Bible." *Zygon* 47 (2012) 875–889.

Wason, Peter C. "Reasoning about a Rule." *Quarterly Journal of Experimental Psychology* 20 (1968) 273–81.

Watson-Jones, Rachel E., and Cristine H. Legare. "The Social Functions of Group Rituals." *Current Directions in Psychological Science* 25 (2016) 42–46.

Waytz, Adam, et al. "A Superhumanization Bias in Whites' Perceptions of Blacks." *Social Psychological and Personality Science* 6 (2015) 352–59.

Westfall, Jacob, et al. "Perceiving Political Polarization in the United States: Party Identity Strength and Attitude Extremity Exacerbate the Perceived Partisan Divide." *Perspectives on Psychological Science* 10 (2015) 145–58.

Wildmon, Donald E. "Principles Which Guide AFA's Opposition to the Homosexual Agenda." http://www.afa.net/faq.aspx?id=2147483680/, downloaded March 7, 2012.

Wilson, David Sloan. *Darwin's Cathedral: Evolution, Religion, and the Nature of Society.* Chicago: University of Chicago Press, 2002.

———. *Does Altruism Exist? Culture, Genes, and the Welfare of Others.* Foundational Questions in Science. New Haven: Yale University Press, 2015.

Wilson, Edward O. *Consilience: The Unity of Knowledge.* New York: Vintage, 1998.

Wiltermuth, Scott S., and Chip Heath. "Synchrony and Cooperation." *Psychological Science* 20 (2009) 1–5.

Wright, N. T. "Mind, Spirit, Soul and Body: All for One and One for All." Presentation at the Society of Christian Philosophers, Fordham University, New York, March 18, 2011.

———. *Surprised by Hope: Rethinking Heaven, the Resurrection, and the Mission of the Church.* New York: HarperOne, 2008.

Xygalatas, Dimitris, et al. "Extreme Rituals Promote Prosociality." *Psychological Science* 24 (2013) 1602–05.

Young, Cliff, and Chris Jackson. "The Rise of Neo-Nativism: Putting Trump into Proper Context." October 9, 2015. http://spotlight.ipsos-na.com/index.php/news/the-rise-of-neo-nativism-putting-trump-into-proper-context/.

Zak, Paul J., et al. "Oxytocin Increases Generosity in Humans." *PLOS ONE* 2 (November 2007) doi: 10.1371/journal.pone.0001128

Subject Index